NO ANGELS

The Short Life and Brutal Death of Brandaline Rose DuVall

STEVE JACKSON

WildBluePress.com

Some names have been altered.

NO ANGELS published by:
WILDBLUE PRESS
P.O. Box 102440
Denver, Colorado 80250

Publisher Disclaimer: Any opinions, statements of fact or fiction, descriptions, dialogue, and citations found in this book were provided by the author, and are solely those of the author. The publisher makes no claim as to their veracity or accuracy, and assumes no liability for the content.

Copyright 2020 by Steve Jackson

All rights reserved. No part of this book may be reproduced in any form or by any means without the prior written consent of the Publisher, excepting brief quotes used in reviews.

WILDBLUE PRESS is registered at the U.S. Patent and Trademark Offices.

ISBN 978-1-952225-30-7 Trade Paperback

ISBN 978-1-952225-29-1 eBook

Cover design © 2020 WildBlue Press. All rights reserved.

Interior Formatting and Cover Design by Elijah Toten
www.totencreative.com

NO ANGELS

PROLOGUE

December 28, 1998

Three days after Christmas 1998, there were few reminders of the holidays in Maria Simpson's Denver apartment. Although her faith remained strong, she didn't feel like celebrating. Her son Danny was sitting in a Jefferson County jail cell, awaiting trial for the gang rape and murder of a fourteen-year-old girl.

Brandaline Rose DuVall. The mention of her name evoked tears from Maria as she sat on a couch in her tiny living room, surrounded by dozens of photographs of family on the walls and every flat surface. "I pray to her all the time ... try to tell her how sorry I am." She tilts her head and looks down, as though the floor might open up and reveal why this had happened. When she is in a contemplative mood, she has a habit of affirming her comments with a nod and a whispered, "Yeah."

"Try to tell her how sorry I am ... yeah."

Danny's trial is set for February. If convicted, he could be put to death. As ashamed and as angry as she is with her twenty-five-year-old son, her oldest son, she doesn't want him to die. She wants him to plead guilty to avoid the death penalty. Even if it means abandoning his best friend, "Pancho," to his fate, and then spending the rest of his life in prison.

"I admit part of that's selfish," she says. "I don't want to sit through a trial and listen to what they did to that poor little girl. And I want him to be alive for his two little boys.

"But even more, I don't want her, the girl's mother, to have to go through another trial. I've told him that, but he's in denial." She pauses, looks down again. "Yeah."

Danny is telling her he can't accept a plea bargain unless Panch—Francisco Martinez—lets him know it's okay. Francisco has already been convicted of first-degree murder and faces a death-penalty hearing in May. He told his lawyer, Dave Kaplan, that it was all right for Danny to save himself. But Danny doesn't trust lawyers—even Panch's lawyer—and he wants his childhood friend to pass the word through Danny's sister, Raquel, or his brother, Antonio.

"He says he doesn't want Panch to think he's leaving him to die all by himself," says Maria. "I asked him when I visited him last week, 'What about my feelings? Don't they matter? And what about compassion for that girl's family?' And he said, 'Yes, but this is about how I feel, too. I can't say something to hurt Pancho.'"

Daniel "Bang" Martinez Jr., twenty-five-year-old Francisco "Pancho" Martinez, and seventeen-year-old Frank "Little Bang" Vigil Jr. are three of the seven members of the Deuce-Seven Crenshaw Mafia Gangster Bloods originally charged with the first-degree murder, first-degree sexual assault, and second-degree kidnapping of Brandy DuVall. Her torn and bloody body was discovered next to a mountain stream west of Golden on May 31, 1997.

The four other members accepted plea bargains in exchange for their testimonies. One of the government's two star witnesses, Samuel "Zig Zag" Quintana, is the twenty-five-year-old son of Maria's sister. He confessed to the second-degree murders of not one but two young women to "save himself," Maria says, "and the prosecutors bend over backward to talk about his *'redeeming qualities'* and believe everything he says about what happened that night."

The murder has frayed a once close-knit family. The government's other key witness is José Martinez Jr., the brother of Maria's first husband, Daniel Martinez Sr., and her boys' uncle.

Frank Vigil Jr.'s mother, Lisa, was one of Maria's best friends when the girls were growing up in Curtis Park. Lisa's cousin, Pam, had been Jose Martinez's common-law wife; Lisa married Pam's brother, Frank Vigil. And Maria's brother, Oney, is married to Nancy Quintana, another childhood friend of Maria's and the sister of Sammy Quintana's father.

Maria still considers Lisa Vigil one of her dearest friends, although they aren't as close as they once were, and Lisa is "coming apart" with her middle son now sentenced to life in prison. Francisco's mother, Linda, who for years blamed Danny and Antonio, and therefore, Maria, for her son's involvement in the gang, wouldn't talk to her for months after Francisco was arrested. "Now we share our grief," Maria says.

But Maria and her sister, Peggy, who's divorced from Sammy's father, are estranged. They haven't seen or spoken to each other since the day Sammy was arrested for Brandy's murder. Maria remains close to Nancy but has "nothing to say" to Nancy's brother, Sam.

And everybody is angry with Jose, "Uncle Joe," but not, as the prosecutors contend, because he's testifying. "Because he allowed our children to get this deep into trouble when he could have stopped it," says Maria.

She knows that what happened to Brandy was horrible and that the killers, including her son, "should pay for what they did."

Fifty-one-year-old Jose, who used to run with bikers and throw himself into bar brawls with his brothers, claims he was afraid of "the Bloods" that night. Now he's emerging from a witness-protection program to label their sons, his own nephew, "animals" and "devils." He may never be welcome, or even safe, in Denver again, but he will walk away unscathed. Jose wasn't charged with anything, including the destruction of evidence. It doesn't seem fair.

And Sammy. The prosecutors have said that when all of the trials are over, they will seek the maximum penalty of ninety-six years in prison for Samuel Quintana. But Maria doesn't believe them. She thinks they will find a way to reward him for giving up the others.

Maria has cut Sammy out of all her family photos. Still, it's hard for her to hate Sammy, who came to live with her and her three kids when his parents were divorcing. She also finds it hard to blame him for what he is doing; she just wishes she could believe he's doing it because his conscience bothers him.

Maria points to a recent photograph of three young children playing—Danny's twin sons and Sammy's daughter. "All they've been told is that their fathers are in jail for something they did," she says. "But they see each other all the time. They don't know what's going on. We take Danny's sons to the jail to see him, and she goes right along." If the boys are visiting Sammy's daughter when that family goes to see Sammy in jail, Danny's boys go, too. "The boys love Sammy and write him letters. And we all love his little girl ... yeah."

It isn't that she is trying to excuse Danny. "He made his own choices." But no one offered him a second-degree murder plea agreement.

Then again, Danny took off when it became clear the police were closing in. "I begged him not to run," Maria says. "I told him, 'Let's give it up to God and go face this together.' But he ran anyway."

Six months later, after Danny was finally caught, he balked at a deal that would have dropped a potential death penalty in exchange for life in prison without the possibility of parole. Danny wouldn't go for it because the prosecution demanded that he write a statement describing not only his role in Brandy's murder, but that of the others. Danny wouldn't snitch.

Nor is he now accepting responsibility. "He says he was drunk and doesn't remember," Maria says. "He says he can't read the transcripts from Frank's and Pancho's trial ... that he tries, but he can't. I tell him he has to if he's determined to go through with a trial. But he won't talk about it.

"He's real down on himself. I tell him, 'The Lord won't judge you for one incident. You have to look back and reflect that you were a very good person at other times in your life and ask for forgiveness.' But he's confused. I got a letter from him today that he probably wrote on Christmas. He talked about his sister visiting him and this and that, then at the end he wrote, 'I want to come home.'"

Danny still thinks there's a chance he can beat the rap. His lawyers tell him he's "fantasizing." Little Frankie didn't beat it. Pancho didn't beat it. It didn't take their juries much longer than the time needed to fill out the conviction papers before they returned with guilty verdicts. But Danny wants to believe that someday he will be free.

Maria stops to wipe a tear off her cheek. "Things are shitty for him," she says, "but nothing compared to what that little girl went through. There is no excuse. I feel for that family and think of her mom all the time." The mother who will be sitting on the other side of the courtroom when Danny goes on trial.

Maria's friends have tried to prepare her for Danny's trial by feeding her bits of information about Brandy's final hours. But they're worried about her emotional state and have tiptoed around the worst of it. So, Maria prepares herself in ways she would have otherwise avoided. She reads the transcripts from the trials of Pancho Martinez and Frank Vigil so that nothing that is said will shock her. She forces herself to watch movies that are violent to women so she'll dull her senses to the shock of brutality, just as she believes an entire generation of kids have been numbed by violent films and rap music.

"I read horror and murder stories," she says. "I don't like them, but Danny's lawyers are afraid of what my reaction will be in the courtroom. They don't want me making any public displays."

Neither does she. In fact, Maria would rather not go out in public at all. There are days when she doesn't want to get out of bed, much less go to work—or much less than that, go visit Danny and try to keep his spirits up while hers drag along the bottom.

At times Maria feels nearly overwhelmed by guilt. Not just for what her son and his friends did to Brandy DuVall. But for whatever deficiencies she had as a mother, for the lifestyle she exposed her boys to that made it impossible for her to fight the gangs for the souls of her sons. If there is anything to be gained in all of this, it's that some young mother might hear about this tragedy and realize that what she does in front of her children does matter.

She thinks back to when she was a young girl, living in the house at 2727 California, the house where Danny and Antonio—Bang and Boom—first gained their gang notoriety. Their grandmother's house, for which they named their particular branch of the CMG. The Deuce-Seven. If she could just go back, back to when her boys were young, when she could have changed their lives—saved Danny's life.

Antonio somehow walked away from his criminal past, graduated from art school, and got a job at a fancy tattoo parlor in another city. He works hard supporting himself, his girlfriend, and her son and also sends money back to Denver to support his daughter. But to move on with his life, he had to distance himself from the brother he loved and from Francisco, whom he loved like a brother.

Maria won't let Antonio come back for the trial. Bad enough that she will have to sit hour after hour on the hard wooden benches of the courtroom, staring at the back of her other son, the little boy who loved people and couldn't stand to be cooped up indoors. Danny. She loves him still and can't abandon him, no matter what he did.

Even if he participated in the rape and then stood on the hillside with Little Frankie, watching while Pancho and Sammy stabbed Brandy dozens of times, then threw her like a piece of trash over an embankment. "The law says that makes him just as guilty, a consequence for their total behavior that night," she says. "But at least I won't have to sit there and hear that my son did the killing."

It's a small consolation on this night, three days after Christmas. "But it helps me feel not quite as bad," she says, then whispers, "Yeah."

CHAPTER ONE

May 31, 1997

It was a great day to drive through the mountains. There were no clouds in the thin slice of sky that showed between the narrow walls of Clear Creek Canyon. The sun was high enough to peek over the edge of the high rock precipices, warming the early afternoon air.

Lance Butler had the windows down as he guided his car along the curves of two-lane Highway 6, a few miles west of Golden. He was enjoying showing the scenery to a visiting friend. They were a couple of clean-cut college grads on their way to Central City for a day of gambling and beer.

A mile or so past the point where Tunnel 1 burrows through a granite shoulder, the friend looked across the highway at the tumbling, rushing waters of Clear Creek. He suggested they stop and dip their feet.

"It'll be cold," Butler warned, as he drove across the highway and pulled into a gravel turnoff at mile marker 296.5. They got out and stretched, then walked over to a narrow swath of grasses. Just ahead, the ground suddenly dropped away to the stream thirty feet below. The embankment was a steep jumble of jagged boulders, too rugged to climb down.

The friend was walking along the edge, looking for another way to the water, when he pulled up short and pointed. "There's a body down there."

Butler thought his friend was joking. But he saw the blue of a pair of jeans and then the body, bare from the waist up, wedged in the rocks almost at the water's edge.

Butler and his friend thought it looked like the body of a small man. They moved along the rim until they were directly above it and were trying to decide if they should get closer still when they saw a dark red stain on the grass. It was a pool of congealing blood a couple of feet in diameter.

They ran back toward the highway and started flagging down cars. This was a busy Saturday, and the highway was jammed with casino buses and other vehicles full of hopeful gamblers. Still, it took several minutes of frantic waving before someone pulled over.

The driver tried to call out on his cellular telephone but couldn't get a signal past the high canyon walls. More cars stopped, and other drivers dialed out but couldn't get through. In the meantime, tourists walked back and forth along the edge, trying to get a look at the body.

Finally, everyone decided to leave and find help. "When you get to a telephone, call the police," Butler yelled as he ran to his car.

A few minutes later, the Jefferson County Sheriff's dispatcher fielded several calls from Central City about a body and "a lot of blood" in Clear Creek Canyon.

Diane Obbema was the first deputy to arrive at the mile 296.5 turnoff. She got out of her patrol car, took a few steps to the edge, and immediately saw the body. Then she began picking her way down through the boulders to see if she could help.

The body belonged to a girl who was past help. She was lying on her back, her face turned to the sky, her eyes closed. Her head was nearly in the water, her bare feet pointed up the hill. A pair of silver-colored handcuffs bound her hands behind her back. She was covered in blood.

Looking back up the hill, Obbema could see a wide trail of blood beginning partway down the slope, smearing rocks, gravel, and plants as it led to the body. The girl had not died where the blood was pooled at the top of the embankment. She'd fought to live—falling and getting up, then falling and rising again, until she fell one final time.

The amount of blood shocked the thirteen-year sheriff's veteran. There were places where it soaked into the ground between the rocks, then came out again lower on the slope.

Obbema scrambled back up to her car and the radio. Soon she was joined by sheriff's investigators, including Allen Simmons, the detective who would take the lead in the case, crime-scene technicians, and an ambulance crew. Television teams arrived and filmed the body of a young, unidentified female being removed from the river's edge in a black body bag.

Simmons was there when Dr. Ben Galloway conducted the autopsy. The forensic pathologist had performed approximately nine thousand autopsies during his career. Few were as disturbing as this one. The girl was young, barely a teenager, only five feet tall and a hundred pounds. She'd been savagely attacked.

The pathologist noted a bruise to the left side of her face that appeared to have been made with a fist. There was a large bruise on her chest, as well as other bruises and abrasions on her arms and legs, which indicated that she'd struggled.

Galloway counted twenty-eight stab wounds, all made with a sharp, single-edged knife. Some were to her chest, but most, including the fatal wounds, were to her back and neck. Her carotid artery and jugular vein had been pierced: She had bled to death.

The most horrifying wounds, though, were not the ones that had killed her. There was an obvious bite mark on her left breast. Her anus and rectum were badly bruised, and purposely cut by a sharp blade.

The last night of the girl's life had been hell.

It took until Sunday, June 1, to identify her as Brandaline Rose DuVall. Brandy's mother had arrived at the Jefferson County coroner's office looking for a missing daughter—and found her on a cold steel table. *Wake up, baby. Wake up.*

Brandy had died two months shy of her fifteenth birthday.

CHAPTER TWO

Maria was six when her mother left her father and moved with her seven children—five girls and two boys—into her grandparents' home near the corner of 27th and California streets. 2727 California.

Maria's grandparents, the Rodartes, were strict. They had both come to the United States from Mexico many years before. Grandfather Rodarte would only speak Spanish, never applied for citizenship, and didn't work, except in his backyard vegetable garden. Grandmother Rodarte, who bore eighteen children, was a nurse and very religious; she went every day to pray at Sacred Heart Catholic Church and belonged to the Legion of Mary.

Although the Rodartes taught their children Spanish, they made no attempt to instruct their grandchildren. Many years later, when it mattered to her, Maria asked her mother why she and her brothers and sisters weren't taught Spanish. "Because everybody thought children who spoke Spanish were slower or dumb immigrants," her mother replied. "And it just caused trouble for them at school." But Maria always suspected it had more to do with the adults wanting a "secret language" they could use in front of the kids.

As a child, Maria thought she lived in the best neighborhood in the world. People took pride in their homes. They mowed the grass, battled dandelions, and raked leaves that fell every autumn from the old shade trees that lined the blocks. It seemed like everyone planted gardens—flowers in front and vegetables in the back.

The collection of small stucco and brick homes had seen a succession of immigrants come and go—Germans, Japanese, Mexicans, Blacks. By the time Maria moved there, it was a mostly black neighborhood, with a strong contingent of Mexican families. Even if the kids usually congregated in racially distinct groups, they still got along with each other.

None of the kids seemed to notice that they were what other people would consider poor. Most of what they did was free, anyway—climbing trees, swinging at the playground at 25th and Stout, walking to the park to catch crawdads in the summer and to the ice rink outside the downtown May D&F store to skate in the winter.

Despite the poverty, there wasn't a lot of crime—at least not crime that affected the children. Five Points, the legendary hub of black cultural and social life in Denver, was still jumping a few blocks to the east. There were no bums shuffling down the sidewalks, no crack dealers standing in the shadows. What drug addicts there were stayed out of sight. Sometimes the kids would hear rumors about a pimp shooting another pimp or beating up a prostitute. Maybe someone's junkie husband, son, or brother would overdose, necessitating a call for an ambulance and sparking a rash of gossip. But it was the grownups doing the crimes, not the kids. Not yet.

And there were always lots of kids. Maria was as close as a sister to some of her neighborhood friends, especially Lisa and Nancy. As the girls grew older, they'd flirt with the boys and size them up for the future. Nancy's brother, John Quintana. Frank Vigil, a distant cousin of Lisa's. And the five Martinez brothers: Rudi, Jose, Tommy, and the twins, Dan and Ben.

Soon climbing trees gave way to hanging out with the other teenagers, kicking back to Motown music blaring over car stereos, drinking beer and smoking pot. A favorite spot was down at the Martinez brothers' house, where the boys were always working on their cars.

Some of the boys were in gangs that took their names from where they lived. They were the 23rd Street or Curtis Park or the Projects. No Bloods. No Crips. And no vice or money involved. If a lowrider drove slowly through the neighborhood, it was to show off, not a prelude to a shooting. Gangs were all about fighting with rivals over dates, insults, and street corners. And it wasn't just the boys doing the scraping.

In the late Sixties, the best place to find action was at the weekend dances sponsored by the Crusade for Justice. Corky Gonzales and other Chicano activists had taken over a huge old building on Downing Street, where they tried to bring together Mexican kids from different parts of town. The Crusade workers wanted to promote unity. What they got were melees out in the parking lot.

The guys would fight over turf. The girls would fight over the guys. Everyone knew there would be fights, no matter how much the Crusaders argued that they had too much in common to try to beat each other up. They just didn't understand it was all in good fun.

Maria and her friends counted on those dances for entertainment. They even dressed for the evening's combat, reminding each other not to wear clothes they cared about. Nothing with buttons. No dangling earrings ... not if you wanted to keep your earlobes from being torn.

The dances took place close to Maria's neighborhood, which meant the kids from the north and west sides of Denver were the invaders and at a disadvantage. The local girls would mess with the guys from another part of town just to get the other girls riled. There'd be a fight, the police or the neighborhood adults would show up to break it up, and everyone would scatter. All through the week, they'd proudly display their bruises, black eyes, and scratches while looking forward to the next dance.

But the Crusade for Justice workers were right about one thing. They did have something in common: Nobody had much money. When they did have cash, it went for groceries or, when the girls started having babies, to buy their kids diapers and shoes. And in that neighborhood, the girls started having babies when they were hardly more than children themselves.

Maria was no different. She was a wild thing who rebelled against her strict mother and grandparents. In their house, drinking and cigarettes were forbidden. So was cussing. So she stayed out until all hours drinking and carousing, hiding when she'd hear her mother walking up and down the street late at night demanding in a loud voice that Maria come home. More than once, she woke up in the closet of a friend's bedroom with her hand still wrapped around a bottle.

Big-breasted and pretty, Maria looked like a woman long before she was one. When she was twelve, one of the Martinez brothers, sixteen-year-old Danny, took an interest in her. She lied and told him she was fifteen, and the chase was on.

Danny wasn't very big, but he already had a reputation for taking what he wanted and not letting anybody stand in his way. What he wanted was Maria. What she wanted was someone who would promise to take care of her ... and get her out of the crowded house at 2727 California. She thought she was in love.

Maria's mother had never remarried. She'd scraped and saved to raise her kids on welfare and never went out except to work after her youngest, Jimmy, was old enough to go to school. Her grandparents slept in separate rooms and seemed to speak to each other only when they had to. There was always plenty of food sitting on the stove, but the family rarely sat down to dinner together.

Ever since she could remember, Maria had envied Danny's family life and adored his parents. She thought they were the perfect couple. She never saw them fight or even argue. He called her *Mama* and she called him *Daddy*. If they were watching television and she noticed him starting to nod off, she'd say, "Daddy, you're sleepy, go to bed." And he'd reply, "Not till you do, Mama." That's the sort of marriage she wanted someday.

Danny's father, Joe, was a hardworking roofer, a good man, fair with his five boys and three girls. He loved to laugh and wasn't afraid to demonstrate his love for his family. Danny's mother, Ida, was a sweet, caring woman who seemed to believe that it was her responsibility to feed any kid in the neighborhood who happened to be there around mealtime. All the family members spent a good deal of time hugging each other.

The Martinezes treated Maria like a little sister, but Danny had other ideas. She was fifteen when they had their first child, Raquel; they married when she was sixteen and pregnant with Danny Jr.

After they married, the young couple moved across the street into a fourplex. Danny worked for his dad. When he came home hot and tired, she'd have a bath ready—then every night they'd go across the street to his parents' home for dinner.

Meals were a crowded, noisy, laughing affair. Everyone—the parents, their boys, their girlfriends, wives, children, and assorted neighborhood visitors—would sit down at the table to eat. They never knew what they were going to get. During lean times it might just be meatloaf, but there were always hot green chiles and a big stack of homemade tortillas fresh off the stove.

It was a rough-and-tumble household. Joe smoked huge cigars, and Ida puffed cigarette after cigarette. They all drank beer. Especially the boys, who would get drunk and wrestle around the house until they were told to take it outside. A favorite pastime was to go to a bar and start a brawl: One minute everything would be quiet, the next, all hell would break loose.

Maria loved it. She'd married into the sort of family she had always wanted and thought her children would grow up safe and well-loved in the arms of that family.

CHAPTER THREE

June 2, 1997

The day after Brandy DuVall's body was identified by her mother, Jeffco sheriff's investigators, Doug Moore and Jeffrey Pevler, visited Patrice Bowman. The fifteen-year-old black girl was one of Brandy's best friends and had been with her on the night of May 30.

Patrice admitted that she and Brandy had smoked marijuana and drunk most of a six-pack of beer, which a man they met at a bus stop had purchased for them in exchange for one of the beers. Brandy had left a little after 11:30 p.m., headed for a bus stop on South Federal Boulevard where she could catch a ride back to her grandmother's house. She'd been wearing a red Chicago Bull's jersey, black shorts, and red, black and white Nike running shoes.

After talking with Patrice, the investigators were five hours closer to Brandy's murder but still had many unanswered questions. Where were her clothes? The light-blue jeans she'd been wearing when her body was found were several sizes too big for her, and otherwise she was nude.

But the trail dead-ended at the bus stop on South Federal and Florida. They hoped someone who'd seen her there could narrow the time gap still further. Maybe that someone had even glimpsed the face of Brandy's killer.

Federal was a busy thoroughfare even at that time of night. A lot of teens, some of them homeless and on their own, hung out on corners and in parking lots. On a Saturday night, lowriders and gang members alike might be cruising the street, showing off and looking for action. Someone must have seen something.

On June 10, investigator Simmons received a call from an informant, who said that a man named Jose Martinez had told him that Brandy DuVall had been assaulted by the Bloods at his home on the night of May 30, 1997.

Two days after receiving that call, Simmons and investigator Ralph Gallegos contacted Jose Martinez at the house he rented at 3165 West Hawthorne Place in Adams County. Martinez quickly confessed to having been the unwilling witness to the rape and torture of a teenage girl. She'd been brought to his house by a Bloods gang member he knew only as "Baby G" and four others he didn't know at all. Already there, getting drunk and high, were his nephew Daniel "Bang" Martinez Jr., Francisco "Pancho" Martinez, Frank "Little Bang" Vigil Jr., and someone nicknamed "Zig Zag."

The gang had "the devil" in them that night, Jose Martinez said, and he'd been unable to stop what they had done to "that poor little girl."

The girl was still alive when they'd finally left his house before dawn, begging to be taken to a hospital. After that, he'd cleaned up his house and found the girl's clothes, as well as her high-school identification card. The name on the card was the same one he'd heard later on the television news.

Simmons asked Martinez if he'd kept any of Brandy's personal effects that would help corroborate his story in court. Martinez shook his head. His nephew Danny and the one he knew as "Zig Zag" had come over and taken the girl's things, including the identification card, a B-shaped diamond pendant, and the bloody mattress of the bed where she had been raped and tortured.

"Nothing?" the investigator asked.

Martinez gave in. He went to his kitchen and removed something from under the sink. It was a small prayer card.

He told the investigators he'd kept it because he liked it and thought he might need something if the police ever showed up asking about the girl.

Now the Jeffco investigators had suspects, but some of them were known only by their nicknames. So Simmons went to talk to Greg Romero, one of the detectives assigned to the Denver Police Department Gang Unit.

Romero identified Zig Zag as twenty-three-year-old Samuel Merced Quintana, Zig Zag, along with twenty-three-year-old Francisco "Pancho" Martinez, twenty-four-year-old Daniel "Bang" Martinez Jr., and twenty-two-year-old David Warren, also known as "Baby G," were all members of the Crenshaw Mafia Gangster Bloods, specifically a subset that called itself the Deuce-Seven.

They were drug dealers suspected of a number of shootings, Romero said, but had done little in the way of jail time to show for it. The DPD's gang unit had Danny Martinez and his younger brother, Antonio, also known as "Boom," pegged as the leaders of the Deuce-Seven along with their first cousin, Sammy Quintana; Francisco Martinez, no relation, was immediately below them in the gang hierarchy.

The Crenshaw Mafia Gangster Bloods had started out as a Black gang near 104th Street and Crenshaw Boulevard in Los Angeles. They'd shown up in Denver in the mid-Eighties, and their power had been growing ever since. The CMG Bloods split Denver by race and territory. CMG on the east side of town was predominantly Black and claimed the Park Hill area down to Aurora and into Montbello; they'd turned some neighborhoods into battle zones in their perpetual fight with the Crips, the first of the two big California gangs to bring their guns and crack-cocaine trade to Denver.

CMG on the west side had come along later. It was mostly Latino, although by 1997 the gang had white, Asian, and black members. Generally, they claimed anything west of downtown to Lakewood and south into Bear Valley.

The police believed that both CMG gangs cooperated in their various criminal activities. By comparison, black and Latino Crips gangs in Denver rarely shared anything other than a name and an affinity for the color blue. In fact, they were often violent rivals.

The Metro Area Gang Task Force had been after the Martinez brothers for some time without much luck. Witnesses to assaults tended to take off or recant; the few charges that stuck had been dismissed by the courts. Antonio had a non-fatal shooting on his juvenile record, and the brothers were both popped on a marijuana charge that hadn't come to much. Otherwise, *nada*.

Now, however, their run seemed to be coming to an end. Danny had an arrest warrant out for failing to participate in a court-ordered drug-and-alcohol rehab program. And, Romero said, his unit was working with a Lakewood Police Department detective, Scott Richardson, who'd been trying for a year to pin the July 1996 murder of a young woman on Samuel Quintana and two other Deuce-Seven members, Alejandro "Speed" Ornelas and his brother, Gerard.

The Denver police had had better luck busting up the Park Hill CMG. In November 1996, a Denver grand jury had indicted ten members for running an "illicit enterprise" that included murder, drug trafficking, and other violent acts. Five of the ten were charged with the murder of Eric Thomas, a Crip who was gunned down in a drive-by shooting in October 1993. Those indictments marked the first time that the Denver District Attorney's Office had used the state's racketeering law—known as the Colorado Organized Crime Act—to go after a street gang.

In May 1997, seven CMG members accepted plea bargains that included dropping the murder charge in connection with Thomas's killing. Denver authorities hailed the convictions as the destruction of the Park Hill CMG.

And now, if the Jeffco investigators' suspicions about who'd killed Brandy DuVall were correct, CMG on the west side was self-destructing. Her death didn't even have the twisted logic of a gangland hit. It wasn't "business"; it was pure brutality. Her body was dumped where it was likely to be discovered; there were plenty of witnesses. Brandy's murderers were practically asking for a date with a lethal injection, compliments of the state.

Jose Martinez was told there'd be no charges if he cooperated and testified. When he hesitated, saying he'd be killed by the gang, Jeffco investigators promised to put him in an out-of-state witness-protection program.

Jose agreed. On June 14, 1997, as the police listened in, he placed a telephone call to Sammy Quintana. "Uncle Joe," as he was known to the gang members, began the conversation by asking Sammy why he thought the police had come to his house.

"What are you talkin' about?" Quintana asked.

"You know what I'm talkin' about," Martinez replied.

"Hey, I know what the fuck you're talkin' about," Quintana growled, "but what are you talkin' about? ... They over at your house or what?"

"You know why they're here ... I told you to leave that girl alone."

"Hey," Quintana warned, "don't start speakin' no shit."

"You got me into trouble," Martinez responded. "Now you got to get me out of it."

Quintana paused, then said, "All right, call Danny boy." He gave Martinez a pager number and hung up.

Martinez paged his nephew. When Danny Martinez called back, he was wary. He asked several times if his uncle was with the "po-pos," the police. He wanted to know where Jose was and, when his uncle wouldn't answer, wanted to know why he wouldn't.

Danny Martinez denied having anything to do with a girl at his uncle's house. "There was a bitch there with Zeebo.

There was a bitch there with Pancho. There was another bitch that came, and there was another bitch there," he said. "I don't even fuckin' know who they were, and I never seen them in my fuckin' life, and I'll never see them again, probably."

After hanging up, Jose Martinez identified Danny Martinez, Francisco Martinez, Samuel Quintana, and David Warren from a photo lineup. A couple of days later he picked a photograph of then-sixteen-year-old Frank Vigil Jr.—Little Bang—out of another lineup.

On June 15, a new informant told Jeffco authorities that he'd been present when several members of the Deuce-Seven CMG sexually assaulted Brandy DuVall. He'd run from the house but assumed the same group had later killed her. This informant added two names to the list of suspects: Maurice "Trap" Warren, the eighteen-year-old brother of David, and nineteen-year-old Jacob "Smiley" Casados.

The Jeffco investigators felt they had enough to move. Sammy Quintana and Frank Vigil were arrested first, followed soon after by Francisco Martinez, who was already in the Denver jail on an unrelated drug charge. A short time later, Maurice Warren and Jacob Casados were picked up. All were charged with ten criminal acts against Brandy DuVall, including first-degree murder, first-degree sexual assault, sexual assault on a child, and second-degree kidnapping.

Still, Jeffco investigators didn't have the whole story. They didn't know who'd actually taken Brandy to the mountains, who'd stabbed her to death.

Then Sammy Quintana started talking. Quintana was facing double trouble. Shortly after his arrest for the DuVall killing, Detective Richardson had charged him and the Ornelas brothers with first-degree murder for the July 15, 1996, death of nineteen-year-old Venus Montoya. That meant he was facing the possibility of two death-penalty murder trials.

To investigator Moore, Quintana admitted his part in the brutality against Brandy DuVall but laid the worst of it, including the stabbing, on Francisco Martinez. Taking a deal offered by the Jeffco District Attorney's Office, he pleaded guilty to two second-degree murder charges, each carrying the possibility of forty-eight years in prison. In exchange, he agreed to testify against the other defendants in both trials.

Zig Zag's confession inspired a flurry of snitching. David Warren was arrested and joined his brother, Maurice, and Casados in pleading guilty to first-degree sexual assault. The other charges were dropped in exchange for their agreement to testify "truthfully" against whomever decided to go to trial.

At the time, that meant Francisco Martinez—District Attorney Dave Thomas had already announced he would seek the death penalty for Martinez—and Frank Vigil Jr., who would be tried as an adult.

The last suspect, Danny Martinez, was on the run. He wouldn't be apprehended until January 1, 1998, five days before jury selection was set to begin for the trial of Frank Vigil.

CHAPTER FOUR

January 6, 1998

Jolene Martinez and her fiancé, Joe Gonzalez, glanced nervously at the crowd moving through the lobby of the Jefferson County courthouse. Jury selection is under way on the fifth floor for the murder trial of Frank Vigil, and they've heard rumors that the Bloods will assassinate anyone who dares appear as a prosecution witness.

The couple has been subpoenaed by the district attorney to report to the courthouse. And now all faces, especially Hispanic and black faces, look hostile. Anyone dressed in anything remotely resembling gang attire is a threat. A bulge beneath a winter coat could be a gun.

"I don't know why they want me," Jolene moans. "My daughter was there that night, staying with my dad. But she's only ten, and she didn't see nothin' or hear nothin'."

Her dad is Jose Martinez, "Uncle Joe." The defendant's mother, Lisa Vigil, and her mother, Pam, who was Jose's common-law wife, are cousins.

Through her father, Danny Martinez Jr. and Antonio Martinez—Bang and Boom—are also first cousins. Making the whole thing even more complicated, Danny's father, Danny Sr., used to live with Lisa Vigil and helped raise "Little Frankie"—the sixteen-year-old now on trial for murder.

It was fear of the gang, including members of his own family, that kept her father quiet until the police came knocking, Jolene says. And it was fear that kept Jose

Martinez from doing something, anything, to save Brandy DuVall that night.

"Dad didn't have a phone," Jolene says. "And he couldn't leave to go get help because he had the kids. He was afraid that if he left, they might kill the kids, too. This has made him sick. He's all tore up and has to take nitroglycerin for his heart. He writes poetry about that little girl. He's always reading his Bible now. He calls her his 'little angel.'"

Her father was asleep with his son and her daughter when he woke up to noises in his home. At first, Jolene says, he thought that whatever was going on with that girl in a back bedroom was consensual. But it didn't take long before he realized he was mistaken.

"He said to me, 'They looked like they had the devil in them.' They were acting crazy, and no matter how much he screamed or yelled at them to take her home—she was begging for her life, you know—they wouldn't listen to him."

"Like animals," Joe Gonzales agrees. "Nobody thinks much about it when these guys in gangs kill each other. They even think of it like they're soldiers, fighting for each other and their 'hood. Only now they're killing civilians. There's no honor. It's sick—killing children."

"At first," Jolene interjects, "I wanted to blame drugs. How else can you explain what they did to that little girl? They just tore her up. But they don't do drugs. They get drunk and smoke some pot, but nothin' like cocaine. They sell it, but they don't do it."

Jolene finds it all very upsetting. She has known Frank Vigil Jr. since he was a little boy. "He was a good little boy, very cute," she remembers. "He's still a little boy. But I hadn't seen him for years. When I did, he was dressed in gang clothes."

She has known Danny Martinez all of her life. "Everybody liked him," she says. "Even when he got older and came over to my house, he was respectful, polite. You'd never know he was in a gang. He was always over at my dad's, who was like another father to him. But I think the money changed Danny—all that money from sellin' drugs. He always had wads of cash he'd throw around. If my dad didn't have any money, Danny'd whip out a few twenties and just give it to him.

"Money is power, and he and his brother, Antonio, had a lot of power on the streets. It's weird. They wanted respect, but the only way they got respect was through fear and guns—they they always had guns on them."

Now fear and anger "has tore us all apart," she says of the extended family. "Just ripped us like someone stickin' a knife in your stomach. Brother not talkin' to brother. My dad wanted to take my little brother over to his grandmother's house, but she told him not to because it wasn't safe. Nobody goes to see each other anymore. It's like the kids don't even have grandparents."

Jolene's voice drops as she looks around to see who might be standing nearby. "And there's a contract out on my dad," she says quietly. "His own family turned their backs on him because he was talkin' to the police.

"But what could he do? What kind of choice did he have? He says he would die if he had to keep it to himself. He wasn't the one who made them do it ... and that little girl needed peace. She didn't ask for what happened to her."

As Jolene starts to cry, her fiancé wraps a protective arm around her shoulders. She shakes her head sadly as she explains that she, too, is afraid—the gang may want to get at her to shut up her father, or just to retaliate. She and Joe will probably have to move out of state in order to feel safe again.

"We have family here," she says, wiping at her eyes. "And it's expensive to move. Until we can afford it, we'll just have to watch out."

Jolene and Joe turn and walk through the security checkpoint. They head to the fifth floor, where they meet

Ingrid Bakke, one of the prosecutors in the case, outside the courtroom.

After all that, Bakke tells them that they probably won't have to testify but that they should be available if they're needed. Relieved, the two hurry back to the elevators before Bakke can change her mind.

As Bakke turns and walks back into the courtroom where jury selection is under way, she passes a small Hispanic woman sitting on a wooden bench with two teenage boys. The woman's eyes are red and shiny from crying; the boys look defensive and frightened.

They are Frank Vigil's mother and brothers. "We don't want to comment," Lisa Vigil says before a reporter can ask a question.

When it's your son, or your brother, sitting in the defendant's chair, you are expected to assume some share of the guilt. There must have been some lack of parental guidance ... maybe even some genetic predisposition to evil. Everything about the trial reinforces that guilt.

While members of the victim's family are comforted by victim advocates, given pillows to ease their time on the hard benches, you're left on your own to sit and stare at the back of your son or brother, lost in private thoughts. *It was them, the bad ones, who led him astray. Please, God, let the jury understand that.*

Finally, the jury is seated. The lawyers will give their opening statements the next morning.

Lisa Vigil and her boys stay close together as they move off down the hall. They look like they expect someone to attack them.

CHAPTER FIVE

1975

By the time Maria gave birth to Antonio, two years after Danny Jr., the old neighborhood was beginning to lose its charm. Others thought so, too.

Her friend Nancy had married Maria's brother, Oney, and moved to Oregon. Her sister Peggy, who'd always wanted more than the neighborhood could provide, decided she'd find it with John Quintana, Nancy's brother.

John was the responsible one of the neighborhood boys, always working, trying to get ahead. He and Peggy married when they were both sixteen and had Samuel a year after Danny was born. A daughter had followed a couple of years later, after they had moved out to the suburbs. Except for special family events, they rarely returned to the neighborhood.

John Quintana had always wanted to be a Denver police officer but couldn't get hired on. There was an offer from the San Diego police, but Peggy had a good job as a secretary and wouldn't leave. So, he took a position with the Denver Sheriff's Department as a deputy at the jail.

Not everyone left the area around 27th and California, though. Lisa stuck around and married Frank Vigil. All of Maria's other friends were married and/or pregnant, and they'd go over to the playground at 25th and Stout and push their kids on the same swings they'd played on themselves just a few years before.

Maria was beginning to wonder what she'd missed by having children so young. Especially when Big Dan, as he was called after their son was born, began spending less and less time at home.

"A lot of guys his age were single, and he wanted to be free like them," she says. "He'd disappear for days and forget that he had a wife and kids. He made good money working for his dad, but he quit and started getting involved with drugs and people I didn't want to be around."

Maria herself was no angel. She and her girlfriends were still on the wild side, only now they took turns watching each other's kids so they could go out and party.

Although Maria and Dan Sr. had only fought twice—physically, that is, and she was nearly his size and just as tough—they argued all the time. Maria began to dream of seeing something more of the world. Raquel was four, Danny three, and Antonio one when the opportunity presented itself.

She was twenty and working as a bartender at Lowry Air Force Base when she caught the eye of Sergeant Bill Rollins, a black airman. Off duty, he wore nice suits and alligator shoes and drove a nice white Monte Carlo. He was just plain jazzy.

What's more, he loved her kids and he loved her. When he was reassigned to an air base in California, he asked Maria to pack up the children and go with him. She agreed and, as soon as her divorce from Big Dan was finalized, they married. On the base, Maria and the kids settled into a solid, middle-class existence. She got a job cleaning houses and thought that at last she'd lost that wild streak.

Bill was a good role model for the boys—honest, hardworking, well-read. And he loved having sons, taking them fishing and camping, coaching their basketball and baseball teams. He was patient, especially with Danny, who could have frustrated Job the way he was forever taking things apart. Instead of getting mad, Bill would buy Danny toys that came unassembled and let him play with all the parts to his heart's content. Then he'd warn the boy, "Once we put it together, you'd better not take it apart."

The children blossomed. Raquel was everything Maria thought a good daughter should be. And she looked after her two baby brothers like a mother duck—until they grew old enough to start looking after her.

The boys' personalities were as different as the sun and moon. Danny was always up at first light, dressed and out of the house before the rest of his family stirred. He hated being indoors, cooped up. It made him nervous—he'd bite his nails and couldn't sit still.

Danny was the athlete, always playing ball or some other game. He was a natural leader, the one picked to be the captain of his baseball and basketball teams. He needed to be around people. And other kids seemed content to follow his example: The boys wanted to be like him, and the little girls wanted to be near him. He was generous to a fault. If another child wanted a toy he was playing with, he would gladly hand it over.

Antonio, on the other hand, was what his mother called "stingy." He hated sharing his toys and found little girls "bothersome." If he couldn't be with his big brother, he preferred to stay in his room with a pen and paper. Left alone, he would draw for hours.

The kids were close. Danny was very protective of Raquel, even though she was older. No one was going to hurt his sister and get away with it. And they were loyal.

There was no better illustration of that than the Christmas when Maria took the kids to Coos Bay, Oregon, to visit her sister-in-law, Nancy. Her brother was away, working on a crab boat, so it was just the women and their children.

With Christmas approaching, Maria took pains to hide the kids' presents in the garage. But she came home one day and discovered that someone had been into them.

She called the boys in and demanded to know which one was the culprit. Neither would admit to it or point a finger at the other. She took a belt to both of them, but they still wouldn't talk.

"Then go to your room and stay there until whoever did it admits it," she yelled.

An hour later, Antonio came out. "If we tell you, will you let us both come out to watch TV?"

Maria agreed to the terms. A few moments later, Danny emerged and admitted he was the one.

She looked at Antonio. "You let me whup you for something you didn't do?" she asked, shaking her head. He shrugged, and she realized that the thought of telling on his brother had never occurred to him. He wouldn't even let Danny confess until he'd secured a plea bargain for television rights for them both.

Danny later told her that he'd suggested they tell her the truth at the beginning, so that Antonio wouldn't be punished. But Antonio wouldn't go for it. They were brothers: Whatever needed to be faced, they would face together.

It was a good life, but Maria still wanted more. Before she'd moved to California, she had once mentioned to Bill and her mother that she might want to join the Air Force. They'd laughed, since she was never one to follow orders and would probably end up in the brig for insubordination.

But in 1979 she decided to join anyway, even though Bill was against it. She packed up the kids, saying she wanted to visit her mother. Back in Denver, Maria went to the Air Force recruitment office and passed the written and physical examinations for placement in the reserves. Only then did she call Bill and tell him. It would mean leaving the boys with Big Dan for six months while she went through basic and then trained to be a flight medical technician.

Bill was angry but quickly resigned himself to the fact that the deed was already done. "Just keep your mouth shut when somebody gives you an order," he warned.

After Maria completed her classes, she returned to Denver and met up with Bill, who drove the family back to California.

Maria eventually applied for active duty and was lucky enough to be assigned to the same base as Bill. She enjoyed flying and seeing different parts of the country.

Unfortunately, by now she'd discovered she enjoyed something else: injecting methamphetamine. It would destroy her marriage to Bill and, many years later, compound the guilt she was feeling over the death of a fourteen-year-old girl named Brandy DuVall.

CHAPTER SIX

January 7, 1998

Frank Vigil Jr. shuffles into the courtroom, shackles around his ankles, hands cuffed behind his back. A large, ill-fitting suit coat can't disguise the bulk of the shock control belt, capable of sending fifty thousand volts of electricity into his body, fastened around his thin hips.

Vigil half-smiles at his mother and brothers sitting in the second row behind the defense table. They smile back, weakly. The exchange is brief, and then Vigil's face goes blank as he turns away.

The first row behind the defense table has been marked off-limits by court security personnel. They don't want to take any chances, considering the rumors of death threats and gang retaliation. But even without barriers, the first several rows on the defense side remain virtually empty, while the three long pews behind the prosecution table are full. No one—not the media, not veteran courtroom watchers, not the casually curious—wants to sit on the side of a defendant charged with such a heinous crime.

The family and friends of the murdered girl take up most of the first two rows on the prosecution side. Sitting in front is Brandy DuVall's mother, Angela Metzger, slim and attractive; beside her sits her husband, Carl. Next to them, Paul Vasquez, Brandy's maternal grandfather, inserts earplugs and pats the knee of the sad, tiny woman next to him: Rose, his wife, from whom Brandy received her middle name.

Deputy district attorneys Hal Sargent, Mark Randall, and Ingrid Bakke sit at the prosecution table, nearest to the jury box. With Sargent in the lead, the same three will stay together to prosecute the cases against Vigil and his co-defendants, Francisco Martinez and Danny Martinez Jr., in separate trials. Seated with the prosecutors are Jeffco investigators Simmons and Moore.

The deputy who escorted Vigil into the courtroom unlocks the handcuffs. He stands behind the sixteen-year-old until he takes a seat next to his lawyer, Randy Canney.

Vigil doesn't look dangerous. His thick, coal-black hair has grown out and is combed neatly back. A spectator on the prosecution side wonders aloud if he even shaves.

Judge Michael Villano, a sixty-five-year-old jurist with twenty years on the bench, enters the courtroom and, when everyone is reseated, addresses the lawyers. One of the male jurors is still trying to get out of serving, he says. The man showed up that morning with a letter from his employer stating that he is "integral" to the business.

Other prospective jurors had tried to evade jury duty, citing fears of gang retaliation. Some of them are on the jury anyway, including a woman who said she'd had to send her son out of state because of problems with a gang. But Villano says he's decided to let this man go, even though there will now be only one alternate juror to fill in if one of the others can't continue or has to be removed at some point.

Villano instructs the bailiff to bring in the jurors: four women and nine men. Then it's time for opening statements. The courtroom, which had been buzzing, quickly grows quiet as Bakke stands to deliver the outline of the prosecution's case.

Bakke has been with the Jefferson County District Attorney's Office since 1990 and with the office's Crimes Against Children unit for almost four years. It will be up to her to begin the process of destroying the defense's expected portrayal of a young, misguided Hispanic youth, replacing it with the portrait of a sadistic and brutal gang member.

Pausing at the lectern, Bakke gathers herself and then, softly, begins explaining to the jurors that what they will hear over the next week or two will be "extremely difficult" to listen to but "is not meant to evoke your sympathy." It is presented, she says, so that they can judge for themselves what happened the night Brandy DuVall was raped and murdered.

Angela Metzger and her daughter were still living with Angela's adoptive parents, Rose and Paul, on May 30, 1997, but were moving into their own place the next day, Bakke says. Angela last saw her daughter at six that evening, when they met on a street corner so that she could give Brandy a little spending money for the weekend. "Brandy reached into the car to give her a hug, and Angela told her, 'I love you,' to which Brandy replied, 'I love you, Mom.'"

Bakke jumps ahead to tell how Lance Butler and his friend discovered the body of an unidentified young woman by Clear Creek Canyon just outside of Golden. And how Jefferson County deputy Diane Obbema arrived at the scene and "saw, literally, a river of blood leading to the creek."

Bakke goes over Brandy's injuries. The stab wounds. The bruises. The bite mark and mutilation of her anus.

The jurors are realizing what Canney meant during jury selection when he said they would be shocked by the "sheer horror" of the case. They sit soberly through Bakke's depiction of Angela's frantic, two-day search for her daughter.

Bakke's voice strains as she describes the misery of a mother knocking on a glass partition at the Jefferson County Coroner's office, begging her daughter to *wake up, baby, wake up.* And knowing that she would not.

Small cries and sniffles can be heard in the spectator gallery, and even some of the jurors wipe at their eyes.

Across the aisle, Canney looks impassively at Bakke, as if listening to an interesting, but not necessarily believable, theory about the creation of the universe. Frank Vigil stares down at the table in front of him. Behind him, his mother bows her head.

Bakke knows that the jury will wonder why a fourteen-year-old girl was wandering the streets at midnight. So she explains that Brandy and Angela were "more like best friends than a mother/daughter relationship." The girl was "independent and in control of her life and did not need a mother to take care of her." She was "street-smart and, like most teenagers, she probably thought she was invincible."

Brandy was no angel, Bakke concedes. She drank alcohol, smoked marijuana, and snorted cocaine. "But this case is not about her lifestyle, but the rape, torture, kidnapping, and murder of Brandy by, among others"—the prosecutor turns and points at Vigil, who keeps his head down—"this man." A member of the Deuce-Seven Crenshaw Mafia Gangster Bloods, known as "Little Bang."

After drinking and getting high with her friend, Patrice Bowman, Brandy was standing at a bus stop on Federal when a car with five young men pulled up. Two of the men are "incidental to the case"; the other three are David "Baby G" Warren, his slow-witted brother, Maurice "Trap" Warren, and Jacob "Smiley" Casados.

"What exactly was said, we don't know," Bakke continues.

But Brandy got in their car and was taken far north into Adams County, to 3165 West Hawthorne Place, near Federal Boulevard and 60th. It was a tiny ranch house, about a thousand square feet of living space. A chain-link fence surrounded an unkempt yard filled with weeds, trash, and discarded automobile parts.

Sleeping in one room was Jose "Uncle Joe" Martinez, who rented the house, as well as his ten-year-old son, Jose, and nine-year-old granddaughter, Rochelle. He was sleeping with the children because he'd done his laundry that day, and his clean clothes were still neatly folded on the bed in his own room.

Hanging out at the home when Brandy arrived were four more members of the Deuce-Seven: Danny "Bang" Martinez Jr., Francisco "Pancho" Martinez, Sammy "Zig Zag" Quintana, and Little Bang.

Bakke briefly outlines the next five hours, a "nightmare," a "free-for-all" of rape, debasement, and savagery. When they were through, there was a young girl, pleading for her life, who made the mistake of admitting that she knew where she was. It was at that point, Bakke says, that the defendant, Frank Vigil, planted the seed for her death by telling the others they were going to have to "dust her" to prevent her from going to the police.

Brandy was taken into the mountains by Bang, Zig Zag, Pancho, and Little Bang. At a turnoff from the highway, "in the dead of night," she was pulled from the car, stabbed, then flung off the embankment toward the stream below.

"There in the dark," Bakke says, just loud enough to be heard, "Brandy DuVall lay ... but she was alive and struggled to get up ... until at last she tumbles ... and falls ... and bleeds to death."

Bakke pauses to take a sip of water. Behind her, the sounds of sorrow are more pronounced.

"Crimes committed in hell do not have angels as witnesses," she resumes. It is an old line, a standard that prosecutors use when they know their witnesses are hardly more credible than the defendant.

The defense is sure to portray these witnesses as liars and worse, making deals and saying whatever it takes to save their own skins. To counter that, Bakke notes that "without angels for witnesses," the only way for the government to give Brandy justice "is to make deals with the devils."

One of these devils is Sammy Quintana, she says. But he confessed to the police before any deal was sealed—not just regarding the DuVall killing, but also regarding his part in the murder of Venus Montoya.

Whether he agreed to talk to save himself from the possibility of the death penalty or to clear his conscience doesn't really matter, Bakke says. In exchange for his testimony against the others, the prosecution has agreed to not ask for more than ninety-six years at his sentencing after the last trial is over.

The Warren brothers and Jacob Casados, who turned off the highway instead of following the others into the mountains, all got deals. "You'll hear from them," Bakke notes. And the jurors will hear from "Uncle Joe," who has known Frank Vigil since he was a baby. Jose Martinez's cooperation earned him a death sentence from the Bloods and placement in a witness-protection program.

Most of the evidence left at Uncle Joe's house was carried away the next day by Danny Martinez and Sammy Quintana, Bakke says. "But unbeknownst to them, there was one piece of evidence Uncle Joe coveted and had secreted ... beneath his kitchen sink."

Although she had rehearsed this many times, Bakke's voice cracks as she describes the little prayer card with the drawing of a hand with a nail hole in it.

There are few dry eyes in the courtroom as Bakke just manages to read the inscription on the card. "See, I will not forget you. I have carved you in the palm of my hand."

CHAPTER SEVEN

By 1985, it was all over between Maria and Bill. Her kids had about had it with her, too. Maria was strung out on meth, her moods swinging back and forth like the pendulum of a grandfather clock.

The children went so far as to call their grandmother and beg to come back to Colorado. Maria's mother sent them money for the plane tickets, then moved the three into the house her parents had left her at 2727 California. Raquel was fourteen, Danny thirteen, Antonio eleven.

Maria soon followed, moving into the house next door. Bill had given up, saddened but unable to do anything for her. She knew that leaving him was a horrible mistake, both for her and the kids, but she couldn't stop. She couldn't get off drugs.

Her kids did their best to cover for her—like the night she overdosed on heroin in the front yard while celebrating her thirty-second birthday. With an ambulance, and potentially the police, on the way, fifteen-year-old Danny ran to his mother's bedroom, found her syringes and drugs and hid them. When the paramedic insisted that they needed to know what Maria had taken if they were to save her life, he ran back and returned with a single used syringe.

That experience got Maria off heroin, but it didn't stop her from shooting up other drugs. She was back running with her old friends and never stopped to think what the repercussions would be for her children.

Family meant a lot to the boys. They split their time between 2727 California, where their mother now lived, and their dad's house, a couple of blocks away. They adopted Frankie Vigil, whose mother was living with Big Dan, as a little brother. Their favorite addition to the family, though, was Francisco Martinez.

"Pancho," as everyone in his family called him, came from a house full of sisters and eagerly assumed the position of long-lost brother to Danny and Antonio. The three were inseparable.

Maria liked to say that Francisco "just kind of showed up one day and never left." She'd barely known his mother, Linda, who was older, from the days before she left for California. But Maria didn't mind. Pancho was a polite, quiet boy and, she soon discovered, liked to keep things neat and tidy. Her own boys were slobs, but Pancho would come over and clean their rooms, even ironing their clothes once they got older and more interested in girls.

Besides, Maria was too busy worrying about her next high to think much about what her kids were doing. It took "divine intervention" to stop her from shooting up. One night, Maria purchased a fifty-dollar bag of cocaine and went to her bedroom, where she'd hidden a brand-new pack of syringes in a box under her bed. She got one out and pulled off the cap that covers the needle, only to find there was no needle to cover. She took out another, and again there was no needle beneath the protective cap. The same was true for every syringe in the package.

Maria had never lost her faith in God. Now she believed the Lord was telling her to quit injecting drugs. She went into the bathroom and poured the cocaine into the toilet.

It was several years before Antonio told her that he, not God, had gone into her bedroom, found her syringes and broken off every needle. Her kids were that desperate to save their mother. But while she would never again resort to needles, Maria continued to get high, especially after she was introduced to the pleasures of smoking crack cocaine.

And that was becoming very easy to find. Like Maria, the old neighborhood had gone downhill. Five Points had fallen on hard times, the nightclubs closed and stores boarded up. Junkies and bums walked the sidewalks past yards and homes that had fallen into disrepair. It wasn't safe to be on the streets at night. And a new threat was just beginning to appear, like the first tiny cells of a cancer. California street gangs selling crack cocaine. Armed and dangerous.

Later, Maria would realize that the drugs hid the fact that her boys were in trouble. The street gangs were metastasizing and in search of new recruits, preferably young ones so they could be indoctrinated early into the gang mentality and commit felonies with relative impunity because of their age.

The three boys—Danny, Antonio, and Pancho—were perfect candidates for the gangs, which appealed to kids by professing to love them more than their own families could. They would die for them, gang members promised, and expected the same sort of unquestioned loyalty in return.

Maria missed the first warning signs. She knew vaguely that Raquel was dating a young black man who had some sort of gang affiliation, but for her, gangs still evoked memories of her youth—nothing too dangerous.

Danny started having trouble at school and was repeatedly suspended for fighting and talking back to teachers. He'd never been a good student, but now every week he stayed home was a week he got further behind his classmates. And Antonio, who loved school and did well, complained that he was having trouble with some of the older kids in the neighborhood on his way to and from Cole Middle School.

Finally, Maria got a sign that even she couldn't miss. Fourteen-year-old Antonio asked her, "If we give you the down payment on a car, can you keep the payments up?"

At the time, Maria was working as a cook at a nightclub that a sister had opened. She often didn't get home until

2 a.m., and the boys worried about her taking the bus that late.

"Where would you get that kind of money?" she demanded.

"Don't worry about where it comes from," he replied.

"No," she said. "I don't want it if I can't understand where you got it."

That opened her eyes to the fact that there was more to all this "Blood this and Blood that" prattle she'd been hearing from the boys, the sort of secret language her grandparents had used when they didn't want her to understand them. She told them they were being brainwashed, but that didn't mean much coming from someone who smoked crack—the very drug that gave the gangs their power.

The boys loved their mother. They would later tell her that one of the things that first attracted them to the gangs was the money, so that they could buy her things. They'd offer her trips, cars, cash. Anything but drugs. They wanted her off the drugs.

Maria realized her sons were right—not just for her sake, but for theirs. If she was going to talk to them, really talk to them, she was going to have to do so from a higher moral ground. So she stopped drinking, stopped smoking crack and pot. She began going to church every day and started trying to learn everything she could about this new type of gang.

The boys had been recruited by Raquel's boyfriend into the Crenshaw Mafia Gangster Bloods run by the Locketts, a family of black brothers who'd immigrated from California and claimed the Park Hill neighborhood. But 2727 California was in the heart of Crips territory, and the Crips were the archenemies of the Bloods. That made her boys targets.

Maria discovered that the gangs tended to recruit boys from families that had some means rather than the homeless or destitute. That way, if the boys were arrested, the parents could pay their bonds. Or if the boys were ripped off for the drugs they were selling for the gangs, they could get their parents to make it up. This lesson she learned firsthand after Danny came to her begging for several hundred dollars. He said he'd been ripped off and was in serious trouble with his gang if he couldn't come up with the money. She gave it to him but said it would be the last time.

Working at night, she found it even harder to keep track of her sons—especially Danny, who began staying out all night. He seemed to have given up on ever being anything but a gang member; he'd fallen so far behind his classmates at school that he dropped out of tenth grade.

Maria would ask Antonio, who preferred to sleep in his own bed, where his brother was. But Antonio always said he didn't know.

She didn't know what to do. She demanded that they stop using gang language in the house and refused to let them listen to rap music that insulted women. "How can you listen to that around me and your sister?" she demanded.

They didn't really have an answer, other than that the music spoke to them about life on the streets. "Things are different now than when you were young," they'd tell her.

Always in the past, she'd been able to talk to her kids. But now all they did was spout gang rhetoric at her. About corrupt cops shaking down gang members ... the brotherhood of Bloods ... an us-against-the-world mentality backed by guns that was particularly frightening when Maria learned her boys had earned nicknames. Bang and Boom—'cause those are the sounds a gun makes.

Maria realized she'd need help if she was going to fight the gangs for her sons. She began attending neighborhood meetings sponsored by the Reverend Leon Kelly, a former convict turned minister who was trying to educate the community about the gangs.

She says she went to every meeting through 1987 and quickly realized that everyone, including the police—

especially the police—had no idea what to do about the problem. Except the one officer who stood up at a meeting and said the department's idea of a solution was to "round them up, put them in Mile High Stadium and shoot them."

It was a big joke, and some in the room even applauded. But Maria was outraged. "Excuse me, but I'm the mother of two gang members," she said. "These people, these Bloods and Crips, moved into Denver and started recruiting our children with their money, and your solution is to corral and shoot them down?"

Los Angeles Police Department gang experts came to some of the meetings. They warned against going after the gangs so hard that they scattered to the suburbs. They were almost apologetic, Maria remembers, about a California program that allowed deferred sentences for gang members provided they leave the state. Many of them had wound up in Denver. The L.A. cops urged everyone at the meetings to learn from their mistakes, to give the kids options and alternatives while they were still young. But Denver wasn't listening.

Maria was often the only parent of gang members at the meetings—at least, the only one who would admit to it. She went to the homes of other parents whose children she knew to be at risk, but had doors—literally and figuratively—slammed in her face. She was ostracized in her own community: Her boys were gangsters, and other families didn't want their children tainted.

She moved to an apartment in Aurora, hoping the distance from 2727 California might make a difference. But the boys just drove to Park Hill. And Danny often stayed with his grandmother, who doted on her grandson.

Maria searched her sons' rooms. When she found drugs, she flushed them down the toilet. When she found guns, she turned them over to Leon Kelly.

"Mom, you can't do that," the boys would complain.

"It's already done," she'd reply.

"Mom, you have to go back and get the gun from Reverend Kelly," they'd demand.

"No," she'd reply. "If you want it, you call him and ask for it back. The gun is gone. The drugs are gone."

But even Kelly disappointed her.

One day he posed with gang members for a photograph that ran on the front page of the Rocky Mountain News to illustrate a story on Denver's growing gang problem. All the other gang members had their faces covered to disguise their identity. But there was Antonio, thirteen years old, grinning like a Cheshire cat for all the world to see.

As she grew increasingly frustrated, Maria began taking more chances. One day she went to the Locketts' house in Park Hill to look for her sons; the mother told her they were at a house three blocks away. As Maria went up to that house, she saw a man being ushered out and money exchanging hands. She knew this was not a safe place to be, and she could see her sons and Pancho through the screen door.

"What the hell is going on?" she demanded, opening the door and walking in. One of the Locketts, his arms as big as hams, looked up in surprise from his chair. Crack cocaine was piled on a table in front of him; an assault rifle lay within easy reach. In fact, everywhere she looked there were guns.

"Let's go," she said to her boys and Francisco, ignoring Lockett's scowl.

"Mom ..," her boys started to protest.

"Don't say a word," she replied grimly. "Go get in the car."

For all their nicknames and growing reputation, Maria's boys weren't about to ignore their mother when she was that angry. They got in the car and let her drive them home.

When she got there, Maria called the police and told them what she had seen. The Locketts were infamous. They'd already had one home seized under public-nuisance statutes for dealing crack. But the officer told her that while they were aware of the current situation, the police had rules they had to follow, and the Locketts didn't.

Maria knew she was losing the war for her sons. Danny, in particular, believed and lived everything he was told by the older members of the CMG. They were family. The cops were the bad guys; women were "bitches" and "hos." Only Bloods could be trusted.

Finally, Maria had heard enough and threw Danny out of the house. In the days that followed, she tried not to think about what he was doing, how he was surviving. Then one evening, Antonio came to her and said, "Mom, you have to go get him."

Danny was living in a motel room on Colfax Avenue, a 9mm handgun on the nightstand, selling drugs for the gang; it was only a matter of time before the police or someone else got to him. Maria wouldn't pick him up, but she told Antonio that Danny could come home.

She had little hope that she could save Danny, but she still thought Antonio might make it. Her younger son had always had big plans. He was going to be an artist, attend college, maybe draw for Disney someday. He knew that to pursue those plans, he had to stay in school.

That wasn't easy, especially because he, too, was proud of his gang affiliation. He'd get expelled for wearing red shoestrings or a red hat, or for throwing gang signs. But he'd always come home and talk to his mother. "Tell them they have to let me back in," he'd insist. And soon Antonio would be back in the classroom.

Antonio managed to stay out of any major trouble until a few days after his fifteenth birthday. But on March 26, 1989, he shot another boy in the alley behind 2727 California. It was Easter Sunday.

CHAPTER EIGHT

January 7, 1998

"When you hear what happened to Brandy DuVall ... the way she was killed and the way she was raped ... it is a natural human reaction to cry out for vengeance."

Randy Canney faces the jury, knowing that he is walking a tightrope on behalf of his client. A criminal defense lawyer for ten years, Canney has never before had a first-degree-murder case. He'd once plea-bargained a death-penalty case—a gang shooting—down to forty-eight years. But this was different, very different.

"But there is only one defendant sitting here: Frank Vigil Jr.," Canney says, pointing to his client. "Frank Vigil did not kill Brandy DuVall. And there is nothing in the evidence you will hear to suggest he did."

Jeffco DA Dave Thomas had opted not to seek the death penalty in this case, primarily because of Vigil's age. But if Canney lost, Frank would spend the rest of his life in prison. No parole. And life in a maximum-security prison was a long, long time for someone not yet old enough to vote.

Canney had always wanted to be a criminal defense lawyer; he liked the idea of fighting for the underdog against the state. His first obligation was to make the state prosecutors prove their case, but he felt his job went further than that. It was up to him to paint his client as a human being, not a monster. And if the government's facts were overwhelming, to find mitigating factors that would explain why a sixteen-year-old boy would have participated in something so sick and brutal.

Circumstances. The word haunts Canney. What circumstances led Frank Vigil to be in that house that night?

"Frank Vigil did not rape Brandy DuVall. There is no credible evidence that he had any sexual contact with her," he continues.

It was Frank Vigil's age that first struck Canney when he was appointed to the case in June 1997. After hearing some of what had happened to Brandy DuVall, he had expected to find some hardened gang member. But what he saw was a scared kid.

It was even hard to deal with the family. Absolutely horrifying to speak to a mother who knew she would probably never see her teenage son in her home again. He had tried to find a balance when talking to Lisa Vigil, a balance that would offer some hope while also making it clear that there wasn't much.

And his work in the courtroom would be another balancing act. What had happened to the girl was horrible; Canney needed to convince the jury that Frank, as the smallest and youngest gang member present, was less involved and, in fact, afraid to speak up or try to stop the brutality.

"He was not the one who picked her up and brought her to the house," Canney tells the jury. "He was not the one who gave her cocaine."

This was another fine line. His client was charged with first-degree murder, sexual assault, sexual assault on a child, assault, and kidnapping. Mere presence at the house wasn't enough to convict him of first-degree murder. But if the jury believed Frank Vigil had participated in any way in the felonies leading up to her death, the way Colorado law read, he was just as guilty as whoever plunged the knife into her neck.

Their only chance, he figured, was to attack the credibility of the defense witnesses, particularly Uncle Joe and Zig Zag. Both would claim that Frank had been the first to urge the others to silence Brandy by killing her. Canney would have to impeach them as liars.

Now, he cautions the jury that when the prosecution presented its case, to "remember where it comes from. For the prosecution to say that these people are not 'angels' makes them guilty of an unbelievable understatement. There is no physical evidence and no reliable witnesses that prove Frank Vigil committed a crime."

It was not some accident that the gang members showed up at Uncle Joe's that night, Canney says. "He is the uncle of Danny Martinez, who was on the run from the law, and he knew that." Nor was it the first time that a similar gang rape had taken place at the home of Uncle Joe, "who got his cocaine from the gang."

Jose Martinez's role bothered Canney tremendously. So many adults could have stopped what happened to Brandy DuVall. The defendant's family, by keeping him away from bad influences. Even the victim's family, by insisting that a fourteen-year-old girl belonged at home in her bed instead of wandering the streets—although he couldn't say that in court without inviting a backlash from the jury.

But Uncle Joe was there. He should have stopped them.

Sammy Quintana was another gem. Admitting to some things but making everyone else look worse than himself. "The prosecution says they'll be asking for ninety-six years. What they forgot to tell you," Canney says, letting a hint of sarcasm slip into his voice, "was he could get as little as forty-eight."

Quintana, he notes, had killed two girls. "In the summer of 1996, Sammy Quintana and a cohort set out to kill a drug snitch, Salvino Martinez," he explains. "Instead, they shot an innocent girl, Venus Montoya."

Canney knew he would have to watch overplaying Quintana's gang activities. That could backfire, since Frank had hung around with these guys voluntarily. Circumstances again. The kid of a single mom. Where was he going to find someone to look up to for strength and protection? It sure as hell wasn't the high-school basketball coach.

The other prosecution witnesses, Canney says, are liars, all liars. When they had to point a finger to save themselves, they pointed it at Frank Vigil, the one they weren't afraid of.

And there are two important witnesses the jurors will not hear from because they are also defendants, Canney points out. Danny Martinez Jr., "the biggest boss," and Francisco Martinez, "who was sicker than anyone can imagine." Bang, Pancho, and Zig Zag were all in their mid-twenties and larger than his client. "Frank Vigil could not have stopped anyone."

"You remember that in *voir dire*, I told you that my great fear was the sheer horror of what happened to Brandy DuVall would make you want to take it out on someone," Canney says, laying it on thick now. "I trust you will not take it out on an innocent sixteen-year-old, who did not commit any crimes."

CHAPTER NINE

Summer 1998

Antonio "Boom" Martinez sits on the porch of 2727 California, a little white house with green trim, fondly looking over the neighborhood that he, his brother, and Pancho claimed as their own. As he remembers it, a bastion of Bloods in the middle of a sea of Crips.

"I loved hanging out over here," he says. "I know we did a lot of bad shit. But I have a lot of good memories about the way things were."

Twenty-three-year-old Antonio is short, barrel-chested, and thick-shouldered; his dark hair has been shorn to a boot-camp stubble. Considering his tough reputation on these streets, his face can be surprisingly soft, with large, doe-like eyes, long lashes, and a smile as white and perfect as a full moon.

But when he's angry, or simply recalling an event that made him angry, those eyes turn hard, almost brittle with suggested violence. The smile may remain, but it loses its warmth and gains a ferocity.

Maybe this face is a mask, something he puts on now that he's chosen to go defenseless in a world where some are still gunning for him.

Maybe not.

Antonio's hands, too, are softer than you'd expect for a street gangster. But then, he's an artist, and his hands are his tools. When he talks about his wilder days, he holds his arms akimbo, his palms up and slightly curled as if loosely holding handguns. A gangster pose. He slips easily into gang slang. Profane. Arrogant. More of the "hooked-on-ebonics" of black gangs than the singsong lilt of the old *cholo* Mexican gangs.

But when he talks about his art, or his daughter or girlfriend, or what he wants to do with his life, he is well spoken and engaging. Confidence replaces arrogance. As he says with what his mother calls his Kool-Aid grin, "I can be pretty charming when I want to—especially with the girls."

He's only a few months shy of graduating from the Colorado Institute of Art. As soon as he's out, he hopes to leave the state and its memories, good and bad, and head to a city further west, where a friend has promised to set him up in a state-of-the-art tattoo studio.

Antonio still considers himself a Bloods gang member; he's just no longer committing crimes. He's a hardworking (two jobs), tax-paying citizen with big plans. He's getting on with life—but he can't leave all of the memories behind.

His earliest are of being with his older brother, Danny. Always together, through thick and thin.

Once, when they were living with their mother and Bill Rollins in a California apartment complex, Antonio was standing next to his brother while Danny threw rocks into the complex's hot tub, clogging the drain. The manager appeared and, seizing the boys by their thin arms, dragged them home. Their stepfather apologized and said it wouldn't happen again. Then he spanked both boys.

Although he'd had no part in the rock throwing, Antonio wouldn't snitch on his brother to escape punishment. "That's the way we were," Antonio says. "We always took our lickings together."

Even if Antonio had told on his brother, he wouldn't be saying anything new. Although everyone loved Danny, they all knew he was a troublemaker.

"I used to steal *Playboy* from my stepfather," says Antonio. "I was only six or maybe seven." He laughs. "I always had a thing for naked women." He hid the magazines under a toy box.

Antonio came home from school one day and heard his mother talking to one of her friends on the telephone. He realized she'd found the magazines while cleaning his room. "It has to be Danny," he heard her say. "He's girl crazy."

Danny never denied it. "All of our lives we took the blame for each other," Antonio says. "We got into trouble together, and we either got out of trouble together, or we didn't get out of trouble, period."

Except this time. Thinking about where his brother is now, awaiting trial for first-degree murder, Antonio grows silent. Stepping away from the gang life when he saw the "craziness" escalating was one of the hardest things he'd ever had to do. Now he's tormented by the thought that if he'd stayed at Uncle Joe's that night, he might have saved them all. Maybe. Maybe not.

Growing up, Danny always wanted to be the leader. "He was charismatic and a good athlete," Antonio recalls. "I always wanted to be with him. We'd be together so much that sometimes people thought we were twins."

Although that was fine with Antonio, it was important to Danny that people knew he was the older of the two—that Antonio was his little brother, a tagalong.

When their mom and Bill broke up, Antonio was lost. "He was the only dad I knew," he says. "I liked him. But he had us call him 'Bill.' He said, 'They know who their father is.'

"One minute, Bill was in my life. He was the guy who spanks you when you did something bad. The guy who buys you toys, who takes you fishing and sees that we have a place to live. Then he was gone, and I didn't see him anymore. What kind of sense is that?"

With Bill gone, Danny became more than a big brother. Even though the boys were sent back to Denver to live with their father, Big Dan, who was living with his parents, "Danny was my father," Antonio says.

Antonio rarely spent any time with Big Dan. "He'd come by and get Danny. I guess it was because he was Danny 'Junior' and sort of knew him before him and mom split up. Me, I was just some kid his old lady had after she left him. In some ways it was depressing," he admits. "I used to wonder, 'How come I never get to go?'"

But on the rare occasion when their father took both boys, Antonio would usually wonder why he'd wanted to go so desperately. "It wasn't like we'd get to be with just him," he recalls. "There was always one of his girlfriends along, and she was always a bitch to the kids. Danny always seemed to have fun with him. But I had more fun with my grandma and grandpa."

And there was always his maternal grandmother at 2727 California to turn to as well. She spoiled the boys, who could do no wrong. The only things the boys didn't like was when she and other relatives would say mean things about their mother, how she wasn't a good mom. That made them cry.

Antonio looks at the house. He notes that the row of bullet holes made when a rival gang fired an assault rifle at the house have been well patched. "You can hardly tell where they were," he says. "Shit, we used to come out of the house some mornings and see a new hole and say, 'Damn. I never even heard the shot.' Guess we kind of got used to getting shot at."

Antonio's first experience with gangs came when they were still living in California. Danny was in a breakdancing group that competed once a week at the local skating rink and, as usual, Antonio would tag along to watch.

One weekend, their friends brought Willy, a black kid just out of juvenile hall. A red bandanna protruded from Willy's back pocket, but Antonio didn't know what it meant.

Another teen did, and he went to call some Crip friends. He told them there was a Blood in town.

A little while later, several teenagers appeared in the parking lot. "They showed the security guard they had a gun, and he came in—didn't call the police—but told us, 'If you're smart, you'll stay inside.'"

But Willy was already outside, checking out the action. Realizing the spot he was in, he took off across the parking lot. "Someone let off a shot," Antonio says. It was his first taste of gunfire.

"Danny and me and our friends were scared," he recalls. "We didn't want to go outside, but we knew we would eventually have to leave, so we went together."

On the way home, they ran across a terrorized-but-safe Willy. "I was thinking, 'Over a red rag? They'll come down here and shoot someone over the color of their bandanna? What kind of fuckin' sense does that make?'"

By the time the boys got back to Denver from California, the gangs were here, too. And they started looking good when Maria moved back home, hooked on drugs. "Life got really shitty," Antonio says. "She'd make dinner and clean the house, but that was about it. I realized that if I wanted something, I was going to have to get it on my own."

A psychologist would one day say that Antonio got involved in gangs because of repressed anger over his mother abandoning him. "That wasn't true," he says. "She was absent a lot of it, but we made our own choices, because it seemed like fun. By the time she knew what was going on, we were too far gone.

"I was like any other thirteen- or fourteen-year-old. You couldn't tell me shit. She'd try to tell us that what we were doing was wrong. But I was like, 'You ain't been livin' right all your life. Don't tell me how to live mine.'"

Gang activity was still pretty loose, Antonio remembers. "The neighborhoods in Denver weren't saturated with gangs, or at least they weren't in control. They were pretty scattered, even on the east side and Park Hill. Fuller Park was the only really established gang territory." Park Hill wasn't "consolidated" by the CMG Bloods until 1987.

That was the year that Danny and Antonio officially joined the gang. But because their sister was dating a Blood and because they were "Mexican kids," they'd already been having constant run-ins with the older Crips and younger Crip-wannabes.

The cops were of no help. "They wrote us off," Antonio says bitterly. "The police knew I was in trouble when I was twelve, but none of the motherfuckers would help. Not an offer of a ride. No one said, 'Hey, I'll watch your back so you can get to school and back home safe.'"

Antonio shrugs. It probably wouldn't have made a difference, "but they didn't even try. If they had tried, then maybe in some later year, I would have been able to say, 'Yeah, there are some who cared.' But I can't."

The way he explains it, he practically joined the Bloods out of spite. When he was twelve, Antonio's favorite football player was Brian Bozworth, who played for the University of Oklahoma. The school's colors were white and red.

For Christmas that year, a relative bought him a red jersey with Bozworth's number on it. He proudly wore it to school. "The Crips were all over me because I liked a particular player who went to a school that wore the color red," he recalls. "I decided, 'Too bad.' I didn't feel like I should have to explain why I was wearing a Brian Bozworth shirt. I told them, 'Fuck you, I don't like you anyway.'"

After that, joining the Bloods and wearing a red bandanna was easy.

"When she found out we were in a gang, Mom freaked out," Antonio remembers. "But we had been around drugs and guns and crime all of our lives, except when we were with Bill. But she got scared, 'cause now we were in it. She was terrified that her sons were now part of all this."

Antonio's mom wasn't the only one who worried. Their cousin, Sammy Quintana, was no longer allowed to visit or spend the night. His parents had built a nice, comfortable life for themselves and their kids, and they didn't want Sammy, a soccer star at school, hanging around with troublemakers.

One day, John Quintana gave Danny and Antonio a warning. "If I ever see you at my jail, you better act like you don't know me. Because that's where you're headed."

If they didn't have Sammy for company anymore, the brothers found someone they liked even better: Francisco Martinez. "He liked hanging around us because girls were always coming over to see Raquel or me and Danny," Antonio says. "He hardly ever went home. Sometimes his mom would get the police to pick him up. He'd go home only long enough to shower, change his clothes, and then he'd be right back.

"He was always straight up with me and Danny. He would tell you exactly what he thought and never lied." Antonio says, then reconsiders. "Except to girls."

The brothers never begrudged Sammy all his advantages. "But we had nothing better to do than be bad," Antonio says before laughing. Even his heroes weren't the regular sort. "I used to tell my mom that I wanted to grow up to be a hit man. I was fascinated with the whole gangster life. I read books about Lucky Luciano, Al Capone, Sam Giancanna, and Carlos Gambino.

"They were my idols. But I wasn't Italian, so I couldn't be in the Mob. I did the next closest thing. I joined a street gang."

Antonio and Danny had been in the gang only two weeks when they were given their first gun, a .22-caliber pistol. "We convinced them that we were willin' to use it. And they were just as enthused—'Hey, some juveniles willin' to shoot.' The violence in Denver was just starting to surface. I think we had a lot to do with that."

Antonio says this with pride. "Part of it was puttin' on a show. We were always smaller than other boys, but we would fight, and now we could back it up with a gun. We got a reputation as being willing to shoot."

Standing in the front yard of an old gang battle zone, Antonio strikes a gangster pose. "If you're not willin' to shoot, then get out of my face," he tells an imaginary enemy, "because I'll kill ya, and I don't care. I got nothin' going for me."

The boys were "beat in" to the gang after their first couple of drive-by shootings. "It was pretty mellow," Antonio says. "I didn't get the ass-whuppin' I should have and have given to others myself."

They already had their nicknames. "Bang and Boom, because that's the sound a gun makes," he says. "We'd already proved ourselves as soldiers, willing to be violent and 'down' for the cause. Willing to do dirt, including shoot people."

But there was more to it than gunplay. In California they'd seen older kids who had things—cars, money, girls—because they were dealing drugs. They wanted some of that for themselves, and also to buy their mother the things she could never afford. Not that she'd take them once she knew the boys were in a gang.

The CMG leadership started giving the Martinez brothers drugs to deal. They defended their turf with bravado and bullets. "You could come buy from us," he says, "but otherwise, you were not welcome on our block. Everyone else was older and bigger, but the word was out that 'them little fuckin' Mexican kids had guns and would shoot.'

"I wasn't stupid about it. I mean, I've seen guys who get all macho and shit and stand there in the middle of the fuckin' street, guns blazing away like they think they're fuckin' John Wayne or something. Those guys usually leave in an ambulance.

"I didn't want to get shot. I might have placed myself in the position to get shot, but when I heard a gun go off, I ducked—and lived to fight another day."

The brothers' reputation grew to the point that every time there was a shooting in the neighborhood, the police blamed it on Bang and Boom. "Sometimes it wasn't even us that did it," Antonio says and grins. "We kind of became established as 'the usual suspects.'"

It was all a big, dangerous game, and they were never caught. Until Easter Sunday 1989.

Raquel, Antonio, and their mother went over to 2727 California to take their grandmother on a picnic; Danny was already living there most of the time. Pancho had dropped by, and he and Antonio were standing in the alley behind the house when they saw three Crips approaching.

The Crips usually knew better than to traipse through the boys' neighborhood. (These three later told police that they were late to a picnic themselves and taking a shortcut.) But to Antonio, they didn't seem to be in a hurry to get somewhere else. "They came lookin' for trouble—and they found it."

The boys flashed gang signs at each other. A challenge. The three Crips were older and bigger, and Danny was in the house. But the other two held their ground.

"They were talkin' shit," Antonio recalls, walking over to the side yard to re-enact the drama. "One put his hand under the baggy T-shirt he was wearing, up near his waistband, as if he had a gun.

"Well, I had a .45 stashed under the trash dumpster," he says, pointing to where a dumpster still stands. "So I bent over and got the gun and says, 'Yeah, muthafucka? Wassup? You think this is a game? Well, if you're carryin', pull your strap and make this a gunfight. I'd like that better.' They took off running."

One of the Crips was trying to climb over a fence when Antonio pointed the gun at him. "I didn't aim—I just let off a shot."

Antonio giggles at the memory. "He caught a hot one in the ass."

The police arrived and forced Antonio and Pancho to the ground, stepping on their necks to keep them from moving as they pressed shotguns against their skulls. They dragged Danny out of the house while photographers snapped away. Danny's photograph would appear on the front page of the *Rocky Mountain News* the next morning, even though the police had already released him by then.

Antonio and Pancho were not so lucky. "To me, I thought it was cool," Antonio says. "I didn't care about the arrest. I know it sounds stupid now, but I was excited that it was going to be on the news and everyone would know I shot a Crab."

It got less exciting fast when Antonio learned that he might be tried as an adult and could face as much as forty years in prison. "I thought gangs were cool," he says. "I got so involved, I was in so deep, that when it stopped being cool, there was no way out."

He stops. Watches a car with tinted windows drive past. Only after it's gone does he relax. "My mom and grandma prayed a lot for Danny and me."

CHAPTER TEN

January 7, 1998

"The people call Angela Metzger."

At those words from prosecutor Mark Randall, Angela rises from her seat in the spectator gallery and makes her way up to the witness stand. She raises her right hand and swears to tell the truth.

She is wearing a black dress. A reminder to everyone in the courtroom that she is still in mourning.

"How is it that you know Brandy DuVall?" Randall asks.

"Brandy's my daughter," she replies, using the present tense.

"Can you give us her full name and date of birth?"

"It's Brandaline Rose DuVall. She was born July 28, 1982."

Randall holds up a photograph and asks Angela to identify the girl pictured in it.

"It's Brandy," she says quietly, as the first tear appears on her cheek.

On May 30, 1997, Brandy was "real excited" about moving with her mother to a new apartment the next day.

"How did Brandy travel?" Randall asks.

"By bus, or she would call me or my brother or her brother—someone to come and get her," she replies. "But most of the time by bus."

"Would days go by where you would not hear from her?" Randall asks.

"Never," Angela replies. Usually no more than an hour or two would go by without Brandy checking in.

"Was she in the habit of staying out all night?"

"Rarely. She liked to sleep at home."

Brandy had paged her that afternoon, soon after Angela got off work. She wanted to go shopping at the mall and needed money.

They met two blocks from Angela's mother's house. "She was very happy. She looked beautiful." Now the tears begin in earnest.

After Angela gave her the money, Brandy had reached into her uncle's car and "grabbed me around the neck real hard and said, 'Thanks, Mom.'"

Angela tries to continue, but she can't speak. She takes a moment, then goes on. "I said, *'You're welcome, baby.'*"

Brandy started to walk away but suddenly turned back. "'I love you, Mom. I love you, Uncle.' She was bouncy, in a good mood."

Angela takes a deep breath. "It was the last time I ever seen her."

At the defense table, Frank Vigil looks up briefly, then back down at the table. Spectators are sniffling on the other side of the aisle. Brandy's grandmother, Rose, is crying, her thin shoulders shaking.

Randall asks how Brandy was dressed. He needs Angela to explain why her daughter was wearing a red basketball jersey that might attract gang members like sharks to blood.

Her daughter liked to play basketball, she explains, "and Michael Jordan was her idol. She got the shirt from her dad, who lives in Phoenix."

"When did you think something was wrong?" Randall asks.

"The next day."

Angela had tried to page her daughter, but there was no response. She tried friends, but no one knew where Brandy was.

At last, twenty-four hours after she'd last seen her, Angela had reported her daughter missing to the police in

Jefferson County and Denver. The next morning, Sunday, the newspaper had an article about an unidentified body found in Clear Creek.

Angela had called the Jeffco coroner. After she described Brandy, she was told to come down to the office. With fear clutching at her like a drowning man, she arrived at the coroner's office. "They told me to come downstairs, where they showed me her jewelry."

Randall holds up a plastic Baggie and hands it to Angela. She opens it and takes out a ring, tries it on. "It's a 'B' ring," she says at last, her voice quavering. "She never took it off."

It's the first time she's seen it since that terrible day at the coroner's office. When she saw it then, she had hoped against hope that her daughter had been robbed. That whoever waited to be identified had stolen these things from her daughter.

But then they had taken Angela to another room and asked her to look through a glass partition. A body bag was unzipped, a face was revealed. *Wake up, baby. Wake up.*

"Who did you see?" Randall asks, as gently as a question like that can be asked.

"It was Brandy," she says, weeping.

Randall takes his seat. Canney has no questions. A mother's grief is left to wash back and forth across the silent courtroom like a scream off canyon walls.

CHAPTER ELEVEN

Summer 1998

Maria Simpson looks at the simple two-story house at 2727 California without much affection.

An uncle she never knew purchased it for his parents, her grandparents, shortly before he died in action during World War II. It was the childhood home of her mother, aunts, and uncles. The address is on her birth certificate and on those of her first and third children, Raquel and Antonio. She was living two blocks away, across the street from her in-laws, when her second, Danny, was born. But he, too, considered this home.

It seems she has spent her life trying to escape from 2727 California. At age sixteen, marrying Danny Martinez Sr. to get out of the house. Moving to California with her second husband, Bill. Moving away again after she ruined that marriage with her drug habit, trying to get her sons away from the gangs.

But something always brought her back. Usually something to do with her sons.

After fifteen-year-old Antonio shot another boy on Easter Sunday 1989 in the alley behind 2727 California, Maria moved back in to live with her mother and seventeen-year-old Danny. She didn't want to, but it was the only way she could keep an eye on her older son.

Danny wouldn't leave—not even after the shooting. It didn't matter that the place was surrounded by Crips, like a fort in a John Wayne western. His grandmother always let him do anything he wanted, bought whatever he asked for. And if Maria complained, her mother would tell her in front of the boys, "You were just as wild when you were young. Leave them alone and they'll grow out of it."

Following their grandmother's lead, Boom and Bang would throw Maria's past mistakes back in her face whenever she tried to lecture them about the gangs. No one seemed to understand that they might not live to grow out of their affiliation with the Bloods—and if they did, it might be behind prison walls.

Even after his arrest, Antonio couldn't seem to grasp reality. "We don't go running to the police every time they shoot at us," he complained. "They shoot at us all the time."

"Why do you think that they're all like you?" Maria retorted angrily. "All this macho, bullshit gang stuff about not snitching. You shot him, Antonio. Why'd you shoot him?"

Antonio just shrugged. The Crips had come up on him and Pancho and threatened them. If he'd backed down, standing in the yard of his own grandmother's house, it would have been seen as weakness. And weakness could get you killed in that neighborhood.

But now Antonio was facing the possibility of being tried as an adult for attempted murder, which carried the possibility of forty years in prison. The police and courts were trying to crack down on gang violence; they'd threatened to make an example of Antonio.

Antonio wasn't the only son she had to worry about. Danny drank a lot—never just a beer or two, always to the point where he was falling-down drunk and sick. He wasn't a mean drunk, just a sloppy one, and Maria was afraid it would destroy him someday. Maybe sooner than later. But there was no talking to him—not about his lifestyle, not about the danger. Even if she found his drugs and flushed them down the toilet, he just hid them better the next time.

Danny was using the house at 2727 California to sell crack cocaine to the addicts who'd wander over from Five

Points. At night they'd come stumbling to the back of the house and whistle. Danny would go to the door and look out to see who they were, then meet them out there in the dark.

"I don't know how many times I tried to tell him, 'Danny, somebody whistles, and you go stand in the door with the light on behind you. What's to keep the Crips from figuring that out and setting you up?'" Maria says, sitting on the porch of 2727 California. "He'd say, 'That's not gonna happen, Mom.'"

She pauses, looks at the large picture window that dominates the front of the house, sees it not as it is but cracked and punctured by bullet holes. "Nothing could hurt him ... yeah."

On the night of June 18, 1989, Maria was in her second-floor bedroom, thinking about Antonio: His public defenders had finally convinced him to plead guilty, saying that as a juvenile with no prior convictions, he'd probably get probation. Sentencing was set for the next morning.

Maria's youngest brother, Jimmy, was asleep on the couch downstairs, his children, Matt and Lisa, nestled into blankets on the floor beside him. Danny was on the telephone in the bedroom next to hers. It was a warm night and she had her window open—and she could hear voices in the side yard. She figured soon there'd be a whistle from below, and Danny would hang up the phone and attend to business.

Suddenly, gunshots—five loud bangs and booms—followed by a high-pitched scream.

Maria hurried down to the living room. "Jimmy, did you hear that?" she yelled.

"Yes," he answered weakly.

She turned on the lights. The picture window had a large crack running through it; five holes had appeared in the pane. She realized then that it was Jimmy who had screamed. He lay on the couch, wearing only his pants, and blood was everywhere. He'd been shot in both arms, both legs and once in the abdomen. Every time his heart beat, blood spurted from the stomach wound.

Danny rushed into the room and scooped up Jimmy's terrified children. He ran upstairs and hid them under a bed in case the shooters returned. Maria's mother took one look and hid in the laundry room, where she ran around in little circles, crying.

Maria rode with Jimmy to the hospital. Although her brother's scream kept reverberating in her mind, all she could think was: *They were trying to kill my son. They thought Jimmy was Danny. They wanted to kill my son.*

The next day, Maria attended Antonio's sentencing. He was given two years at the Lookout Mountain juvenile detention center.

Still sleepless, Maria returned to 2727 California and worked with Danny to clean up the blood. But for a case of mistaken identity, she kept thinking, on this day she could have had one son in the hospital fighting for his life, the other incarcerated. Her worst fears were coming true, and she had no idea what to do about it.

The boys' father, Danny Martinez Sr., was no help. Under a variety of aliases, he's been arrested thirty-one times—beginning with simple assault in 1974 and then going on to seven more assaults, five driving-under-the-influence citations, burglary, drug charges, auto theft, and weapons charges.

"He was as much a part of the gangster lifestyle as they were," Maria says. His nickname, "Bird-dog," was "as familiar on the streets as 'Boom' and 'Bang.' He never tried to stop them; he went right along with them."

Maria called Bill Rollins, her ex-husband in California, and explained the situation. Despite their breakup, they'd remained friends, and she knew he still cared about the boys. Bill suggested that she send Danny to him.

Surprisingly, Danny went without much fuss. He knew as well as she did that the bullets had been meant for him. And the only two members of his gang he could count on to watch his back—Antonio and Pancho—were locked up at Lookout Mountain.

Jimmy survived his injuries, but Maria's mother never returned to 2727 California. She said she couldn't stay there, not with the memory of her son's life spurting out of him. She moved in with another daughter and had the house boarded up. She said she was going to get rid of it.

When Danny and Antonio heard about their grandmother's intentions from their sister, they begged her not to sell the house. It was the closest thing to a permanent address they'd ever known; it was their house. "If you don't want it, give it to our mother," they said.

After their grandmother gave in, they called Maria. "Grandma says you can have the house if you want it."

Maria didn't want it. There'd been too much blood. Too many shots and sirens. But her sons begged and pleaded, promising to turn their lives around, to get out of the gang. So, Maria agreed to keep 2727 California.

She glances at the new picture window. Her reflection stares back. "It took me a lot of years to get the sound of Jimmy's scream out of my head." She shakes her head. "I hate this house ... yeah."

CHAPTER TWELVE

January 14, 1998

Before they begin their deliberations, the jurors in the trial of Frank "Little Bang" Vigil Jr. observe a moment of silence for the murdered girl, Brandaline Rose DuVall.

Never in their worst imaginings, not even after warnings from both the prosecutors and defense attorneys at jury selection, did the four women and eight men expect to hear anything so grim.

* * *

"Pancho, he told Danny Boy to get out of the way and put that broom in her butt. He was laughing. She was crying, 'It hurts, don't do that.'"

During a break in Jose "Uncle Joe" Martinez's testimony, the jury didn't witness Brandy's grandmother, Rose Vasquez, moaning in the hallway outside the courtroom—"Oh, dear God, dear God"—as her family tried to dissuade her from going back in to skip the rest of his bizarre, nauseating, podium-pounding account of the gang rape of fourteen-year-old Brandy. "There was blood everywhere. ... I thought the bitch was on the rag."

Rose had waved them off. Brandy was her youngest granddaughter; they had been particularly close. She had to be there, no matter how much it hurt.

But day after day, the jurors couldn't help but see the grieving family weeping in the front rows as the prosecution paraded its witnesses—dressed in jail jumpsuits, handcuffs, and shackles—in and out of the courtroom.

The gang members who'd found the girl at a bus stop on South Federal Boulevard a little before midnight on May 30, 1997, and invited her to a party: the Warren brothers, David and Maurice, and Jacob "Smiley" Casados. They had all pleaded guilty to first-degree sexual assault and agreed to testify in exchange for first-degree-murder charges being dropped.

As well as Sammy "Zig Zag" Quintana, who'd pleaded guilty to two second-degree-murder charges for the same deal. In a month he'd be taking the stand again, this time against Alejandro "Speed" Ornelas for the murder of another girl, Venus Montoya, a year earlier.

"I did not look at her face. I didn't know her name," Quintana had testified.

"What was she to you that night?" Deputy District Attorney Hal Sargent asked. "What was she to your gang?"

"She was a girl that supposedly was going to be down to screw everybody."

"You care much about what she thought that night?"

Quintana shrugged and shook his head. "Other people took control of that situation if she didn't want to. We were all in agreement to take her out."

"When you say 'take her out,' you're not talking about taking her someplace?" Sargent clarified. "You're talking about killing her?"

Quintana nodded. "Not out to dinner."

"What do you think about your role in the killing of a fourteen-year-old girl?"

"I'm guilty," Quintana said, as he tried to wipe tears from his face with his manacled hands.

"How does that make you feel?"

"Shouldn't have happened," he said, his voice hardly louder than the sounds of sorrow in the gallery.

And finally, there was Jose Martinez, the uncle of Daniel Martinez Jr., who'd be tried later for the same crime. He testified as Vigil's family, his friends from the old neighborhood around 27th and California, glared at him. "They was possessed by the fuckin' devil," he told the jurors.

Although Judge Michael Villano admonished Jose to quit the theatrics and just answer the questions, he managed to squeeze out some tears as he described how much he loved "little Frankie." Then he accused the same "little Frankie," as had all the others, of being the first to say that Brandy must die.

"Where was Little Bang?"

"Standing there, laughing, like this was a big old fuckin' joke."

But in the end, Frank Vigil sealed his own fate—with a letter he'd written from his jail cell to Antonio Martinez before the trial:

Hey dog wats up. ... I guess that bitch ass nigger Zig is tryin' to pin that other shit on Speed. He's trying to sing. I'm the one going out like a trix-ass bitch, Blood. I'm a real nigga like you and Pancho.

I gest that only God can judge me now. ... This is still Westside till I die.

Lil Bang

Defense attorney Randy Canney called no witnesses. There was no one who'd been at the house that night left to dispute the claim that his client had been the first to suggest they kill the girl.

In closing, he could argue only that sixteen-year-old Frank Vigil was too drunk and too intimidated by the bigger, older members of the Deuce-Seven Crenshaw Mafia Gangster Bloods to try to stop what happened. That the prosecution witnesses were lying to "save their own skins." That the prosecutors had "cut deals and brought five witnesses in here while truth and justice went out the door."

But in his closing, Deputy District Attorney Mark Randall countered: "Frank Vigil was not afraid of them; he is one of them. In his letter, he proclaims himself a Blood. He's protecting the organization. 'I'm a real nigger, like you and Pancho.'"

* * *

It takes the jury less than six hours to reject Canney's assertions. As they shuffle back into the courtroom one last time, many of the jurors are in tears. They gaze sympathetically at Brandy's family and avoid looking at Frank Vigil, who sits staring at the table in front of him, pale and mute. He lifts his head only when the judge asks for the verdict forms.

"In regard to counts one and two ... first-degree murder ... guilty," Villano says.

Brandy's mother, Angela Metzger, stifles a sob and buries her face in her hands. Rose Vasquez cries quietly, her shoulders quivering as her husband, Paul, puts an arm around her and wipes at his own eyes with his other hand.

Across the aisle, Frank Vigil's mother, Lisa, fights to maintain her composure while tears roll down her cheeks. Other family members and friends cry out and collapse in each other's arms.

Then, strangely, Frank Vigil turns to the jury and begins to smile and nod. Is he frightened and trying not to show it, as his lawyer thinks? Or is this his idea of going out like a "trix ass bitch?"

CHAPTER THIRTEEN

Summer 1998

While Antonio was locked up at Lookout Mountain, Maria remembers, she visited him at least once a week. She'd come to realize that only at Lookout, under her friend Lonnie Lynn's watchful eye, was her son able to finally just be a boy.

She'd never forget the day she arrived and saw Antonio outside playing. He looked so young and carefree, running back and forth across the field, yelling and laughing with boys he'd probably exchanged bullets with on the outside. *This is the way it's supposed to be*, she'd thought.

Maria had met Lynn, a six-foot, nine-inch former pro-basketball player, several years before when she was working as a cook. At the time, she'd asked him to speak to her sons, particularly fourteen-year-old Danny, who was getting in trouble at school. But it hadn't done much good. There'd been too little of Lonnie Lynn in their lives, just as there'd been too little of Bill Rollins and far too much gang pressure. *We're your family. We're your homeboys. We're the ones you can trust. Who else is going to give you the means to money, hos, and clothes?*

After Antonio was sentenced, Maria had again called on Lynn, now a counselor at Lookout, and begged him to watch out for her boy.

The first reports from Lynn were frightening. The Crips at the detention center outnumbered the Bloods two to one, and they were waiting for Antonio. "Hey, there's the motherfucker who shot our homeboy!" someone yelled when they brought him through the gates in handcuffs and shackles. The boys inside the dormitories had begun beating on their windows. "It sounded like a storm," Lynn told her. "'We gonna git you, Boom.'"

But Lynn, who'd started Lookout's first gang counseling group to find common ground between Bloods and Crips, skinheads and blacks, arranged a truce. And so, Antonio had quietly done his thirteen months, going to class every day and working on his art.

Danny, too, was doing better. Living with Bill, he'd even received his high-school equivalency degree. But Danny got homesick and returned to Denver when Pancho was getting out of Lookout Mountain in early summer 1990.

When Danny enrolled at the Colorado Institute of Art to study broadcast journalism, Maria dared to hope. He had always been a people person with a gift for gab; she even secured a federal grant to help him pay for school. But before she could put it in his bank account, she had to send it back: Danny had dropped out of school.

His girlfriend, Terry, was pregnant with twins. Her family thought the right thing for him to do was to go to work to support their children. So he got a job working as a busboy, but that didn't last long. There was more money in dealing drugs.

"He had the connections," Maria recalls. "Even when he'd say, 'Okay, that's the last one, I'm not doing this anymore,' there'd be a telephone call for 'just one more time.' It was appealing—go pick something up from Point A and deliver it to Point B and make a thousand or five thousand dollars."

So Danny was up to his old tricks when Antonio was finally released from Lookout Mountain in August 1990, after thirteen months. As he got in his mother's car to go home, back to 2727 California, Antonio scooted over next to her. He suddenly lifted his hand to cover his eyes. She asked what was wrong.

"Mom, I can't do it. I want to go back."

Maria pauses to let the memory pass. Her dark-brown eyes are wet and shiny. Behind her stands the house that symbolizes all that has gone wrong.

They named their gang after that house. The Deuce-Seven. And now where were they? Little Frankie sentenced in February 1998, just three days shy of his seventeenth birthday, to spend the rest of his life in prison. Pancho going on trial that fall, maybe to face the death penalty. And Danny set for trial a few months after that ... all for what the Deuce-Seven had done to that little girl.

Now Antonio was out there, trying to stay out of trouble. Unprotected, most of the members of his set dead or in prison.

"He was safe and happy when he was locked up," Maria remembers. "You know, I sometimes believe that a lot of these kids think that way."

CHAPTER FOURTEEN

March 1, 1998

"What do you say after you kill the nineteen-year-old mother of a four-year-old boy? What do you say after you've blown the right side of her face off with a semi-automatic assault rifle?

"What do you say if she's someone you did not even know?"

Deputy District Attorney Sargent pauses in front of the jury, then walks over toward the defense table and points at Alejandro "Speed" Ornelas.

"If you're this man, what you say is, 'I smoked the bitch.'"

Twenty-two-year-old Ornelas watches Sargent like a hawk watches a field mouse. Only this time, he is not the predator but the prey.

Ornelas is on trial for first-degree murder, with the added sentence-enhancer of "with extreme indifference for human life." The life of Venus Montoya.

"Why did Alejandro kill Venus?" Sargent asks, then answers. "Tragically, the fact is, this had absolutely nothing to do with her. He was looking for an informant named Salvino Rojas."

On July 19, 1996, after a night of heavy drinking, Sammy "Zig Zag" Quintana and Alejandro Ornelas had changed into dark clothing and gone hunting for Salvino. Alejandro's older brother, Gerard, was driving.

Word on the street was that Sal was the "confidential informant" who'd turned in the Martinez brothers, Danny and Antonio, for selling marijuana. And on these streets, a snitch had to die, even if he was another Blood.

The Ornelas brothers had their own reasons for going after Sal. They were sure that the hefty six-footer had opened fire on their mother's house with an assault rifle and that he'd threatened their sister with a shotgun.

Add to that the fact that they just plain didn't like him. Salvino may have been a Crenshaw Mafia Gangster Blood, but he wasn't a Deuce-Seven. Now they referred to him as "Sal Snitcho."

The hunters drove to a low-rent apartment complex off Sheridan Boulevard in Lakewood. An uncle of the Ornelas brothers had reported seeing Salvino at one of the apartments. Number 52.

That apartment was rented to Venus Montoya, a pretty, nineteen-year-old high-school dropout who'd moved in with her four-year-old son, Angel, and a roommate. Venus had been there only two weeks, but already she was complaining to her twin sister, Vanessa, that she wanted out. The complex had a reputation as a gang hangout, and she was beginning to think she'd made a bad choice.

The girls' grandmother, Becky Estrada, had raised them and their youngest brother after their twenty-one-year-old mother died of an overdose when the twins were just eight months old. Becky had watched out for the girls for almost two decades now, and she wasn't about to stop. She'd told Venus she didn't like the apartment's location, but Venus wanted to make a life on her own.

On July 15, Venus called her grandmother. She'd had a frightening dream about "two devils" trying to get at her, and even after waking up, she'd been unable to shake her fear. "I want you to come and pick up Angel," she'd said. "I don't want my baby to get hurt."

So Becky had taken the child back home. A few days later Venus had come by; she and Vanessa were going house hunting. As she got ready to leave, Venus had held her arms open to the woman she called Mom.

"I want a hug," she'd said, pouting. "Don't you love me no more?"

Becky had pulled the pretty girl to her and held tight, strangely reluctant to let her go. "I will always love you," she said at last.

The devils arrived at 3 a.m. the next morning, just minutes after Salvino Rojas left the small party that was winding down inside apartment Number 52. Venus was sitting on a daybed, in full view of the screen door, as Quintana and Alejandro Ornelas approached carrying a 9mm handgun and an SKS assault rifle.

"Also sitting on the bed was her boyfriend, John," Sargent tells the jury. "He had asked her to marry him, and she had accepted. It should have been the happiest night of her life, but it was her last."

There was the sound of a blast. Instinctively, John dropped to the floor and reached up to pull his fiancée down. "At about the same time, Venus's head exploded," Sargent says. "Brain matter and blood filled the air."

In the gallery behind the prosecution table, Vanessa lays her head on her grandmother's shoulder.

Across the aisle at the defense table, Alejandro studies his fingernails. His attorneys, former judge Michael Enwall and co-counsel Toby Cleaver, scribble notes on a legal pad. Behind them, Ornelas's friends and family listen impassively. Several of the young women have babies with them.

Nineteen shots were fired into the apartment, all from the assault rifle, some passing through the walls into bedrooms where other people were sleeping. Ten of the bullets struck Venus. "Miraculously, of the eight people in the apartment, she was the only one killed," Sargent says.

Listening at the prosecution table is Sargent's co-prosecutor, Brian Boatwright, and Lakewood detective

Scott Richardson. The detective had been assigned to the case the night of the murder and had seen for himself what a high-velocity 7.62-caliber bullet could do to a human head. The girl was unrecognizable. Her family members, who heard the news from a neighbor, were kept away from the body when they showed up *en masse*.

Working with the Denver Police Department Gang Unit, Richardson soon identified the suspects through informants. He seized the assault rifle from the home of the Ornelases' mother; ballistics tests had proved it was the murder weapon. But Alejandro Ornelas and Quintana had their alibi ready. Some "Baby Gs"—young gangster wannabes—had taken the gun and later returned it.

The detective turned up a couple of independent witnesses who had seen two men lurking outside the apartment complex. Their identification of Ornelas and Quintana was shaky—the witnesses were frightened of getting involved in a gang killing—but combined with all of the other evidence, it was pretty damning.

Still, Richardson wanted a conviction, not just a trial. What he needed was for someone in the gang to get in trouble and roll over on his comrades. For all their big talk about loyalty, most of them could be counted on to snitch as soon as they started looking at time behind bars. That was how the gang unit had gotten Salvino to set up Danny and Antonio Martinez in the first place.

Richardson even called Danny Martinez to see if he could shake something loose. In the background, he could hear Danny telling other gang members, *"Lakewood po po's want to talk to me about Zag and Speed and that shit."*

Then Danny turned his attention back to the detective. *"I don't want to talk to you,"* he said. Taunting him, he added that he knew about the murder but would go to prison before he turned into a snitch.

Then on June 16, 1997, almost a year later, Sammy Quintana and some of his pals were arrested for the murder two weeks earlier of a fourteen-year-old girl, Brandy DuVall. Quintana sat in jail for two days and then started talking. Not just about DuVall, but about Venus Montoya, too.

Alejandro fired the assault rifle, Quintana said. He himself had pointed the handgun, but the clip fell out before he could shoot. That clip had been found at the scene.

At Alejandro Ornelas's trial, Richardson sits within reach of the SKS assault rifle that's been marked as People's Exhibit 38. Pinned to the detective's tie is a small, gold figurine: an angel given to him by Venus's family as thanks for his efforts in catching the killer of Angel's mother.

"There's no question Sam Quintana's motivation was the possibility of the death penalty in not one, but two murders," Sargent tells the jury. "He also told us that his conscience was bothering him."

The prosecutor knows that as bad as his witness will appear to the jurors, he must make the defendant look worse. *No angels for witnesses ... deals with the devil.* He contrasts the image of Quintana wrestling with his conscience and Ornelas bragging that he'd "smoked the bitch" when Ornelas didn't even know who she was.

Sargent warns the jurors that during this trial, they will hear about the "ugly side of life. I don't expect you to like it, but you'll be exposed to a world where someone can kill an innocent nineteen-year-old mother of a little boy and not be ashamed."

Alejandro Ornelas scowls but doesn't look up as Enwall objects to the prosecutor's characterization of his client.

CHAPTER FIFTEEN

Spring 1998

"BOOOOM!" A young white man emerges from the back of Mixed Up Creations, a Colfax Avenue T-shirt shop, to greet Antonio. After a brief flurry of hand jive, they get down to business.

"I like this ... and this," the store's owner says, looking through one of Antonio's drawing portfolios. A sleepy-eyed fish. A cluster of mushrooms reminiscent of Fantasia, except these are more obviously the hallucinogenic kind. Big-breasted, scantily clad comic-book women. Hip-hop characters.

"You ought to do this one," Antonio says. It's a gangbanger with a smoking .45-caliber handgun.

The shop owner shakes his head. "I don't want to sell violent T-shirts to kids."

"Then I suppose you won't want this one?" Antonio says, and laughs. Another alien-looking gangster, this one holding an AK-47 assault rifle.

The shop owner turns the page to a pencil drawing of two hands templed in prayer. "Jesus sells good in the ghetto," Antonio suggests. "Everybody's lookin' for the Lord in the ghetto."

Instead they settle on a skateboard/snowboard character for a new line of T-shirts. Antonio tells the store's owner to be expecting an invitation to a party when he graduates from college in June. "I'll be leaving a couple days later," he says. "A friend's goin' to set me up in a new tattoo shop."

The party will be at 2727 California.

"Sounds cool, Boom," the shop owner says. In this setting, the nickname carries no threat. It's not Boom the gangster but Boom the artist.

When Antonio got out of Lookout, he went to live with his aunt and grandmother in Westminster. He enrolled in high school there, only to find that the school wouldn't accept any credits from the classes he'd attended so religiously at Lookout. He'd have to start where he left off. But even that wasn't enough to deter him.

Then one of the metro gang-unit officers spotted him in class. "Did you know that you've got a notorious gang member sitting here?" he asked the students. "This is Boom."

Soon after, Antonio's mother was notified that he'd have to withdraw from school. Although Antonio hadn't done anything wrong, but school authorities said they had an obligation to protect the other students. If a rival gang found out Antonio was there, they might try to shoot him and hit an innocent bystander in the process.

It seemed so unfair. Antonio was a good student, got good grades, followed the school rules. To Maria, this was just another way the system had of trying to force gang members out of the mainstream. The further they fell behind at school, the more likely they were to drop out and be left with nothing but gangbanging. Like Danny.

Antonio wasn't so easy to get rid of, however. He moved back to 2727 California—Danny was living there now, along with Raquel and Maria—and enrolled in the Denver Public School's Career Education Center, an alternative school that stresses vocational education.

"Being locked up made me smarter," he explains. "I didn't like having to knock on the door to be let out to go to the bathroom. I didn't like other people making decisions for me. I knew that if I went to prison, I would die or become worse than I already was to survive. I'd have to do so many crimes in prison, they'd never let me out."

Antonio was smarter, but he was no saint. He wanted to make money, and the only way he knew how was by selling drugs. Since he was still in a gang, it would be easy. But he decided he wouldn't "shoot someone for no reason," he remembers; it drew too much attention from the police.

"Now, if you're my homeboy and someone is giving you trouble, then I have nothing better to do than shoot someone for you," he adds. "Or I'd shoot you if you threatened me. But I stopped doing stupid things, like violence just for the sake of violence."

He played it low-key. Wearing a red bandanna in his back pocket, he concluded, was advertising to the cops and other gangs. He didn't need to do that; he already had a name. "I didn't need to be letting people know 'I'm a gangster—stay away.' They already knew it."

But things had changed while Antonio was in Lookout. The Mexican boys weren't as welcome in the black Park Hill gang anymore. Back before Antonio got locked up, he, Pancho, and Danny had referred to themselves as the Deuce-Seven in honor of the house at 2727 California. They'd even tattooed their arms with "Deuce-Seven," under which they wrote "CMG," followed by "Bloods."

Now the CMG was getting too big. "No one knew anybody else," he recalls. "There was no way to get everybody together." Small groups were breaking off, forming their own subsets under the umbrella of CMG Bloods, or B-dogs, as they called themselves.

So Antonio, Pancho, and Danny did the same thing. Like the rest of the gangs, the members of the Deuce-Seven made their money selling drugs. And when they weren't selling drugs, they were robbing each other. It wasn't just fighting with the Crips or the Inca Boys, or whatever other group they came in contact with. They were even robbed a couple of times by other Bloods—friends of the friends who'd brought them into the gang in the first place.

"It got worked out," Antonio says. "I mean, it was all dirty money, anyway. It wasn't like whatever we had belonged to us. So, we weren't going to go kill some other Bloods over money we had taken from somebody else."

Although the house at 2727 California was ransacked a couple of times and shot at more frequently, they didn't worry. Until one night, when the violence boiled over a few minutes after the boys left to visit their uncle, Jose Martinez.

Their sister, Raquel, was alone in the house with her newborn daughter, Danielle. She was walking down the stairs with the baby when a gunman in a car outside sprayed the house with an automatic weapon, sending bullets and bits of wood, plaster, and glass flying inside.

Maria arrived home a few minutes before her sons. Police cars surrounded the block. There was a neat line of bullet holes stitched across the front of the house above the porch awning. It was a miracle that neither Raquel nor the baby had been hit.

Danny and Antonio seethed. They knew the police wouldn't even look for whoever had done this; they'd never found whoever shot their Uncle Jimmy a couple of years earlier. Instead the family was told that if someone shot at their house again, the property would be seized as a public nuisance.

The boys were plotting their revenge when Maria confronted them. "There will be no retribution," she said. "You're the ones who joined the gang."

When her sons protested that they couldn't just let someone shoot up their house, she retorted, "What did you expect? This is the consequence for what you do ... you put us all in danger. Jimmy. Raquel. Danielle."

Remembering this, Antonio pauses. "We felt bad, knowing we brought this on our family. We were doing a lot more to our mom than we realized.

"I mean, we were used to her going into a rage about the things we were doing. She'd hit us and throw things and break them ... and we'd just say, 'You're being silly, breaking your own shit when there's nothin' you can do about it. It's already happened.' We were glad that she had straightened her own life out, that she was going in the right direction, taking care of herself. But me? I was too far gone to listen."

Maria recognized that, and she'd had enough. "That's it. That's it," she said. "I'm getting rid of the house." No amount of pleading from her sons could change her mind.

Once again, 2727 California was closed up. While Maria moved into her own apartment, the boys went searching for a place of their own. Antonio wanted to live near the Career Education Center so he could walk to school. When they found a place, it seemed like a sign.

The address: 2727 Clay Street.

Not that they always stayed there. "We lived the high life. Money, ho's, and clothes," Antonio remembers. "We stayed, sometimes for several days at a time, in the presidential suites of Denver's best hotels. We'd be drunk and high the whole time. They didn't care who we were. Our money was green, and we paid for everything in cash."

Their neighbors on Clay cared. They called the cops and their city councilwoman.

"They didn't like all these young guys, who didn't seem to have jobs but drove nice cars and sat in the backyard talking on cellular phones," Antonio recalls. "We weren't doing nothin' wrong. I mean, we weren't dealin' drugs out of the house. We weren't shooting anybody in the front yard or the backyard.

"What I think they really didn't like was all these black guys, some of them pretty obviously gang members, comin' over to visit."

The Denver cops had been after the Deuce-Seven for a long time, without much luck. "Some fool would accuse us of something, and somebody'd go visit them and say, 'I hear you talked about Bang or Boom or Panch. Well, you fucked up, and you better change your mind. And since you gave a statement, now you better go tell the motherfuckers that you did it.'

"There were a few fools who decided they would rather take the blame for something they didn't do than stand by their statements about us," Antonio remembers. "So, we were beating a lot of dumb-shit counts on account of 'mistaken identity.'"

He smiles. "And there were a couple of times we really weren't guilty."

Then Antonio was awakened one Saturday morning in July 1992 by loud knocking on the back door. He went to see who was there and was met by police officers with guns drawn who ordered him back into the house.

"Some of the kids in the neighborhood were shooting off firecrackers," he says. "But, of course, our neighbors reported that we were shooting guns in the backyard. And there we were in our boxers and T-shirts, trying to wake up."

The occupants of the house were taken to the backyard in handcuffs and placed on their stomachs. Meanwhile, five officers went into the house without a warrant and began searching the premises. "They found a paintball gun under the couch and acted like it was some sort of nuclear weapon." But no one was arrested, and the cops told Antonio and his friends that they were free to go back inside.

The next night the police began pulling over cars that stopped by the house. This time a few people were arrested on outstanding traffic warrants, but most were let go.

Then, a day later, Antonio, his Uncle Jimmy, and a cousin were in the house when they saw police cars suddenly appear at the front and back. This time the cops kicked in the back door and arrested everybody ... for trespassing.

The police took their time searching the house. Some even sat on the couch to watch television while their prisoners waited in the kitchen with handcuffs on. But one of the officers climbed into the attic and found a shotgun. Antonio concedes that the gun was his, but, he says, "Who cares? They didn't have any business in my attic. We're supposed to follow the law, but they're not?"

"The cops never had any warrants," he says. "They kept saying that the neighbors' complaints gave them 'probable cause.'"

The trespassing charge was dropped when the property manager said they had a right to be in the house. Antonio and the others were bonded out by midnight. The next morning, Antonio returned to the house to get his things. He was still trying to go to school every day, and all of this police attention was threatening his graduation plans.

As he drove away, he was pulled over by a motorcycle patrolman who'd been waiting in the alley behind the house.

Antonio had slipped up. "I don't know why, but I had a 9 millimeter on the seat next to me," he says, shaking his head. "It wasn't even hidden. I had bought it from a crackhead who stole it from someone's house. So now I was lookin' at felony theft by receiving."

Back in a jail cell, Antonio realized that, legally or not, the police were going to keep coming after him until they could put him in prison for a long time. And he wouldn't be able to attend school or be an artist if he was spending all his time in a cell or a courtroom.

"I finally said to myself, 'You know what? I give up. I'm gonna stop sellin' drugs. I'm gonna stop bangin' and doin' any kind of illegal shit. I give up. I quit.'"

CHAPTER SIXTEEN

March 1998

The trial of Alejandro Ornelas lasts four days. After Sargent's opening, defense lawyer Enwall gets his turn. He begins by attacking Sammy Quintana, "the state's star witness." The evidence, he says, will point to Quintana, who "held the head of another girl while her throat was slit," as the man who also shot Venus Montoya.

"He lied to get a deal," says Enwall, peering at the jury over the half-glasses perched on the end of his nose.

After a night of drinking, Quintana and his client had come up with a "half-baked" plan to kill Salvino Rojas. It was Quintana who carried the assault rifle, Enwall says. "Alejandro Ornelas is guilty of a crime. He is not guilty of first-degree murder."

After Enwall takes his seat, the prosecution uses a series of witnesses to paint an emotional portrait of violence:

Vanessa Montoya in tears as she's asked to identify a photograph of her twin. Survivors from the apartment who vividly recall the acrid gunsmoke, the sight of brain matter hitting the wall, the smell of blood. The image of Venus's fiancé, Johnny, lying across her body, crying, "No, don't do this to me," then taking off before the police arrive because there are warrants out for his arrest.

The second day begins with the defense lawyers asking, outside the jury's presence, that prosecution witness Max "M-dog" Archuleta be reminded that he is not to say anything about first meeting Ornelas when the latter was in prison "for killing a Crip."

Then Archuleta, tattoos visible on his neck and wrist, is brought in and warned to avoid the topic of Ornelas's prison record. He nods nervously. He's in a witness-protection program and feels he's risking his life talking at all—much less testifying that he often saw Ornelas with an assault rifle.

Sargent picks up People's Exhibit 38 and carelessly swings the muzzle past Venus's family. They cringe. "That's the gun," Archuleta blurts out. He then identifies the gun in a picture from a gang photo album that Detective Richardson found; Ornelas is holding the rifle in his mother's backyard.

Alejandro Ornelas and Danny Martinez had talked almost daily about wanting to get Salvino Rojas for snitching. "They said, 'The rat's gonna get it,'" Archuleta testifies.

"Why would Speed care if Sal snitched on Danny?" Sargent asks.

"That's his OG," Archuleta answers, using the gang expression of respect for an older gangster.

A couple of days after the killing, Archuleta says, he was visiting Alejandro at his mother's house when his friend bragged about shooting up the girl's apartment. "He said he 'smoked the bitch.'" Speed was upset with Quintana because he'd dropped the clip from the 9mm and was afraid the police would find fingerprints.

At the beginning of the third day, Ornelas comes into the courtroom and smiles at a well-dressed middle-aged man sitting with the rest of his family members, who seem to defer to him in the hallways and courtroom. The man nods and smiles back, a benediction.

After Ornelas is seated, Sammy "Zig Zag" Quintana enters. He's dressed in a jail jumpsuit, hobbling along in shackles. The defendant sneers as his former friend passes and stands before Judge Thomas Woodford.

Quintana has difficulty raising his right hand to be sworn in because his cuffed hands are connected by a short lead to a chain-link belly band. As he takes a seat at the witness stand, the well-dressed man sitting with Ornelas's family raises his hand and makes a shooting gesture toward Sammy.

Quintana's father sits in the back of the courtroom, a dark blazer covering his Denver County sheriff's deputy uniform. He's already had to listen to his son, during the Frank Vigil trial, describe his part in the killing of one girl. Now he must hear about his boy's role in the murder of a second.

Zig Zag Quintana now testifies that he was sitting in his jail cell after his arrest for Brandy DuVall's murder when he decided to approach the authorities. He was facing a first-degree-murder charge and knew the likely consequences were life without parole or the death penalty.

"Was that the only reason?" Sargent asks.

"Prior to being arrested," Quintana says, "my life was going downhill, and my heart was speaking to me to break free—to do what's right for once."

One night he and Alejandro had gone to the house of another CMG Blood, Jevaun "Gangster J" Ivory. It was obvious that someone was going to get shot that night, beginning with Gangster J's Rottweiler, which tried to take a bite out of Alejandro's leg while they were standing on the porch.

"Speed pulled out his gun, a .38, and pointed it at the dog," Quintana recalls. "He said, 'I'll shoot your dog.'"

"'You shoot my dog and I'll shoot you,'" Quintana says Ivory responded, going into the house to get a 9mm handgun in case he had to do just that. But Quintana stepped between the two. "We got problems with other people; let's not take out ourselves," he said.

Gangster J then loaned them the 9mm, and they took it with them as they searched for Salvino Rojas. They drove to one address where they thought he might be, and Alejandro emptied the gun into a car parked there. Then they drove to the apartment complex where one of Alejandro's uncles had reported seeing Salvino hanging out.

They saw a large, shadowy figure standing in one doorway that they thought might be their target. But first, they decided, they needed more weapons, so they went to Alejandro's mother's house to get the assault rifle and change into dark clothing.

Then they returned to the apartment complex. Twelve feet from the screen door to Number 52, they could see a young woman sitting on the daybed. "Alejandro began to fire," Quintana testifies. "It was very loud. I saw a woman taking many bullets. There was a lot of screaming."

As he sprayed bullets into the apartment, Alejandro walked toward the door. Quintana raised his gun, but it wouldn't shoot.

"Were you pointing at the girl?" Sargent asks.

"No," Quintana says, shaking his head. "Just pointing."

After he emptied his gun, Alejandro turned and ran. As Quintana moved to follow him, the clip, which had been meant for a different gun, fell to the ground. He couldn't find it in the dark, panicked, and left it behind.

Although the prosecution can't bring up the defendant's past, the defense is bound by no such restrictions regarding witnesses. During cross-examination, Enwall points out that Quintana's first felony was in 1992 for assault with a deadly weapon. He hammers away, trying to get Quintana to admit that he was the one carrying the assault rifle. Quintana's deal isn't just that he has to testify truthfully; he also can't be the one who shot Venus or stabbed Brandy DuVall. Otherwise, the deal is off.

But Quintana won't budge. "I'm not lying, sir."

After Quintana steps down, Richardson is called to the stand. Informants have reported that a "hit" was put out on the detective while he was investigating the case. He's spent a good part of the trial staring down Ornelas family members and supporters who've tried to stare down the prosecution's witnesses.

The detective recounts how he caught Ornelas in fifty-seven separate lies over several interviews. The defendant denied having anything to do with the killing, he testifies, but also complained about Salvino Rojas being such a good friend of the police.

Salvino had pulled a "gauge," a shotgun, on his sister and blasted his mother's home, Ornelas told Richardson. "Salvino shoots at us and nothin' happens. All the bullet holes in my mama's house are from him."

Reading from a transcript of one interview, Richardson recalls how he told the defendant he knew he was lying: "You're sinking, Alejandro."

"I'm not lying," the defendant had protested. "I was not the triggerman, and I don't know nothin' about it."

CHAPTER SEVENTEEN

Late Spring 1998

Antonio sits at a drawing table in his garden-level apartment. The shades are drawn, and the only light is the lamp that illuminates his work.

He rubs his face as if he could wipe away the stress he feels when he thinks about his brother and the others. "When I was a youngster, I didn't care a lot about what happened to me. I didn't think about how my grandmother and my mother would miss me if I died or went to prison.

"But sitting in that cell, I realized that I did care. I didn't want to spend my life in prison. I didn't want my children or my mother to have to visit me there. I didn't want to die."

Still, stopping was much harder than starting. Antonio was still a Deuce-Seven, and even though he knew Danny and Pancho would back him up, they couldn't always be around. Antonio found himself constantly looking over his shoulder.

After he'd bonded out of jail on the gun charge, he moved in with his mother. There he was joined by his first cousin, Sammy Quintana, whose parents had divorced.

The Quintanas had tried hard to get their children away from the old neighborhood, to give them the best of everything. Sammy Jr. was a soccer star and a member of the all-city marching band. But he still ended up in a gang.

"That was, of course, all our fault: 'If Danny and Antonio had left him alone, he would have been okay,'" says Antonio. "But Sammy was his own fault. We didn't even know it when he first got into a gang. He was selling drugs and doing a lot of acid with his high-school buddies out in the suburbs.

"Then he takes a shot at somebody in a car over in Bear Valley. Gets probation, then gets caught with a gun and does ten months in Buena Vista. This is all long before he starts hangin' with us ... but it's our fault. Then his dad kicked him out of the house, and he had nowhere else to go, so he moved in with Mom and me."

Because Sammy was family, he was allowed into the Deuce-Seven without the usual pain of getting "beat in." He liked the trappings of gangbanging—the gold chains, the red shirts, pants, and sneakers—that the others had mostly grown out of. "He wanted everyone to know he was a B-dog," Antonio remembers. "A violent gangster."

The Deuce-Seven had begun to attract other Hispanic Bloods who felt out of place with the black sets. Many were related to the original members: Danny, Antonio, and Pancho. David and Maurice Warren, more weekend warriors than hardcore gang members, were cousins of Pancho's.

Frank Vigil Jr. was just a kid, like they had been, when he asked to be let in. "We didn't encourage him," Antonio says. "In fact, we tried to discourage him. But he was going to do it no matter what—better he do it with us, where we could kind of look out for him."

Other gang members came and went—sometimes not of their own accord, like Alejandro Ornelas.

"Alejandro was a friend of a friend," Antonio recalls. "He got sent to Lookout after I got out, two years on a manslaughter rap. Some Crips jumped out of a car and started chasing him down an alley, so he smoked one of them. The Crips originally thought it was me that did it. They was callin' and sayin' what they were going to do, and I was like, 'Yeah, whatever.' So I wanted to meet him when he got out."

But Ornelas wasn't free more than a few days before he got caught with a gun on school property and sentenced to a year in federal prison. When he got out, he aligned himself with the Deuce-Seven and was soon joined by his older brother, Gerard.

"The problem for a lot of guys who want to be in a gang is, they can't handle the stress and the danger," Antonio says. "The Ornelas brothers were more like us. No fear. And they were willing to be as down and violent as us."

Antonio was still going to school every day. The shotgun charge was dropped, but he was fighting the handgun charge from the arrest at 2727 Clay as well as two attempted-murder charges. "Some guys got shot at a car wash," he says. "They knew who the driver was and thought I was the shooter. I wasn't."

Although he had sworn off criminal activities, his reputation nearly got him kicked out of school. He credits Career Education Center vice principal Debbie Williams and commercial-art teacher Brad Vickers with keeping him in school.

Once word got out that the infamous Boom was no longer gangbanging, some other students tried to take advantage of that by trying to run him over with a car. "Fuck 'em," he says. "I wasn't hiding. I just wanted to go to school and be left alone.

"But I was still from the set, and some of my homeboys went over and fucked 'em up. Debbie Williams pulled me out of class and said, 'I hear you're with a gang' and that she wouldn't put up with it.

"I told her that I was a gang member when I woke up and when I went to sleep at night. That I was a gang member who goes to school and gets good grades, but I could not stop being a gang member. It's who I was. But that I wanted to stay out of trouble and stay in school."

Antonio rubs his face. "She could have suspended me, a lot of others would have. And I know it wasn't easy on her.

A lot of the teachers didn't like me, not even my counselor. But she took a chance."

Vickers saw something special in Antonio, too. "He said, 'I'm not just blowing smoke up your ass, you got real talent,'" Antonio remembers. "What he said stuck with me, and I went from drawing pictures of gangsters blowing the heads off each other to commercial art."

The teacher's confidence in Antonio paid off when his work took first place in a regional commercial-art contest. "I always thought that maybe I had talent," he says. "But here was someone who knew what it took, telling me that I could do it.

"He was the first person outside my family and my homeboys who ever tried to help me. Fact is, until him, all I ever got from the police and district attorneys was that I was a piece of shit—that I was going to be in prison or dead."

Antonio doesn't like to appear weak. He has to blink a few times and rub his face before he can go on. "I began thinking about tryin' to get into a good art school." He pauses again to blink. "I owe a lot to Ms. Williams and Mr. Vickers."

The attempted-murder charges were dropped after Antonio agreed to take a lie-detector test and passed it. He was given a deferred sentence on the gun charge on the condition that he leave Colorado for a year.

That was fine with Antonio, who hoped to go to art school in California.

In June 1993, Antonio Martinez finally graduated from high school. He considered it his revenge toward those who told him he'd never amount to anything, who had tried to keep him out of school.

"I had seen my name on walls and police papers that I would be dead before I was eighteen," he says. "But here I was, graduating from high school, and I was nineteen years old.

"I think it scared them—the cops and the DAs—because I had done so much shit, and here I was alive and doing just fine."

CHAPTER EIGHTEEN

March 5, 1998

The final day of the Ornelas trial begins with the jury out of the courtroom while Gerard "G-Loc" Ornelas attempts to withdraw his guilty plea to a charge of conspiracy to commit first-degree murder in exchange for the murder charges being dropped.

Prosecutor Brian Boatwright angrily denounces the attempt as "gamesmanship. Obviously, we think this is ridiculous." The judge says he'll consider the matter and get back to the attorneys.

As Gerard Ornelas is led away, he steals a look at the well-dressed man who's back in the spectator gallery. The man gives him a thumbs-up and a smile. Gerard nods weakly and hobbles out of the courtroom. (But he will later accept the plea agreement.)

The prosecution has a few issues of its own. Apparently, Alejandro Ornelas has told one of the deputies working security that if he's convicted, he plans to force them to shoot him. Told that they'd just zap him with his security belt, he smirked and said, "Not if the belt's not on."

Ornelas, who has already been reprimanded for scratching 2-7 on a wall while waiting to be brought into the courtroom, is still smirking. Judge Woodford says he'll leave it to the deputies to take whatever security measures they deem necessary.

Finally, the defense presents its case, mostly witnesses who testify to discrepancies about which of the two dark figures—the bigger one, Quintana, or the smaller one, Ornelas—ran from the scene with the assault rifle.

The surprise of the trial comes when Ornelas decides to testify. He's already in tears when he takes the stand, and his family cries along with him.

Carefully questioned by defense attorney Cleaver, who does not want to open the door for the prosecution to discuss "character issues," particularly his "peacefulness," Alejandro tells the jury that he was born and raised in Denver. He has an older sister, a younger sister, and an older brother, Gerard. He also has a girlfriend and had two children at the time of Venus Montoya's murder.

That night began with an orgy of alcohol, he says. He drank a six-pack of sixteen-ounce beers, four shots of Remy Martin, two Amaretto Sours, part of a bottle of tequila, and smoked some marijuana. He remembers only brief snatches of what happened after that. He doesn't remember changing into dark clothes or fetching the assault rifle from his mother's house, he says.

"Do you recall having a gun at Venus's apartment building?" Cleaver asks.

"No, I don't," he says, his voice breaking.

"Do you have a recollection of shooting Venus Montoya?"

"No, I don't."

"Did you shoot Venus Montoya?"

"I don't remember," he claims, sniffing loudly and reaching for a tissue.

"Are you afraid you might have?"

He nods, blows his nose. "Yes, 'cause I was there in the parking lot that night."

After Cleaver sits down, Sargent launches right in. "As far as you know, you shot Venus Montoya with an SKS assault rifle?"

"I don't remember."

"But you have no memory of not doing it?"

"No."

Sargent nods, then asks, "You shed tears when you took the stand?"

"Yes."

"But you never shed tears for Venus Montoya." It's a statement, not a question.

"How do you know that?"

"Answer the question," Sargent presses.

"Yes, I have," he says.

"Do you consider yourself an honest man?"

"Right now?"

"In general," Sargent says.

"Before this situation, no."

Ornelas looks confused by this line of questioning, but it suddenly becomes clear where Sargent's going as he begins to recite the long list of lies Ornelas told Richardson when first asked about the killing and his gang affiliation.

"You lied fifty-seven times," Sargent notes. "You lied because you didn't like the consequences of telling the truth."

"I was always taught, 'Don't tell the police nothing,'" Ornelas says.

In the spectator gallery, the well-dressed man nods and says, "That's right" loud enough to be heard throughout the courtroom. As his running commentary continues, the judge stops the proceedings and tells him to be quiet.

Sargent now brings up a rap song Ornelas wrote in prison in response to remarks Salvino Rojas had made to a newspaper reporter.

In the article, Salvino denied that he was a police informant. That rumor, he said, was spread by the police to set the gang members against each other and by members of the Deuce-Seven who were jealous of his drug-dealing enterprises. He accused the Deuce-Seven of showing up at parties and not only robbing those present but putting "a gun to a girl's head and saying, 'You're gonna fuck me and all my homeboys.' I told them that shit with the women was going to catch up to them one of these days."

He claimed that the Deuce-Seven shot at him and that he may have returned fire. "Some of their cars got shot up, and somebody blew up Ornelas's mom's house. It might have been me, and maybe it wasn't.

"The funny thing is, they're all rollin' over on each other. They said I was a snitch, but they can hardly wait to snitch on each other."

Ornelas addressed his song to "Sal-snitcho:"

Well, I'm back to set the record strait [sic] *to that punk ass snitch you know I hate.*

Your [sic] *watching your back, now you gotta watch your front.*

Sooner or later you'll end up in the back of my trunk.

I'm gonna start by telling the true facts and not fiction.

About Salvino who ain't no good for nothing but snitchin'.

Sargent also introduces another "song" that Ornelas had intended for Sammy Quintana, in which he wrote about:

(putting) *a shank through the homey I thought I knew.*

It's not my fault you were facing the death penalty.

You should of [sic] *handled it and left out the homeys.*

And now you want to take us all down with you.

Damn blood, you're through.

"I wrote that, yes," Ornelas concedes. "It's just a rap song; that's all it was."

The tears are gone; he's angry.

A baby cries in the gallery. Venus's family keeps reaching over to touch her twin, Vanessa, as if to connect with the girl who's no longer there.

"As far as you know, Sam Quintana is telling the absolute truth about everything that happened at that apartment?" Sargent asks.

"How can I say that?"

"So if I understand you, you were so drunk you didn't even hear gunshots."

"No, I didn't." After one more round of tears, Ornelas says, "Ever since this situation happened, I've tried to forget about it."

"I'll bet you have," someone in Venus's family says quietly.

Then it's over. Ornelas sits at the witness stand, his head down, until he's told to step down. The defense is done.

It takes this jury even less time to reach its verdict than the jury in Frank Vigil's trial. After just four hours, they send a message to the judge that they're ready. Word is sent to gather the lawyers and families.

After everyone is seated in the courtroom, the Jefferson County sheriff's Special Operations Team quietly assembles in the hall outside. They're in full riot gear.

When the judge says the word "guilty," the section behind Ornelas erupts. Alysha Abeyta, the mother of his children, begins screaming as other family members and supporters shout.

When Woodford orders that Abeyta be quiet or be removed, Ornelas yells, "Fuck you! What the fuck did you expect her to do?"

Deputies quickly subdue Ornelas, who continues to shout profanities.

As the riot squad enters the courtroom, the jurors are quickly escorted out a back door—and Ornelas's supporters vent their anger at Venus's stunned family.

Detective Richardson moves to protect them, knocking over the drinking water on the prosecution table in the process.

One of Ornelas's female relatives uses both middle fingers to flip them off. "The fuckin' bitch deserved to die if she was hangin' out with snitches!" she screams as she's pulled from the courtroom by the riot squad.

CHAPTER NINETEEN

April 1998

Just as California pawned off its gang members on Denver by giving deferred sentences and bus tickets to those who left the state, Colorado gave the same deal to Antonio Martinez. His mother moved first, a week after his graduation; it took Antonio a couple of months to follow.

When Maria asked what was keeping him, he had to admit that a girl he'd been seeing was having a baby. "I think it's mine," he said. He wanted to be there for the child's birth.

In California, Antonio got a job working at Kmart, selling shoes. It was the first real job he'd ever had. "I didn't even need it," he recalls. "I had plenty of money. But Mom got tired of me just hanging around, doing nothin' but drawing."

Of all the members of the Deuce-Seven Crenshaw Mafia Gangsters, Antonio was the only one to ever visit Crenshaw Boulevard in Los Angeles and introduce himself to the Bloods there. But the California gangs were not nearly so welcoming of strangers—especially a Mexican kid—as the gangs in Denver.

Antonio soon had company, though: Danny, now split from his girlfriend, and Pancho moved out to California. Maria marveled at how relaxed they were, walking unarmed and unafraid down the street to go to a store, something they could never have done safely in Denver. She hoped they'd all make new lives for themselves.

But Antonio, who'd made a lengthy visit to Denver to see his baby, Patricia, was still homesick. After his application to art school was denied, he was done with California. "Okay, let's go home," he told Maria. Danny and Pancho followed soon after.

Back in Denver, Antonio was accepted to the Colorado Institute of Art, even receiving a federal grant to study. He was warned, however, that any felony drug charge would result in the forfeiture of the grant—no other crime, just drugs.

Danny, Pancho, and Antonio had often talked about "going legitimate"—maybe starting a commercial-art company with Antonio doing the art, Pancho doing the grunt work, and Danny using his people skills in "marketing."

It was a fun dream. "But Danny always wanted to be the older brother, in charge, the president of the company," Antonio says. That grated on Antonio, but he figured that someday his brother was going to need him worse than he needed his brother. That was part of the reason he'd refused to let anybody stop him from getting an education.

While the brothers sometimes talked about Danny getting away from *"the life,"* it was increasingly clear that "the life" was all he had. There had been no Ms. Williams to keep Danny in school, no Mr. Vickers to encourage him, and no Lonnie Lynn, whom Antonio kept in touch with when he needed someone to talk to about making the right decisions.

He was working hard in school, but Antonio still hung out with Danny and Pancho—which meant he hung out with other members of the Deuce-Seven and CMG Bloods as well. But he found himself liking few of them, especially guys like Salvino Rojas, who talked big.

And then Antonio made the mistake of letting Danny use his apartment when he went off to school during the day. Danny made it his headquarters for drug sales, and one of the people he sold to was Salvino Rojas.

"They called him a 'confidential informant,'" Antonio scoffs. "But you'd have to be a moron not to know who the 'confidential informant' was once the attorneys got the paperwork. 'Confidential informant bought this amount, at this time, on this day.' Jesus."

Antonio was at school when the police kicked in his door and arrested Danny. They left a note in the apartment, telling Antonio to turn himself in.

The "confidential informant" said Antonio and Danny had sold him pot. "It was a lie," says Antonio. "I never sold him anything. But I think they didn't want just Bang—they wanted Boom and Bang, and that's what he gave them.

"It was fucked up, anyway. Salvino was trying to get out of some charges he was facing, so they get him to give up Danny and me. I mean, what kind of a system of justice is it that the police let someone off who they know had done the crime for someone they think has done a crime?"

Antonio was desperate and went on the run for almost a week. If he was convicted of a felony drug charge, he'd lose the grant and he could kiss his dreams of graduating from art school goodbye. But he also realized he couldn't go to school while he was a fugitive, so he got a lawyer. "I told him, 'I can't live on the run, I got shit to do,'" he recalls. "I turned myself in."

As angry as he was at Salvino, Antonio was just as mad at Danny. "We were in jail and I told him, 'This is fucked up, dude, and it's your fault.'"

Danny tried to shrug it off. "Nah, blood, it's cool." After all, they'd always taken their lickings together.

Antonio realized then that as much as he loved his brother, as much as they had been through together, he was going to have to keep a greater distance. Still, he couldn't stay mad at Danny too long.

"I was getting out and he wasn't," says Antonio. "But we were still brothers," he says. "We were still Boom and Bang."

Fortunately, his lawyer convinced the prosecutors that they didn't have a good case. He got another deferred sentence provided he attend drug and alcohol counseling and submit to drug testing for three years.

After Venus Montoya died, Antonio says, the police hoped they could pin the murder on Danny and say that he ordered the hit. "A snitch is a snitch, and a snitch has to die," he says, switching back to his gangster mode. "No one had to order anybody. Salvino had shot up the Ornelases' mom's house when his sister was inside. What if she'd been killed, and not Venus Montoya? The cops knew it was him. But did they care? Fuck, no. He was their boy, and it was just a gang member's house."

Antonio turns off the light on his drawing table. It was all about choices and living with the consequences of those choices. Whether you were Danny, Pancho, Frank, Alejandro ... or even Venus Montoya.

"She was no innocent bystander," he says. "She was smart enough to make decisions not to be around gang members. Gangs are synonymous with violence, and she damn well better have known that what she was doing was life-threatening.

"Everyone sees her as this innocent little girl. Well, fuck that, dude. If she had died in a drunk-driving accident, everyone would have thought she was an idiot. But because she's hanging out with gang members getting drunk, that's different?"

Antonio realizes how harsh he sounds. It's part of the duality of his nature—the war that rages within him between the angels and the devils. He sighs. "Whose fault is any of this?" he asks. "The cops, because they set us against each other and sometimes innocent people get hurt?

"Hers, because she thought it was cool having a big gangster around, and she wound up dead on the floor?

"His, for not telling her that she was in danger because of him?"

In the dark, he's a silhouette against what light comes through the window. He rubs his face and rubs again, but a conscience is something that can't be rubbed away.

"Or is it our fault for hating so much that we shoot moms in their houses?"

He closes his portfolio and nods his head. "That's our fault," he says, then quietly repeats himself. "That's our fault."

CHAPTER TWENTY

May 1998

A month after Alejandro Ornelas's trial, Becky Estrada prepares herself to speak at his sentencing. There has been so much death in her family already—a daughter and a son who'd overdosed on drugs, another son murdered whose killer still walked the streets, then Venus.

Some days she sits on her porch and looks for her granddaughter to come waltzing down the block, swinging her hair out of her eyes. When Angel asks where his mother is, she points to the stars. But how now to explain to the man who killed her, a man who didn't even know her, the crushing devastation of his senseless act?

She walks to the podium and addresses the judge without looking at the young man who sits glumly at the defense table. Now he looks just like all the others who came to court to testify against him. No more trying to fool a jury by dressing him in civilian clothes; no more pretense that he's some innocent boy.

"He hurt my family," she tells the court, "and he hurt my baby. I'm sure his family hurts as much as we do.

"Now your family has to suffer, too," she says, as she at last turns to face Ornelas. "But at least they can see you. I can't see my daughter. But I have her in my heart."

Ornelas says nothing. There are no more tears, no outbursts.

Then Woodford sentences him to life in prison without parole. "You have caused the very violent death of a very young mother, fiancée, and daughter," the judge says, "and I have seen no remorse on your part."

CHAPTER TWENTY-ONE

June 1998

Antonio Martinez negotiates his way through a maze of boxes scattered across the living room of his small apartment as a massive stereo system pulsates with gangsta rap. Except for the stereo, he's almost packed—and ready to get the hell out of Denver.

The night before, his mother threw him a party at the old family home. 2727 California. It's not theirs anymore, but the new owners were gracious enough to allow one last hurrah in honor of Antonio's graduation from the Colorado Institute of Art.

Now he's laboring under a haze of too much tequila. Antonio isn't much of a drinker, hasn't been since he gave up gangbanging nearly five years ago. Even in his wilder days, he didn't like losing control to alcohol, not like Danny and Pancho and the rest.

I was raised in this so-ci-et-ty, Martinez raps along with Tupac Shakur, who was gunned down in 1996.

So they-ah's no way you can 'spect me to be a perfect person ...

Antonio's round head bobs with the beat. He strikes his gangster pose—arms out to the side, hands curled around the grips of imaginary pistols. He's wearing the uniform: baggy T-shirt and knee-length shorts hanging halfway down his butt.

"Life made us crazy," Antonio says after the song is over. "Life made us this way." He thinks for a moment, then adds, "And rap music ... coming from where I come from,

I can relate to that shit. Tupac. Snoop Doggy Dog. They're successful, and they been around gangs and in prison and shit, and they ain't nobody's good role models.

"I don't understand these kids in the suburbs who say they're into rap music and wanna be gangsters. What do they know? My mama didn't buy me no new car when I was sixteen. I didn't get to sleep safe in my pajamas at my parents' home in the country.

"To tell you the truth, I resent them comin' to my 'hood and trying to act like me. It's a good way for them to catch a hot one in the ass, know what I mean?"

Despite his hangover, Antonio has to keep packing and cleaning. He's leaving this evening for a new life in a city where hardly anybody knows him. Not the cops. Not the gangs. Only a friend and fellow art-school graduate with whom he'll be opening a high-end tattoo shop, putting his drawing skills to use.

Things are changing, not just for Antonio "Boom" Martinez, but for all of the members of the Deuce-Seven Crenshaw Mafia Gangster Bloods. He's escaping. Most of the others who made up the core group—including his brother, Danny "Bang" Martinez Jr., Francisco "Pancho" Martinez, Frank "Little Bang" Vigil Jr., Sammy "Zig Zag" Quintana, and Alejandro "Speed" Ornelas—are not. They're doomed, brought down by an insanity that ate them from within.

Alejandro and Frank have already been tried for murder and convicted: twenty-two-year-old Alejandro for his part in the July 1996 shooting of nineteen-year-old Venus Montoya; seventeen-year-old Frank for the May 1997 rape, torture, and murder of Brandaline Rose DuVall. They will both serve the rest of their lives in prison. No possibility of parole.

Pancho faces a death-penalty trial in late August for the DuVall slaying. Danny's trial for the same crime is set for later in the fall; the Jefferson County district attorney hasn't yet said if he will seek the death penalty in Danny's case.

Antonio scowls. "And all because of snitches," including his cousin, Sammy "Zig Zag" Quintana, who has pleaded guilty to second-degree murder in both cases in order to avoid a potential death sentence and is now a star witness for the prosecution.

That's the way Antonio sees it. But a moment later, he concedes that the gang was already coming apart. Things were spinning out of control. Danny was "falling-down-in-the-mud" drunk most of the time; Pancho was getting more and more aggressive.

By the time Venus Montoya was murdered, the Deuce-Seven's heyday—of fine hotel suites and nice cars, of big-time drug deals and rolls of cash the size of fists—was over. Dismantled by internecine warfare with other gangs and nearly constant pressure from the police.

Antonio was smart enough to see that it was only going to get worse, and he got out. The others, well, they saw no way out for themselves. "Or maybe," he says softly, "they didn't want an out if all it meant was no place to go."

No one made getting out easy for Antonio—including Antonio himself. He'd been suspended and expelled from school, sometimes for good reason, sometimes not; he'd spent a year in Lookout Mountain after shooting a Crip; and there'd been other charges.

Most would have quit trying. Danny did. Pancho did. Frank did. Alejandro did. Antonio didn't. He had dreams and a few teachers who believed in him. And he had Lonnie Lynn.

Lynn had been the counselor who'd helped Antonio at Lookout, and then, as head of the local Amer-I-Can program, he'd helped him again. In the gang group at Lookout, Lynn had talked to kids like Antonio and Pancho about taking responsibility. The Amer-I-Can program was an extension of the same message.

It had gotten through to Antonio. He'd even had custody of his young daughter, Patricia, while he was going to art school and asked Lynn to help him get a job in order to provide for her—and meet the conditions of a deferred sentence on a drug charge.

But in the long run, what he got from Lynn was better than a job. It was a new way of looking at how he arrived at decisions that either got him into trouble or helped him stay out of it.

"Amer-I-Can gives you the idea that if you don't like where you're at, go somewhere else," Antonio says, as he scrubs dishes and loads them in the dishwasher. "It says there's always more than one option and points out how if you're sitting in a cell or lying in a casket, it was probably because of a bad decision you made days ago.

"Lonnie didn't lecture about right and wrong. He talked about living with the consequences of whatever decision you make. No blaming it on somebody else."

The program's doctrine of personal responsibility was an antidote to the "all for one" rhetoric of the gangs he'd been hearing since he was twelve years old. There is no *we*, there is only *I*. No "my homeboys did this or said that." Only what *I* do or say.

It took a long time for the antidote to take hold. Antonio still lapses into the thinking that captivated him for so long, although not nearly as much as he used to. He can laugh one minute about a gang rape—with a nervous *I can't believe we used to do that sort of shit giggle*—and the next minute rush to a back bedroom to take care of his girlfriend's invalid son.

The child was born without the part of the brain that controls motor functions. He is wheelchair-bound, helpless. Antonio, the (formerly) antisocial, violent gangster, works with the boy to understand what it is he wants, gently wiping his face and caressing his head.

Antonio lost custody of his daughter when her mother wanted her back, and after he'd raised her for two years. Letting Patricia go was one of the roughest times of his rough life. He'd accept the responsibility of raising her again in a heartbeat.

A little later, four-year-old Patricia is brought to the apartment by Antonio's sister, Raquel, to say goodbye. She wants to know if she can take Snacks, a Cabbage Patch doll, that's at the apartment for when she spends the night.

No, Antonio says. The doll goes with him and will be waiting for her when she comes to visit.

"You know I love you," he says. His eyes are moist as he demands and receives a hug. "I love you," she murmurs back. He watches her leave with some apprehension, knowing that the world can be a dangerous place for girls. He's reminded others of that.

After Antonio graduated from the Amer-I-Can program, Lynn paid him to teach it at a middle school. Lynn was impressed with how much time he put into the assignment, staying late to play basketball or just talk with the kids. He also noted that Antonio didn't come into the classroom telling war stories about his days with the gang, but the kids found out who he was as soon as they talked to their older brothers and sisters. They'd come back to class the next day, their eyes wide, suddenly respectful. "You didn't tell us you was Boom!"

He wouldn't deny it, but he pointed out the price he'd paid: "I can't go to the mall with my little girl without looking over my shoulder. I can't go to a concert without taking six or seven other guys. And if somebody comes after me, I might have to kill him and that would ruin my life."

One day, a thirteen- or fourteen-year-old girl, the most disruptive kid in the class, was bragging to her classmates about how she would be hanging out on Federal Boulevard, going to parties with older guys. She tossed around the names of known gang members like they were her best friends.

Antonio brought her up short. "One of these times you're gonna get in a car with the wrong guy," he said. "It might be some of my friends or someone just like the way we were. It's gonna get rough, you're gonna get scared, and you ain't gonna make it."

The girl sat still, blinking and swallowing hard as Antonio dropped the kind smile and soft voice he'd used as their teacher. She saw the ferocity and hardness that had made him a feared gang member.

Although the girl remained subdued through the rest of the classes, Antonio doesn't know if she really got the message. And there are always other girls out there who think gangs are glamorous, that there's something romantic about criminals.

"They want to party. They do our drugs, drink our liquor, but when it's time for the panties to come down, they panic," he says. "Even the older girls—seventeen, eighteen—have a hard enough time trying to get out of it. The younger ones ..." He lets the rest of the words go unspoken.

It was only a month or so after he frightened the girl in the Amer-I-Can program that Brandy DuVall, for God knows what reason, got into a car with five young men who took her to a home in Adams County. Antonio rubs his face and picks up Snacks, carefully placing the doll in a box to keep her safe.

CHAPTER TWENTY-TWO

August 20, 1998

Maria Simpson peeks through the double doors of the fifth-floor courtroom. There are no seats available, so she sits on a bench in the hallway. She's just come from a hearing for her eldest son's girlfriend.

The Jeffco DA's office arrested the girlfriend for helping Danny when he was on the run for the murder of Brandy DuVall. Today's hearing was to make sure she understood the charges against her.

It is also the third day of jury selection for the trial of Francisco "Pancho" Martinez, a slow, agonizing process made more so because if this jury finds him guilty, it will send him on to a subsequent trial. One for Pancho's life.

Maria had hoped to watch the questioning of prospective jurors for a few minutes to show her support for his mother, Linda. She still remembers the quiet boy who never seemed to leave her house at 2727 California, who slept on the floor of her sons' room rather than be parted from Danny and Antonio, his adopted brothers. The polite little "neatnik" who picked up after her messy kids.

She recalls a story her friend Lonnie Lynn told her about when Antonio and Pancho were incarcerated at Lookout. Lynn was conducting a bed check of the dormitory when he noticed that sixteen-year-old Pancho was not in his bed. He found the boy sleeping at the foot of Antonio's bed: the good soldier, watching the back of his fifteen-year-old friend.

Maria had called Lynn a month ago after meeting with Danny's lawyers, Forrest "Boogie" Lewis and David Lindsey. They wanted her to use her influence to get Danny to accept a plea agreement. It wasn't much of a deal: Plead guilty to first-degree murder and the DA wouldn't seek the death penalty, just life in prison. No parole.

Lynn told her that he'd heard Pancho was going to try to "take the weight off Danny" for his role in Brandy's murder. "He's willing to take the death penalty if it helps."

Maria doesn't know these new attorneys appointed to Danny's case. It seems to her they just want to get it over with; they flat-out told her there's no chance of an acquittal, not even a slim possibility that a jury might go for a lesser murder charge. It's the death penalty or life without parole, they said.

She doesn't think Pancho will be able to help Danny, either. Her son, like Pancho and Little Frank, had been charged with two counts of first-degree murder, as well as first-degree sexual assault, sexual assault on a minor, kidnapping, and assault.

The first murder count is murder after deliberation. She knows there will be testimony that several of the young men, including Danny, Pancho, and Sammy Quintana, actually held a little council to decide what to do with the girl after they'd raped her. But even if Danny can somehow claim he was too drunk to have deliberated that night, there's the second count: first-degree murder/felony murder. Essentially, it means that if Danny participated in any of the many felonies that led up to the girl's death—the sexual assault, the kidnapping—then he's just as guilty as the man who stabbed her to death.

Maria wishes that Danny had been able to keep his first attorney, David Lane, who at least seemed willing to fight if that was what her son wanted. "It's his decision," she told the new lawyers, but she agreed to talk to Danny about the plea deal.

Danny had listened to her and also talked with his grandmother and girlfriend. He'd decided to accept the agreement. "But at the last minute, they wanted him to sign an affidavit that what all these other witnesses were saying is the truth, so they could use it against Panch," Maria says. "He wouldn't. He'll admit what he did, but he won't say anything to hurt Pancho."

That was nearly a week ago, a Friday.

On the following Monday, Jeffco DA Dave Thomas gave official notice that his office would seek the death penalty if Danny is convicted of first-degree murder. The next day, they'd arrested Danny's girlfriend and charged her with being an accessory after the fact.

"Danny says she's a good girl," Maria says, "that she didn't know about this. She wouldn't let him tell her, she didn't want to know. He says, 'They're hurting her to hurt me.'"

The family is worried about what the prosecution will do next. Will there be more warrants? Maria prays the prosecutors won't go after others.

But a trial isn't what Maria wants, either. All along, she thought Danny should just own up to what he'd done. Maybe if he had in the beginning, he could have swung a deal like his cousin Sammy. Quintana got off with second-degree murder and has a chance of someday getting out of prison.

That thought brings on a wave of guilt. Maria thinks all the time about the murdered girl and what her mother must be going through. She even feels ashamed for hoping that the state won't kill her son after what happened to Brandy.

If only Danny hadn't run—twice. "Danny isn't prison material. He won't make it," Antonio had warned her after the 1995 drug bust. Danny has always hated being cooped up. Her elder son had never spent more than a few hours in jail; he'd had no convictions on his record.

Maria fought to keep Danny out of jail after that drug arrest, had even made a personal appeal to the judge to let Danny serve his sentence at Cenikor, a treatment program. She thought the worst of Danny's problems were related to his drinking.

While Danny was in jail awaiting trial on the drug charge, two members of the Deuce-Seven Bloods, Sammy Quintana and Alejandro "Speed" Ornelas, had gone looking for a fellow Blood, Salvino Rojas. They believed that Salvino had turned in Danny and Antonio on the drug deal. And in July 1996, Sammy and Alejandro poured nineteen rounds of high-velocity rifle bullets into an apartment where they thought Salvino was visiting, but he had already left. They killed nineteen-year-old Venus Montoya instead.

The police believed that Danny was the leader of the Deuce-Seven and must have ordered the hit. "It didn't make no sense," Maria remembers. "He was waiting for sentencing, hoping everybody would stay cool so that I could work out the Cenikor deal. That was the last thing he needed."

But if Danny wasn't guilty of the crime (and charges were never formally filed), neither was he honest with her about what he knew. "He told me that he didn't have anything to do with it and didn't know who did," Maria says.

So she'd had no clue that Sammy, her sister's son who she saw with his baby daughter in church every Sunday, was a killer. "He knew Danny would never tell on him," she says. The family ties were stronger than ever: The mother of Sammy's child and the mother of Danny's twin boys are sisters.

On December 30, 1996, Maria won, and Danny was sentenced to Cenikor. Again, Antonio warned her that his brother didn't have the discipline necessary. And he was right. Danny, upset that he wasn't allowed to use the telephone, walked away from the program the next day.

In the hallway of the Jefferson County courthouse, Maria begins to cry. She should have let Danny go to prison. If he was in prison, none of the rest of this tragedy would have happened, at least not this way to that little girl.

After Danny left Cenikor, Maria had her telephone disconnected so that he couldn't call her. "I felt that after everything I had done, he had turned around and stabbed me in the back," she says.

Fighting for control of her tears, she grows angry. "Danny is not the victim here. He had his chances, just like Antonio," she says. "He could have stayed in college. He could have given up the gang life. He could have stayed at Cenikor.

"He chose to mess up his life. That little girl did not choose what happened to her."

The Deuce-Seven was in a downward spiral. The violence, the way they viewed women as "bitches and hos," all the antisocial values of gangsta rap were dragging them down.

Venus Montoya was just unlucky enough to have been in their path. As was a fourteen-year-old girl, a year later.

While on the run from Cenikor, Danny lived at least part of the time with his uncle, Jose Martinez, his father's brother, at a house in Adams County. 3165 Hawthorne. It was a house where the gang got together to party. It was the house where they brought Brandy DuVall on the night of May 30, 1997.

CHAPTER TWENTY-THREE

August 1998

"The People call Angela Metzger."

For the second time in a year, Brandy's mother rises from her seat in the spectator gallery and goes to stand before Judge Michael Villano. She's again wearing a black dress. She ignores the husky young man with the brooding features at the defense table: Twenty-four-year-old Francisco "Pancho" Martinez.

Before the jury was brought in, defense attorney Pat Ridley had asked the judge not to let Angela sit with her family until after she appeared on the stand. The defense didn't want the emotional impact that would have on the jurors. "We'd ask that Mrs. Metzger, like all other witnesses, wait outside."

Prosecutor Mark Randall labeled the request "silly ... they're going to see her sitting there for the next two weeks." The judge denied Ridley's request, the jurors were brought in, the opening arguments presented, and Angela was called to the stand.

Brandy's mother looks like she's caught in a recurring bad dream. Randall again yanks tears from her by asking that she identify Brandy in a photograph—a shot of her daughter hamming it up at Continuation, the ceremony marking her passage from middle school to high school—and then Brandy's jewelry. The "B" necklace. The engagement ring Angela's first husband had given her. Another ring with the letter "L," for the nickname Brandy had given herself. Logic.

Angela is asked the same questions she was asked at Frank Vigil's trial. Why was Brandy wearing a red Chicago Bulls jersey the night the gang picked her up?

"She loved Michael Jordan and wanted to be like him," she says. "Her father, who lives in Phoenix, bought it for her."

Didn't she know that Bloods wore red? That Chicago Bulls jerseys and jackets were a favorite of the gang?

"I know," she replies. But Brandy wore it only because of Michael and because red was the color of her birthstone.

Angela doesn't get a chance to explain that shortly before her death, Brandy had complained to her mother that she couldn't wear her favorite color in public because of the gangs. And Angela had told her to wear what she wanted. If you can't wear red or blue or purple or whatever, then the gangs have really taken over.

Angela knew now that she was wrong. It wasn't safe. And although she will have to live with that for the rest of her life, it isn't something she's allowed to tell the jury.

There are so many things she would like to tell the jurors. Especially how much her daughter had meant to her. After her son, Tim, was born, Angela wasn't supposed to have any more children. But she wanted a daughter so desperately that she "sneaked" another pregnancy.

It was a difficult delivery, and the doctor opted to put her under. When she woke, she asked her then-husband about the sex of the child. "A girl," he said.

"Is she beautiful?" Angela asked.

"Yes," he answered. Then she passed out. When she woke up, she asked the same questions.

A baby girl ... and yes, she was beautiful.

In her opening statement, prosecutor Ingrid Bakke had again described Angela as being in a transition period when Brandy died. She and her husband, Carl, had separated, but she'd secured a good new job, and Angela and Brandy were going to move out of the home of her adoptive parents,

Rose and Paul Vasquez, the very next day into a place of their own. Nothing much, a converted, one-bedroom motel room, but it had a tiny kitchen and a pool. It represented a fresh start.

They were "more friends than mother-daughter," Bakke had said, adding that Brandy was an independent girl.

Bakke had to say something, in answer to the unspoken question that stuck like an ice pick in Angela's heart: What was a fourteen-year-old girl doing at a bus stop on South Federal Boulevard a few minutes before midnight?

Angela wanted to answer the question: Brandy was trying to get home from her friend Patrice Bowman's, as she had many times before. She didn't have to take the bus. She could have called her brother for a ride. She could have called her grandparents or uncle. But she was an independent girl who didn't want to trouble her family when the bus would drop her off just a couple of blocks from her grandparents' home.

The prosecutors had warned her early on that they wouldn't be able to defend Brandy's memory from everything its own witnesses would say about her, although Bakke did admonish the jurors in her opening that "this isn't about her lifestyle, but the rape, torture, kidnapping, and murder of Brandy."

But the girl they would describe was not the girl Angela knew. The girl she knew was an honor-roll student who agonized over a single B when all her other grades were As. The girl she knew was not a virgin, but she still asked a lot of innocent questions about sex and didn't understand the promiscuity she saw on television shows. The girl she knew was so shy about her body that she wouldn't wear a swimsuit to the pool, or a dress to school, or even shorts that showed too much leg. The girl she knew wouldn't wear mascara.

Angela didn't have many answers to the questions she knew she would be hearing—and she blamed herself that they had to be asked at all. She didn't know why her daughter got in the car with those boys. Or why she allowed the man sitting at the defense table to strip her naked and carry her to a back bedroom.

Was she offered a ride home? Was she given more drugs and liquor than her small body could handle? At what point did she realize she was in way over her head?

And was what the prosecution witnesses were saying true? Or were they trying to minimize their involvement by claiming that, at least at first, Brandy had been a willing participant?

Angela would never know the answers. The only person in the world she could trust to tell her the truth was dead. *Wake up, baby. Wake up.*

The courtroom is packed. The man accused of raping and stabbing her daughter has many supporters on his side of the aisle. A baby cries among them. Otherwise, the room is quiet except for Angela's voice and that of prosecutor Randall.

He asks her about the last time she saw Brandy alive. She can feel the emotions building as she describes her daughter reaching in the car to hug her.

"Did she say anything?" Randall asks.

Angela looks down. Only a month has passed since Brandy's birthday, when they erected a four-foot-tall steel cross on the hill above where she'd died. Visiting her daughter's spirit there was about all she had left, except for memories and photographs and tears. Sometimes it seems she'll never run out of tears. She doesn't try to stop them as she looks back up. "I love you," she says softly.

CHAPTER TWENTY-FOUR

August 1998

The trial of Francisco Martinez unfolds much like the trial of Frank "Little Bang" Vigil Jr. There are strategic differences, however.

In Vigil's trial, prosecutors concentrated on Frank's position as the protégé of reputed gang leader Danny "Bang" Martinez Jr. (hence the "Little Bang" moniker), and on the then-sixteen-year-old being the first to suggest that Brandy had to die to protect their identities.

At this trial, the prosecution is contending that of all the gang members there that night, Pancho was the worst. On him will be laid the most brutal aspects of Brandy's rape and torture; he will be accused of doing the actual stabbing.

In his opening remarks, Pat Ridley makes it clear that the defense position will be that prosecution star witness Sammy Quintana is accusing Pancho in order to "protect" his cousin Danny and himself. That Pancho was "merely present"—a legal term that's the only defense against the felony murder count—while Danny was giving the orders and Sammy was doing the killing. "Blood is thicker than water," Ridley says.

It's nonsense, the part about Sammy protecting his cousin. Danny and Antonio were always closer to Pancho than they were to their blood relative. Pancho had joined the CMG Bloods at the same time the Martinez brothers did, and he had helped establish the Deuce-Seven subset. That was several years before Sammy got involved.

But the jury doesn't know that. And Pancho, who's not exactly trying to "take the weight off Danny," just sits there and lets his attorneys do the talking.

Otherwise, the trial follows the Vigil script. Lance Butler, who with a friend discovered Brandy's body on the afternoon of May 31, 1997, lying next to Clear Creek, is called to the stand. He holds his arms in a circle to describe the pool of blood he nearly stepped in. "We saw more than we intended," he says of that day.

Jeffco sheriff's deputy Diane Obbema recalls her arrival at mile marker 296.5. Of looking back up that hill at a river of blood that led to the body of a young woman.

Then come the gang members, the three who have pleaded guilty to sexual assault and agreed to testify against the others in order to avoid the murder charges. David "Baby G" Warren, who answers each question as though the answer is being pulled ever so reluctantly from his mouth, testifies about walking through the door of 3165 Hawthorne with a box of booze, proclaiming that he and his pals had brought a girl who was "down to have sex" with the gang for some cocaine.

There is testimony about how Warren's brother, Maurice, walked into the home with an arm around a young girl. Two other girls, one Pancho's girlfriend and the other Danny's girlfriend, were already in the house, getting high with Jose "Uncle Joe" Martinez. One will later testify that the girl with Maurice kept her head down and appeared drunk or high. She wasn't introduced. She wasn't offered a beer. She was taken to the bathroom, where she was given cocaine by Quintana and stripped by Pancho, who then carried her to a back bedroom.

Through all of this, Pancho rarely shows emotion. The jury sees a clean-cut young man in a loose civilian shirt that conceals a shock belt as well as his tattoos.

On the first day of the trial, an attractive young woman is seated on one side of Pancho, his lawyers on the other.

The more cynical court observers note that placing an attractive young woman—who otherwise seems to serve no purpose, since she takes no notes and participates in none of the courtroom questioning or discussions—next to the defendant in cases where sexual assault is a component has become common at defense tables. As if to say, "See, he's not a danger to women." But she looks uncomfortable when Pancho leans over to whisper something to her. The next day there is a lawyer between the woman and the defendant. By the end of the trial, she is at the opposite end of the table from him.

During a break the first day, when the judge and the jury have left the room, Pancho reveals something more of himself. As Brandy's family rises to leave, he turns toward them and with a smirk nods his head at each one. Angela. Her husband, Carl. Grandma Rose and Grandpa Paul. Brandy's brother Tim. The cousins and friends. It's not a friendly act.

When Sargent angrily notes this to the deputies providing security, Pancho lashes out at the prosecutor. "Fuck you, you fuckin' pussy." Then he turns to prosecutor Bakke and adds, "And fuck you, too, bitch."

When Villano returns to the courtroom, lead prosecutor Hal Sargent is still seething. "I don't care what he says to me," he tells the judge. "But the victim's family shouldn't have to put up with that sort of thing."

Villano, who's been on the bench for twenty years, looks at Dave Kaplan for his response. The defense attorney shrugs. "I wasn't present. It may have been a staring contest."

Sargent shakes his head. "It was not a 'staring contest,'" he says. "He has the right to a public trial, but he doesn't have a right to try to intimidate the victim's family."

Villano agrees. From now on, he'll stay in the courtroom until the prisoner is removed. "I won't put up with it," he says to Pancho, who stares at him with no visible reaction.

"If the problem persists," the judge adds, "he'll be excluded from his own trial."

There will be other incidents, although not all involving Pancho directly. One afternoon, with the court in recess, Rose and Paul Vasquez walk out to their new car only to find it surrounded by a dozen young men, two of whom sit on the hood. A relative goes to fetch a deputy, but by the time he arrives, the young men are gone.

Driving out of the courthouse complex later with several other family members in his car, the relative finds himself boxed in on two sides by young men in cars. He drives as fast as he can until the others finally tire of their game and turn off.

The day Jacob "Smiley" Casados is scheduled to testify, a mistake by the escorts allows Pancho to see him in a hallway. "You aren't going to be Smiley much longer," he tells the young man whom he beat into the gang on the night Brandy died.

CHAPTER TWENTY-FIVE

August 24, 1998

"The People call Jose Martinez." Deputy District Attorney Mark Randall, the worrier of the three prosecutors, turns toward the door at the back of the courtroom.

The spectators turn in their seats to follow his gaze. An angry muttering rises from the defense side of the gallery as "Uncle Joe" saunters in wearing a tight white T-shirt and blue jeans. His black hair is greased and combed back.

Uncle Joe is still living out of state in a witness-protection program. If he's frightened now, he doesn't show it. His posture is all insouciance as he stands before Judge Villano and raises his right hand. He even stifles a yawn as he climbs up into the witness stand.

It's mildly disappointing for some courtroom observers who sat through Frank Vigil's trial. During that testimony, Uncle Joe was all over the place. Pounding on the witness stand, rising out of his seat, cussing and muttering diatribes.

Out of the jury's hearing, Randy Canney, Vigil's attorney, had questioned whether Jose Martinez was high on crack cocaine and should be allowed to continue testifying. When Uncle Joe stayed on the stand, Canney had asked the same question.

"No, sir," Uncle Joe had replied, his antics calmed only momentarily by Villano's admonitions that he "stop doing that."

But today he's much calmer. His voice is singsong Mexican-American, and even a word like "sir" comes out polysyllabic.

"Some people call you Uncle Joe?" Randall asks.

"Sometimes."

"Let's talk about that." Randall begins trying to lay the groundwork for the convoluted familial nature of this case. "What is your brother's name?"

Jose Martinez has four brothers, but he knows what the prosecutor wants and offers only one name. "Danny Martinez."

"Who are his sons?"

"Antonio Martinez and Danny Martinez."

"Danny Junior?"

"Yes."

"Does Danny Junior have another name that he goes by?"

"Bang."

"He is your nephew?"

"Yes, sir."

"Is Bang involved in a gang?"

"Yes, sir."

"Do you know what gang?"

"Crenshaw Mafia Bloods."

"Any certain block or sect?"

"27th Street Gang."

"Do you know who is in charge of that gang?"

"I think Danny Martinez."

Randall asks who else is considered powerful in the gang. But before Martinez can answer, Kaplan objects. The attorneys gather before the judge, where Kaplan argues that testimony about the gang connections is supposed to be limited. The mere mention of the word gangs, he fears, is prejudicial to his client.

"I am just asking who is in control here," Randall responds. "It is in the discovery that they've been in his house before and assaulted people there before. I am just going to talk about how often he has seen Danny and Pancho together and how they interact."

Villano allows him to ask questions about Uncle Joe's observations of the two together.

"Is Francisco Martinez a member of the 27th Street Bloods?"

"Yes, sir."

"Is Francisco Martinez in the courtroom?"

Uncle Joe points to Pancho, who looks up briefly, then goes back to staring straight ahead into space.

"Does Francisco Martinez have any other names?"

"Pancho."

Uncle Joe describes how in May 1997 he was living in a rented house at 3165 Hawthorne Place with his son, Jose, who was nine at the time. His nephew Danny Martinez had asked to stay with him "about a month before all this."

"Did he have any clothes there?"

"No clothes. He just comes and goes. He is my nephew. I love him." The last line elicits snorts of derision from the defense side of the gallery.

"Were you at home on Friday, May 30, 1997?"

Martinez says he was, with his son and granddaughter Rochelle.

"Anybody else there?"

"Later on, yes. There was Pancho, Zig Zag, Bang, and Little Bang."

Randall nodded. "Who is Little Bang?"

"Frankie Vigil."

"Who is Zig Zag?"

"Sammy Quintana."

"Did anybody else show up that day?"

"Boom showed up."

"Who is Boom?"

"My nephew, Danny's brother, Antonio."

"Is he part of the same group?"

Martinez hesitates, then answers, "Yes. It seems like he is trying to get away from it, though."

Two girls showed up. One named Jamie.

"Who is Jamie?"

"Danny Boy's girlfriend."

He didn't know the other girl's name, only that she was with Pancho. In the audience, Pancho's wife doesn't react to the testimony about her husband's dalliances.

After a while, Uncle Joe says, Antonio and the girls left. About eleven, he went to bed in his son's room, where his granddaughter was also sleeping.

"Why didn't you go to bed in your bedroom?"

"Because I had done all my laundry," Uncle Joe replies. "I did about five big old bags of clothes. I had them folded on my bed, on the small single bed. They were all neat, ready to be put away the next day into the closet, into the dresser."

He was awakened by a door slamming. "I looked out the window. I see some guy running down the street, running as fast as he could, like there was a ghost behind him."

"After you saw this guy running, what did you do?"

"I told my granddaughter to go back to sleep. I laid down with her. Then I heard my TV slam against the wall, hard. I heard things being knocked over."

"What did you do?"

"Peeked out the door." He says he saw his nephew Danny standing over someone who was lying on the floor. He plays his nephew's role: "'You want to be initiated? I am going to initiate you.'"

"Could you see who he was standing over?"

"No, sir. I thought it was a guy. I went back in my room. I seen them initiate people before. I want no part of this."

"What happened next?"

"Pancho comes over by the door. He said, 'Do you want some head, Uncle Joe?'"

"How long have you known Pancho?" Randall asks.

Martinez shrugs. "Nine, ten years." He says he laid back down on the bed for another few minutes until Pancho issued the same invitation.

This time Uncle Joe got up and opened the door. "I seen five guys standing there in red shirts," their backs to him, watching whatever was going on in Uncle Joe's own bedroom across the hallway.

"I didn't like all that stuff bangin' around," Martinez continued. "They were going to initiate somebody in my house."

"Did you recognize any of the five guys?"

"Frankie."

"Little Bang?" Randall wants to get the gang nicknames in front of the jury as often as possible.

"Little Bang," Uncle Joe nods.

"Did you recognize anybody else?"

"Monkey Boy," he says, using his term for Maurice Warren.

"Why do you call him Monkey Boy?"

"Because he looked like a monkey?" As he had at the previous trial, Uncle Joe smiles at his joke. When no one else does, the grin drops off his face.

Randall asks what he saw when he went to his bedroom. "I opened the door," Uncle Joe says. "The door was closed, the light was off."

"Did you turn the light on?"

"I turned the light on." He seems reluctant to go on.

"What did you see?"

"Zig Zag was getting head."

"What does that mean?"

"She was giving him oral sex."

"Who is she?"

"I didn't know who it was then."

The girl was on her back on his bed, a mattress on top of a box spring on the ground. "And then Danny was on top of her. I don't know where he had his thing at, but he was having sex with her. Pancho was standing right around on the side. I was real mad. My clothes were thrown everywhere. There was blood on them. They threw my clothes anywhere they wanted to, like animals."

Jose shakes his head over what they had done to his clothes.

"Was there blood on the bed?"

"Blood on the bed, on the sheets," he says, disgusted.

"You are looking at this girl here and you're concerned about your clothes. Are you concerned about her?"

"No."

"Why?"

"I thought she was doing it for free, you know," Jose Martinez says. "I thought she was on the rag."

He doesn't appear to notice the tiny cries from Brandy's family. But the jurors are starting to look uncomfortable and squirming a bit in their seats. It will get worse.

"You said you saw Pancho in that room, too. Did you see what he was doing?" Randall asks.

"Standing there, acting stupid."

"What happened next?"

"I told him to get the fuck out of my house. 'You're fuckin' up my house,' and 'Get this bitch out of my house. She's fuckin' up ever'thin'.'" Uncle Joe shrugs and repeats himself. "I thought she was on the rag."

"Are they listening to you?" Randall asks.

"They're not listening. It was like talkin' to somebody that don't understan' English."

Randall asks a series of questions about whether he saw Pancho have sexual contact with the girl. Uncle Joe screws up his face and thinks for about thirty seconds before saying he can't remember. Defense lawyer Kaplan wants it noted on the record that it appears Uncle Joe is "trying to remember his story" rather than respond to the question.

Randall tries to get Uncle Joe back on track by asking if he recalls a conversation he had with Jeffco investigator Al Simmons, the bullet-headed detective who sits at the prosecution table. "Do you remember at that time,

Investigator Simmons asked you, 'He is getting head from her?' And that you recalled Pancho saying, 'My turn.' And Pancho was getting head now.'"

"I don't want to lie," Uncle Joe says, inspiring snickers behind the defense table. "I don't remember."

"What did Danny do?"

"Danny got off her."

"Describe what Danny looked like."

"Like a sickening man," Uncle Joe says. He's starting to work himself up to the dramatics of the last trial. Randall asks again, "Tell me what he physically looked like."

"His pants down to his ankles," Uncle Joe recalls. "His underwear all bloody. He was wearing white boxers. They were red. He is walking with his legs wide open, walking away from her." His voice is at once robotic and singsong. "He's going towards the bathroom. He takes a shower."

"What happened after Danny got in the shower?"

Uncle Joe begins to recount his "heroics" in the face of the gang. "I am telling everybody, 'Get out of my house.'" Danny told the girl to go take a shower.

"Who took the girl to the bathroom?"

"Danny and Pancho went to the bathroom together with her."

After the shower, Pancho went back into the bathroom and carried her out. "He takes her to the bedroom. He body slams her."

"What do you mean?"

"Like wrestling, you throw somebody on their back on the floor. He slammed her on the bed. Her leg hit the windowsill."

"Did he throw her hard?"

"As hard as he could," Uncle Joe says, nodding. "I started calling him all kinds of names. It was fun, fun to him, fun to them. They're all laughing."

"What was their reaction to you?"

"There was no reaction. They didn't care," Uncle Joe is almost yelling. "They didn't hear me. They didn't want to hear me."

Randall holds his hands out, makes a calming motion. "How old are you?"

"I'm fifty-two years old."

"How big are you?" Randall wants the jury to compare the much smaller man to Pancho's broad shoulders and six-foot frame.

"I'm five-six."

"How much to do you weigh?"

"155."

Randall returns to the scene of Brandy on the bed, fourteen years old, five feet tall, a hundred pounds, and in trouble.

"Then they put her on her hands and knees. I am at the doorway lookin' towards the bed. Danny Boy puts her on her hands and knees. Baby-G tries to get some head. I am looking."

"Did anyone say anything at that time?" Randall asks.

"One of them young kids says, 'Somebody fucked her up.' Them are his words."

"What did you see?"

"I seen the back of her butt. It was about this big," he says, his hands out as though holding a large grapefruit. "It was swollen. She was bleeding from there, from her rectum. I told myself, 'This is no freebie. This is a rape.'" He pauses, then adds, "I hated it even more, and Danny jumps on her from the back."

With that, Randall indicates to Villano that this would be a good place to stop for the day. The judge admonishes the stunned-looking jury, "Let me remind you, until this trial is completed, do not discuss this case with anyone, including members of your family, anyone involved with the trial, other jurors or anyone else. Do not read or listen to any news reports."

They will have to be alone with their thoughts. And still, it will get worse.

CHAPTER TWENTY-SIX

August 1998

She was one of them. A female member of the CMG Bloods on the west side of town. She has followed the story of what happened to Brandy DuVall with a heavy heart.

Although she was "beat in" to the gang, she and her friends were "homegirls" and thus treated better than the young girls they'd locate for the Bloods. "We used to find girls like Brandy for them," she says. "We'd look for them at bus stops and parking lots and ask if they wanted to go party—drink and smoke a few joints and make some money."

The young girls they picked up were particularly interested in the money. What they didn't know was that they were going to be raped by the gang. "Me and the homegirls would be in one room getting high, and the guys would be in a back room pulling a train," she says. "We knew what was going on, but I guess we just kind of got caught up with the guys calling these other girls 'bitches' and 'hos.'

"We sat back and didn't think too much about it, 'cause the guys respected us. They'd take us shopping and buy us things. I liked all that money. We'd steal and rob for them, and if the girls wouldn't go along, we'd beat them up for them."

Some of these young girls were used by the gang for prostitution. "They'd call these Chinese guys who liked young girls and have them come over for sex or oral sex.

We'd sell them to the Chinese guys. If the girls didn't want to, we'd beat them up."

When the gang got tired of the girls, the female Bloods were in charge of dropping them off on some street corner with a warning. "Don't talk or we'll come looking for you again."

Brandy was not the first young girl raped at Uncle Joe's house, the female Blood says. "It went on at least weekly a couple years ago. The guys would give him drugs and money to use the back bedroom, and he'd turn his back."

It was all "crazy and sick," she says now. But it took getting older and having children of her own to realize just how low she and the others had sunk. "It was like other people weren't real."

She mostly hung out with younger members of the CMGs, particularly the Warren brothers, though she knew the older guys in the Deuce-Seven subset. Of them, Pancho was the "most aggressive," she says.

"He's the one who would give us orders, like 'deal with that girl,' which meant beat her up."

The former Bloods member pauses. "What we did to young girls affects me really badly," she says. "I pray to Brandy and ask her to forgive me.

"I don't know if I'll ever be able to forgive myself."

CHAPTER TWENTY-SEVEN

August 1998

Inside the courtroom the next day, Randall picks up where he left off, with Brandy on her hands and knees, her rectum swollen and bleeding.

"Danny got on top of her from the back. He had sexual relations with her," Uncle Joe says. "I don't know what kind it was. I don't know where he had his penis at."

"What happened next?"

"Pancho ... I don't know what was wrong with him. It was all a big, funny thing to him."

"What was Pancho doing?"

"He was laughing. He took off to the kitchen. He comes back with a broom. He tells Danny, 'Get out of the way. Move.'" Uncle Joe gestures with his hand. "Danny moves over to the right."

Randall interrupts in order to introduce a new piece of evidence: a straw kitchen broom purchased at Safeway. The real broom disappeared after that night, but Uncle Joe had told investigators where to buy one just like it. Now the prosecutor leans the broom against a table in front of the witness stand and asks Uncle Joe to continue his account.

"He came from the kitchen," Uncle Joe says. "He laughed like a little kid with a new toy in his hand. He was laughing."

"Danny moves to the side, and what happened?"

"Danny held her down from the back. Pancho puts it in her rectum. She is hurting anyway." Several of the jurors have gone white. Rose Vasquez cries quietly, her head on her husband's shoulder.

Uncle Joe looks at the new evidence with distaste. "Could you please remove this broom out of here?" he says weakly.

Randall complies, then asks, "How did he put it in?"

Uncle Joe demonstrates a two-handed shove for the jury and says, "She goes, 'Don't do that. It hurts.'"

All of Brandy's family members are crying. But they keep their seats and continue to listen. Pancho still stares straight ahead.

"I am calling him all kinds of names," Uncle Joe says.

"Describe the force he used?"

"Hard. He was laughing about it. He took the broom out. I went over and grabbed it. I grabbed it and threw it." It was the last he saw the broom.

"Did you hear anybody say anything?"

"Danny says, 'I got shit on my shoes.' Pancho goes, 'You got shit on his shoes. That's my friend, bitch,'" says Uncle Joe, his voice rising. "She is still on her hands and knees, and he kicks her in the chest."

"How?" Randall asks.

"Like a football, as hard as he can." Then Danny and Pancho took her back into the bathroom.

"Did you see what was happening in the bathroom?"

"Yes, I was trying to get in there to help her." This statement brings forth sighs and groans from Brandy's family. No one believes Uncle Joe acted in the least bit heroic that night.

"What did you see?"

Breathlessly, Uncle Joe recalls the scene. "Danny was sitting on the toilet with his legs open. His penis was out. He was making her give him head. I see Pancho with the toilet plunger now. I am tryin' to get in. 'Leave her alone.' She said, 'Take me to the hospital.' I am tryin' to push the door open. Pancho is right there by the door, and he has the toilet plunger. I don't know what he is going to do with that." He never did see, he adds, because he was pushed out and the door closed.

Uncle Joe describes walking out to the living room where Zig Zag and some of the others were milling around. "I said, 'What are you guys doing, man? What's up? Why don't you guys go? Leave. Get the fuck out of here.'"

"Did Zig Zag tell you anything?"

Uncle Joe imitates Sammy Quintana holding his hands a foot apart and saying, "Uncle Joe, she did a line this long."

Then Danny came out and went to the kitchen. "Danny comes back with some handcuffs that my cousin's daughter left in a big old box from her house."

"With metal handcuffs?"

"Metal," Uncle Joe agrees. "There's not a key for it. He grabs her arm. He puts one on her wrist. And I am going, 'What are you doing?' I went at him, 'Don't be doing that.' I got pushed back about four feet."

"Who pushed you back?"

"Mostly Danny pushin' me back. She was right there, still naked. Then he put the other handcuff on her with her hands behind her back."

"What did they do then?"

"Then that other guy, Monkey, says, 'My turn, my turn.' I said, 'Get the fuck out of here.' Danny Boy takes her by the handcuffs and pulls her to the living room and throws her in the corner by the front door. She lands on her butt on the floor. I am standing right there by the TV, lookin' at all this in amazement."

Uncle Joe is quiet for a moment. Softly, he recalls her saying, "'Take me to a hospital.'" Then he grows agitated again. "Pancho jumps up and kicks her in the back of the head with his foot. Real hard."

At last, Angela Metzger bows her head. She knows that what will follow is the test that Brandy failed by passing.

Frank Vigil asked if Brandy knew where she was. "I was hoping she didn't say 60th and Federal," Uncle Joe says. He sighs.

"What did she say?"

Another sigh, then, "'60th and Federal.'"

"What was Little Bang's reaction to that?"

"'She knows where we're at. We are going to have to dust her.'"

"How far was he from her when he said those words?"

"Probably three feet away from her. He was close to her."

"Did Frank say that loud enough for her to hear?"

"Yes."

The courtroom is quiet except for a few sniffles. The image of a girl sitting naked—bloody, battered, in pain and afraid—on the floor with her hands cuffed behind her back, trying her best to figure a way out is in every mind. She gave the right answer, but it's the wrong answer.

"I told them, 'Why don't you put some pants on her?' Monkey went and got a pair of pants I was wearing the day before," Uncle Joe continues. "They were light blue, like these pants I am wearing now. He comes back and throws them at her and says, 'Put these on, bitch.' I said, 'How in the hell do you expect her to put them on when you got her handcuffed, you dumbass.' So he put them on her, Monkey Boy did. She is standing up then.'"

Angela has had enough. She gets up and leaves in a rush, tears streaming down her face. Those sitting on the defense side of the gallery pretend not to notice.

"Were other articles of clothing put on her?"

"Danny comes back with his pullover winter sweatshirt with a hood on it. He puts it on her backwards. It covered up her face. She says, 'Let me go. Let me go.'"

"What happened then?"

"Little Bang, Frankie, hit her."

"How?"

"With his fist, his right hand, the left part of her face. He told her, 'Shut up, bitch.'"

Then there was a new terror. "Here comes Zig Zag with a knife going at her. I say, 'No.'" For the first time this trial, Jose Martinez hits the witness stand. The judge scowls.

"I attack him," Uncle Joe says. "I take the knife from him. I am wrestling. You get strength when you are in a position like that. I took the knife, and I threw it."

Zig Zag went for the wires of a Sega video game in the living room. "I like to take care of my boy," Uncle Joe says as an aside. "I'm not like other people."

Zig Zag doubled the wires and wrapped them around his hands. "I attack him again. I take that from him. The other guy goes in the kitchen, and he gets in the top drawer where I got my knives."

"Who?"

"Frankie."

"Did you see what he got?"

"He stuck it in his pocket. I don't know what he got." There was no time to find out. Zig Zag was back with another set of the video-game wires. "I fight him and took that away from him. What the other guys are doing, I don't know. I am concentrating on this one fool."

After the battle with Zig Zag, the core of the Deuce-Seven gang left the room. "Danny Boy, Pancho, Zig Zag, Frankie, and Baby-G."

"Who stayed in the living room with you?"

"Monkey Boy and that young kid," he says, referring to Maurice and Jacob "Smiley" Casados. "There was Monkey Boy watching me. There was another boy watching her."

"What are you doing?"

It's time for more Uncle Joe heroics. "I am thinking about hitting this guy, gettin' the strength to knock him out. And I was going to go after the other one and knock him out and run out with her," he says, then shakes his head. "But I have two kids in the bedroom still sleepin'. My main concern is them. If they weren't there, it would have been a different story, let me tell you."

"Did people come out of the back room?"

"They came out. They went to the front, by the front door. They go out except for Danny Boy. They went out like there was somethin' chasing them."

"What did Danny do?"

"Danny stayed there. I tell Danny Boy, screaming at him, 'You better not mess with her. You better take her to the hospital. You better drop her off at her house. Don't fuck with her.'"

"What did Danny tell you?" Randall asks quietly.

"'Oh, Uncle Joe, I am going to take her home,'" he says. "Like a good little boy."

The gang left with the girl about 4:30 a.m.

"Let me ask you, what did you do then, after they all left and you closed the door?"

"I started praying."

Kaplan objects to the statement on grounds that it isn't relevant. "I'd ask that it be stricken," he says, and Villano complies.

"Did you call the police?"

"No, sir."

"Why not?"

"I was scared."

"Scared of who?"

"The Bloods."

The next morning, Uncle Joe cleaned up his house. He found a lot of beer and liquor bottles and the girl's clothes and her Nikes. "I looked inside the pants. There was a pack of Marlboros, and I smoked one."

"Anything else in the pants?"

"I found a prayer card. It broke me up."

As he was cleaning up, his son woke. "I said, 'Come here, *hijito*. Look at what these Bloods did. I don't want you to be part of no gang.'"

About 10 a.m., Danny returned to the house. "He tried to get my boy to put them shoes on. 'Here. Try these on.'"

"What did you do?"

"I said, 'Don't put those shoes on. Don't try them on. Danny is going to take them back to the girl. Them are hers.'"

Danny took the clothes and shoes, as well as a bag of bloody sheets, out to a dumpster in the alley.

"You told us earlier you found a prayer card in her pants. Did Danny take it?"

"No," Uncle Joe says. "In case I got shot, they dust me, I stuffed it under the sink."

Randall holds up a plastic bag with a card in it. "I show you what has been marked as People's Exhibit 30. Can you tell me what that is?"

"That is her card." The prosecutor lets this sink in. Only a few days ago, Bakke read from the card in her opening. 'See I have not forgotten you. I have carved you in the palm of my hands.'

Uncle Joe continues. Several days later, Zig Zag and Danny returned to take the mattress. He helped them.

"Why did you do that?"

"I am not going to say no to them guys. I'm not crazy."

In fact, Randall points out, Jose Martinez said nothing until the police came looking for him.

Uncle Joe explains that he had been asking his family what to do. "This doesn't happen every day. I asked my sister, my other sister, my daughter, her husband, one of my other daughter's husband." But no one would help. "They turned their backs on me. I am trying to figure out what to do. I have the police on this side. I've got the Bloods on that side. I am right in the middle."

As for the witness-protection program he was put in after he agreed to testify against the Bloods, "I was given a thousand dollars; a U-Haul was loaded up," Uncle Joe says.

"Wherever a thousand bucks would take you, which ain't too far, that is where I went."

PHOTOS

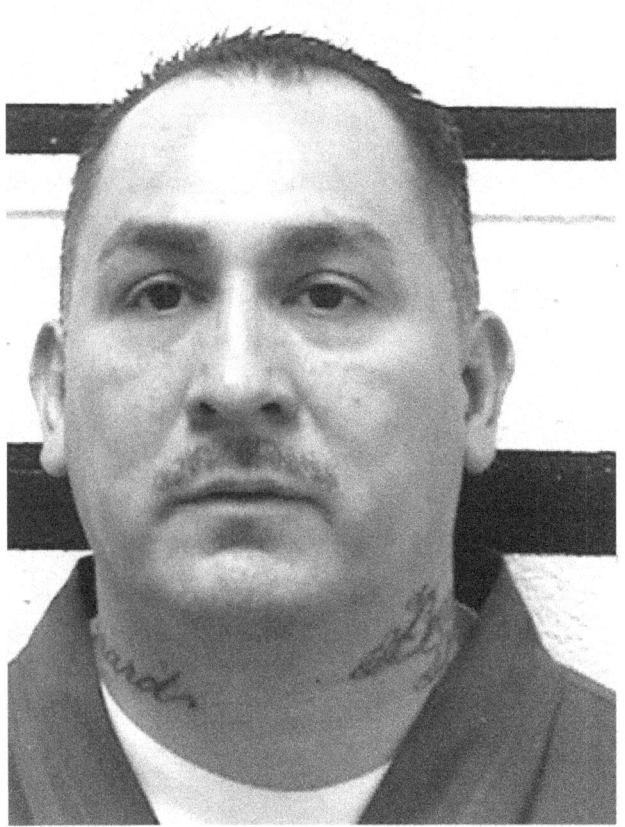

Alejandro Ornelas was convicted of premeditated murder for the shooting death of Venus Montoya and sentenced to life without parole. *Most Recent Colorado Department of Corrections Photograph*

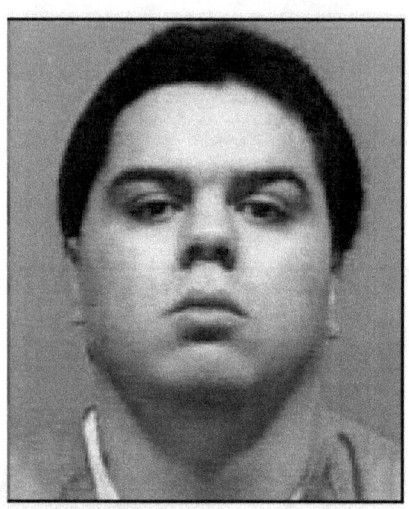

Francisco "Pancho" Martinez received the death penalty for his vicious role in the murder, but the sentence was commuted to life without parole. *Photograph 1997 Jefferson County Sheriffs Office.*

Brandaline Rose DuVall was a petite, 14-year-old girl when she was brutally raped, tortured and murdered by the Deuce-Seven Bloods.

Top-Daniel Martinez, Francisco Martinez, Frank Vigil.
Bottom-David Warren, Maurice Warren, Jacob Casados.
Photographs Colorado Department of Corrections

A steel cross for Brandy was erected on the side of Highway 6 in Clear Creek Canyon at mile marker 296.5

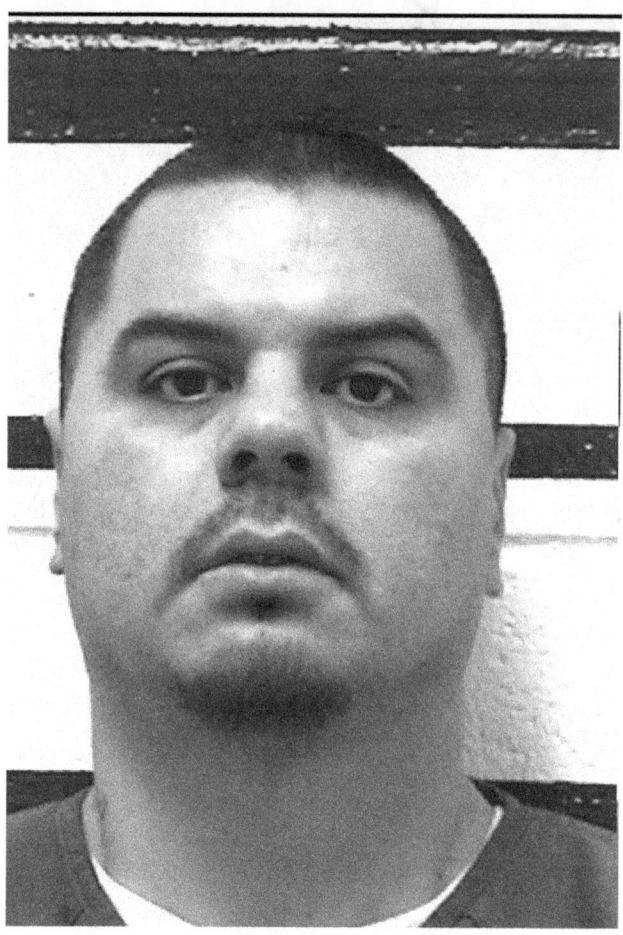

Francisco "Pancho" Martinez led the depravity that night. *Most Recent Colorado Department of Corrections Photograph*

Frank Vigil was just 17 when he participated in the rape, torture and murder of Brandaline Rose DuVall. He was sentenced to life without parole. *Most Recent Colorado Department of Corrections Photograph*

Brandy's headstone. She was a fan of basketball star Michael Jordon and was wearing a Jordon jersey the night the gang killed her. *Photograph Find A Grave*

CHAPTER TWENTY-EIGHT

August 1998

All day long, the courtroom has been packed. Loraine Bartles and her sixteen-year-old son sit on the bench outside, waiting for someone to leave so they can take their seats. As a woman exits, Bartles sends her son inside.

"Pancho is my husband's nephew," she explains. "I talk to my son every day about staying out of gangs. I brought him here because he wanted to see Pancho and because I wanted him to see how serious this really is.

"It's so hard to raise kids now. There's nothing for them to do. He wants this and he wants that. I tell him to get a job. He had one at the beginning of the summer but lost it."

Long ago, Bartles recalls, she used to babysit for the defendant and his sisters. "Pancho was a good kid, always happy. They're a good family, always together. He has like five uncles and six aunts.

"But I think he was affected when his grandfather got killed in a construction accident. I remember it was November 12, 1981, and he was working in downtown Denver when a concrete slab fell on him and cut off his legs."

This trial has been even harder than that on the family. "It used to be you'd go over to their house and they'd keep you laughing the whole time," Bartles says. "Now it's like going to a funeral."

The sun is beginning to sink behind the barren hills to the west of the courthouse. As the light strikes the window, an image appears.

Apparently, one of the courthouse pigeons had tried to fly through the glass, striking the pane so hard that dust from the feathers—down to the tiniest ones on the chest—left a perfect imprint with two outstretched wings. Only where the head struck was the detail lost, and there's a single bright smear, like the flash of a camera strobe light.

As the sunlight strikes the impression, Bartles whispers in awe. "Oh, my God, it looks like an angel. Like maybe the girl was trying to get in."

Others are thinking along the same lines. During a break in the horrific testimony of Jose Martinez, other spectators notice the apparition as they exit the courtroom.

They make the sign of the cross.

CHAPTER TWENTY-NINE

August 1998

Kaplan's cross-examination of Jose Martinez is angry, confrontational.

"Let's talk first a little bit about the evidence that you helped get rid of," he begins. "When you were collecting the materials in your home, at that point you had known that there was a serious assault that had taken place, isn't that right?"

"Yes, sir." Uncle Joe knows he has nothing to fear. He broke the law by helping cover up a crime but has been assured he will not be prosecuted.

"At that point you had known that a rape had taken place?'

"Yes, sir."

But he wasn't so afraid of the Bloods, Kaplan points out, that he got out of the house.

"I wasn't going nowhere, sir."

"That is right. After you collected all these things in the morning, you didn't immediately wake up your son and your granddaughter and say, 'Let's get out of the house, before anybody comes back,' did you?"

"No, sir."

Kaplan points out that Uncle Joe wasn't afraid of Danny Martinez harming his son.

"He is my nephew, sir."

"He was there sometimes when Joe Junior was there, right?"

"Yes, sir."

"And that was okay by you?"

"Yes, sir."

"And you weren't scared when he was there just with your son Joe, were you?"

"No, sir."

"You didn't call the police, did you?"

"I did not call the police. I am not stupid. I'm not going to call the police on a man. I didn't ask no questions. I didn't want no part of it."

"Frank Vigil you have known for a long time?"

Uncle Joe nods. "Since he was born. I held him."

"As a matter of fact, your ex-wife, isn't her brother Frankie's father?"

"Yes, he is my good friend, too."

"So there are some relations there?"

"I love Frank Vigil. I love his son," Uncle Joe says, turning partly to face the hard stares coming from the gallery behind the defense table.

"And you said that Danny Martinez is your nephew?"

"Yes."

"And Sammy Quintana, Zig Zag, is actually related to Danny, isn't that right?" This goes back to Ridley's opening gambit, that blood is thicker than the bonds that tie Pancho to the Martinez brothers.

"So all those people are related by blood or by marriage somehow. Isn't that right?"

"Yes, sir."

Kaplan is trying to build a case against the others as the true killers. It's Danny who handcuffs Brandy. Danny who throws her to the floor. Frank Vigil who suggests they have to kill her.

"And the person who responds to that is Zig Zag, Sammy Quintana. Isn't that right?"

"One of them."

"He is out of control, is he not?"

"They are all out of control."

"And you have been telling Danny, 'Take her home,' right?"

"Take her home, take her to the hospital, drop her off, do something with her, but don't hurt her. I told all of them."

"But you were telling Danny because you thought Danny would follow your orders?"

"They all heard me. I was telling all of them, plus Danny."

"Danny is who you're the closest with?"

Uncle Joe nods. "That is my true blood."

CHAPTER THIRTY

September 3, 1998

Word that the jury has reached a verdict goes out shortly before 11:30 a.m. The jurors had made their decision in just a couple of hours.

The last of the government witnesses, including Sammy Quintana, had testified the day before. "Who was stabbing her?" prosecutor Hal Sargent had asked.

"Francisco Martinez," Sammy had replied.

When Kaplan then accused Quintana of being the real killer on cross-examination, Sammy had retorted that "but for one man's actions"—Pancho's—the girl would still be alive. "It wasn't my actions that led to murder."

Courtroom 5-B fills quickly. Except for Francisco Martinez's family, most of the spectators who enter try first to sit on the prosecution side, as if by doing so they cast a vote along with the jury. But court personnel and district attorney employees have already claimed most of the seats in the rows behind Brandy DuVall's family. A couple of spots in the first row remain open for Angela and Carl, who have yet to arrive.

Latecomers peer at the pews behind the prosecution, hoping space will miraculously open up. They glance nervously, even distastefully, at the rows behind the defense table where there are still a few seats left near Pancho's family. Everyone is aware of what happened after the Alejandro Ornelas verdict was read and his supporters went off.

A deputy in plainclothes directs members of the press to sit in the first row between the defense table and Martinez's family and supporters, a row previously kept empty by court security. Behind the reporters, family members gasp as they try to hold back their fear. Many are red-eyed from crying or lack of sleep; they look around without hope. Several of the young women clutch babies who were not even born the last time their cousin/uncle/father "Pancho" Martinez was a free man.

Three deputies stand at the door next to the defense table through which prisoners are brought in. Two deputies stand by the jury door, and two more guard the public entrance.

Just before noon, Martinez is led into the courtroom in handcuffs, the shock belt bulging beneath his shirt. His appearance elicits a new round of cries from his family. He glances at them but gives no sign of recognition before he takes a seat at the defense table. He leans forward, propping his chin up with his right hand, a finger extended along his cheek.

All of the main players in the courtroom drama seem used up, their energies drained. At the prosecution table, investigators Al Simmons and Doug Moore slump in their seats, lost in their thoughts; the prosecutors occasionally speak softly to one another but for the most part seem content to watch spectators arrive.

At the defense table, Kaplan and Ridley sit between the attractive young woman and Martinez. Ridley scribbles notes. Kaplan just stares off into space.

Judge Villano enters the room and sits down. A few minutes later, the jury is escorted in. The seven women and five men take their seats—some look at Villano, some stare straight ahead, others glance curiously at the crowd.

Villano asks, "Members of the jury, have you arrived at a verdict in this case?"

The jury foreman answers, "We have."

The indictments are handed to Villano, who takes a few minutes to read through them. Only the tiniest of whimpers can be heard from Pancho's family. Everyone in the courtroom seems to be holding his breath.

At last Villano looks up from the papers and addresses the jurors. "Members of the jury, listen now while I read your verdicts in the case 97-CR1697 regarding the charges of murder in the first degree after deliberation and murder in the first degree felony murder, we the jury find Francisco Martinez Jr. ..."

The word "guilty" is hardly out of the judge's mouth when the gallery behind Francisco Martinez erupts in despair.

"Noooo," his wife wails, and other members of the family join in. Their wracking sobs wash over the reporters sitting in the row directly in front of them.

A deputy moves to place himself between Martinez and the gallery, and the other deputies take up positions closer to the crowd. But this time there is no violence, just black, bottomless grief as the judge reads the verdicts on the other seven counts.

Second-degree kidnapping. Guilty. First-degree sexual assault. Guilty. Sexual assault on a child. Guilty.

Pancho drops his hand and bows his head, rapidly blinking his eyes. Then he gathers himself together, places his hand back on his chin, and sits without showing further emotion.

Conspiracy to commit first-degree murder after deliberation. Conspiracy to commit second-degree kidnapping. Conspiracy to commit first-degree sexual assault. Guilty. Guilty. Guilty.

When he finishes, Villano asks Kaplan if he would like the jury polled. Kaplan says "yes" just as Angela and Carl Metzger rush into the courtroom and take their seats in the front row. Villano polls the jurors, then thanks them and adds, "This was not a pleasant case to hear."

Francisco Martinez is ordered to stand and is handcuffed. "We love you, Pancho," family members yell. "We love you." Finally, he looks back, tilting his chin ever so slightly and raising a hand as best he can. Then he quickly turns and heads out the door with his escort.

A few minutes later, Pancho's family members run through a gauntlet of television cameras and reporters. The women try to hide their faces with pillows.

Outside the victim assistance center on the first floor of the courthouse, Angela Metzger, with Carl at her side, holds up a photograph of Brandy. "I don't feel any better," she tells reporters. "It won't bring Brandy back. I know that she isn't in any pain, and it's my hope that what happened to her will help other little girls live—that this won't happen to them."

Angela says she has mixed feelings about whether Martinez should get the death penalty. "I don't really care, as long as he can't hurt anybody else," she says. "No parent should have to go through what we went through."

CHAPTER THIRTY-ONE

October 1998

Antonio Martinez has settled into his new life when Patricia comes to see her father on her birthday. 'Snacks' the doll is waiting for her. It's nice to be able to take his daughter places without having to look over his shoulder.

Antonio's been busy attending to all the details of opening his business. Taking the local board of health exam and getting his tattoo license. Making sure the shop will get through inspection. Buying supplies. Getting the word out.

News of Pancho's conviction didn't surprise him. He knew a long time ago, before "that girl's" death, that it was inevitable that his childhood friend, as well as his "little brother" Frankie Vigil and his blood brother would end up in prison or dead.

Going legit was too much work. They liked the easy money, the power, and the fear they instilled in others because they were the Deuce-Seven. In the straight world, they would be nobodies.

After Venus Montoya's murder, with Danny on the run from Cenikor, Antonio had begged his brother to give up gangbanging, or at least lie low. "But he said he wouldn't even slow down. If anything, they speeded up. They were drunk all the time, and they'd talk crazy shit, like going out in a blaze of glory, shooting it out with the police."

Antonio's efforts led to an argument with Danny that spring. "He said I was no longer down with the homeboys," he remembers. "I said, 'How can you say that after all we've done? What I've been through?' We could still be B-dogs, but the gangbanging wasn't leadin' nowhere."

They got through the fight. After all, they were brothers, no matter what. Thick and thin.

But there was now a gap between Bang ... and Boom.

On the evening of May 30, 1997, Antonio had stopped by his Uncle Joe's house to see Danny, Pancho, Sammy, and Frank. The four seemed intent on getting as drunk as possible, and Antonio didn't like it when they got that way, talking and acting like fools. And he didn't like the two girls who were there. They were the sort to drop names, and he didn't need the attention.

Antonio was having a difficult time accepting it, but he didn't belong in that world anymore. He had worked too hard to let his dreams be destroyed in an end he could sense was coming.

Antonio left, angry and alone. A few hours later, a fourteen-year-old girl named Brandy DuVall was brought to the house, and the others stepped over a line from which there was no turning back.

"What they did was insane. It made no sense," Antonio says. "To tell you the truth, I think they wanted to get caught. I think they were tired. They knew they weren't going anywhere."

Maybe if he'd stayed, he could have stopped the madness. It's nice to think that he would have. But Antonio, tormented by guilt, doesn't take the easy out and leave the thought there. "Or maybe I would have made sure they didn't get caught," he has to add.

He loves his brother. He loves Pancho and Frankie. They aren't monsters to him. They were lost and made bad decisions that had inevitable consequences. He went another way.

But sometimes he still feels the need to remind himself that he will always have some of the gang member inside him.

"I'm Boom," he says. "I ain't no little motherfucker who wants to be 'like Boom.' I get up in the morning, look in the mirror and say, 'I am Boom.' And that will never change."

CHAPTER THIRTY-TWO

December 1998

Antonio Martinez has some last-minute Christmas shopping to do. He buzzes through Kmart, picking out a serving bowl for his grandmother, a video game for a cousin. In Denver just for the holidays, he shivers as he steps outside. He got rid of his winter clothes when he moved west to start another life. A new life.

He's making good money at the tattoo shop. "I'm one of the two best drawers in the city," he says. Humility has never been his strong suit.

Antonio's transition from "Boom," the notorious gangbanger, to Boom, the working artist, is an ongoing process. He charges a hundred dollars an hour for his work—part of which goes to the shop's owner—and is doing well enough to complain that he needs an accountant to help figure out his quarterly taxes. He drives an economy car and is thinking about making a down payment on a house.

But every time he's feeling up, he's brought back down by thoughts of the friends and family he left behind. His big brother, Danny, the "Bang" to his "Boom." His childhood pal, Francisco Martinez, "Pancho." And Frank "Little Bang" Vigil, who was like a younger brother. He thinks about "my homie," Alejandro "Speed" Ornelas—even his cousin, Sammy "Zig Zag" Quintana, "the snitch." Thinks of where they are today—behind bars—and agonizes about how they'll spend every Christmas for the rest of their lives behind bars.

He understands that they put themselves there. Long before the murders of Venus Montoya and Brandy DuVall, starting when they were boys just recruited into a gang, they made decisions that led to this consequence. It's like climbing in the car of a rollercoaster: Once the guy releases the brake, you can't get off until the end of the ride.

Except that somehow, Antonio did. This compounds the guilt he feels. He found a way out, but "they didn't bother to think life could be better than this."

Antonio understands there has to be retribution for the deaths of the two women. It's one thing when gang members kill each other—the authorities jump on those crimes only if it fits their overall plan for attacking the gangs. But the two girls weren't gang members. They were innocent victims.

Still, the deal Sammy, the star witness for the prosecution, got for pointing the finger at Frank, at Pancho, and, soon, at Danny, is tough to swallow. "It hurts my heart," he says. "It's like he's dead to me now.

"What kind of fucked-up justice system is this?" he asks. "The guy who helped kill Brandy DuVall gets sixteen to ninety-six years because he told on everybody else around? When it happened, he was just as involved, even more involved than they say my brother was. It's no wonder gangs think the system is just as corrupt as they are."

He's angry at other members of his extended family, too, for turning their backs on Danny. When the gang was making a lot of money in the drug trade, Danny was particularly generous toward his relatives. Buying clothes and shoes for the kids. Handing out money to any relative who asked. "There weren't a lot of people standing around with their hands in their pockets," Antonio remembers. "You know what I mean? But now it's all our fault. We influenced the others, like Frankie. What they did, they did on their own. We were who we were."

If it weren't so serious for his brother, Antonio would laugh at the prosecution team presenting the DuVall case "like a big Godfather movie," with Danny portrayed as the capo, the boss and unquestioned leader of a large and sinister crime syndicate, the Deuce-Seven.

"I suppose there was a time a long time ago when we might have been considered 'leaders,' because we started the Deuce-Seven," he says. "And I suppose some of them little 'busters looked up to us because we had been around for so long. But that didn't make us leaders. It made us survivors."

By May 30, 1997, the Deuce-Seven was at the end of its ride. Still dangerous, as the gang members proved to Brandy DuVall, but more a band of a few relatives and friends than an organized-crime empire.

"By the time all of this happened," Antonio says, "there was about five or six guys that hung around together. We were all equals. We just liked doing the same things.

"It wasn't like we had rules or told people what to do."

In fact, Antonio had long since given up gangbanging and just enjoyed hanging with friends. And Danny, he says, was an alcoholic, hiding from the police because of a drug-dealing charge, with no money and little power on the streets except by reputation.

If anybody was angling to be the leader, it was Sammy, who'd joined the gang later and was still enthralled with the trappings of gangsterhood. "He wanted it so bad," Antonio says. "It was changing his whole persona. He went from this nice kid from the suburbs, the soccer star and all-city band guy, to always going to clubs and wanting to be the high-roller. He didn't need any of this. He had a good job, a girl, a nice place, and a brand-new car. He wanted it."

Antonio thinks of Danny, of Pancho, of Frank locked down in their cells all but a few hours every day. Of the three, seventeen-year-old Frankie seems in the best spirits. "He still holds out a little hope that someday he may get out," Antonio says. "He may be an old man when he does. Still, he's awake to the possibility. More power to the kid."

Pancho isn't afraid, even with a death-penalty hearing looming in May. "He was never scared of anything," Antonio says. "If he is now, he's not showing it to anybody. Everybody keeps sayin' what a monster he is, but he's taking this like a man."

But Danny is not used to being locked up. When he writes, he talks about missing the streets. He can't hide his envy of Antonio's freedom, and future.

Back when Antonio was struggling to stay in high school, part of what drove him was the belief that he was going to have to "be there" for Danny someday. Now he feels an obligation to continue down the road he's on, to become a success, so that he can look out for Danny's twin boys.

"I want to be there to tell them about their dad," he says. "His kids are going to have to deal with a lot of shit. I don't want them to assume their dad was all bad. I won't hide what we did from them, but they should know that he was also a good man who did a lot of nice things for the people he loved. But that he got caught up in some bad shit."

Danny's first-degree-murder trial is set for February. If he's convicted, the district attorney has promised to go for the death penalty. Antonio says Danny's lawyers have warned him to stay out of the process. His mother worries that if Antonio makes any attempt to speak out on behalf of his brother, the DA will look for ways to go after him.

When Danny went on the run after Brandy DuVall's murder, Antonio faced the toughest decision of his life: to help his brother or stay away. Although Antonio had been at Uncle Joe's earlier that night, he'd left before Brandy DuVall arrived—even the government witnesses agreed on that. And those who'd stayed didn't tell Antonio what happened. "I didn't know they were even involved until people started getting arrested," he says.

The police were looking for Danny, and the district attorney's investigators had made it clear that they'd charge anyone who helped him. So Antonio told his brother he couldn't help. He couldn't hide him or even take his phone calls. After that, other people had to tell him that his brother was okay.

Danny said he understood. For one of the few times in their lives, they would not be facing the consequences together.

"I had to protect myself," Antonio says. Now back at his mother's apartment, he picks up his daughter, Patricia, squeezes her until she giggles and protests. "There were others who weren't smart enough, or loved Danny so much, they placed themselves in harm's way.

"I love him, too. But it would have been like trying to save him by chasing out after him into traffic. We both woulda got hit."

CHAPTER THIRTY-THREE

Spring-Summer 1997

Six days after Brandy DuVall died, with Francisco Martinez already in jail on drug charges, Danny Martinez and Sammy Quintana robbed several other drug dealers at gunpoint.

The pair then returned to Jose Martinez's house at 3165 West Hawthorne in Adams County—Uncle Joe's—to divide the spoils. That's when they decided to get rid of the mattress soaked with Brandy's blood.

A few days later, an informant called the police and talked about a young girl who'd been raped at Uncle Joe's on May 30—the girl whose body had been found the next day.

The cops visited Jose Martinez on June 12, and Uncle Joe started talking. "They had the devil in them."

Jefferson County Deputy District Attorney Hal Sargent was in a meeting discussing where to go with the Venus Montoya homicide when another investigator came in and asked what they knew about these guys in the Deuce-Seven.

They were looking at the same names. One in particular, Samuel Merced Quintana, aka "Zig Zag," had been implicated by informants in the deaths of both Venus Montoya and Brandy DuVall.

Quintana's automobile was impounded for tests. Although Sammy had cleaned and detailed the car, a tiny amount of blood was found on the backseat. Brandy's. More was found on the front passenger-door handle. A mix of Brandy's and Pancho's.

The gang knew someone was talking. But who? Sammy and Danny questioned David "Baby G" Warren, who had been there that night. They warned him about the hazards of snitching and told him to warn the others.

On June 16, Sammy Quintana and several others who'd been at Uncle Joe's that night, including Frank Vigil, were arrested for the murder of Brandy DuVall. Two days later, Sammy began to talk. He filled in the gap in the story of what had happened to Brandy after she was taken from Uncle Joe's house before dawn on May 31.

Sammy implicated himself and his fellow gang members in Brandy's death. He also talked to Lakewood police detective Scott Richardson about the Montoya killing a year earlier, a conversation that resulted in murder charges being filed against Sammy, Alejandro Ornelas, and Alejandro's brother, Gerard. Next to have at Sammy were the Denver police, who wanted to discuss the criminal activities of the CMG Bloods.

By August 5, 1997, Sammy had a deal in place. He'd plead guilty to two second-degree murder charges, each worth a possible forty-eight years. The first-degree murder charges and the potential death sentence were dropped. But there were two conditions. When he testified against the others, he had to answer everything truthfully—and it could not turn out that Sammy had shot Venus or stabbed Brandy.

Two days later, Sammy was again interviewed about Brandy's murder. This time he gave up the details, including his role in Brandy's death.

Locked up in jail, neither Frank Vigil nor Pancho Martinez were talking. Danny Martinez and David Warren were on the run. Warren was soon caught, though, and admitted that he'd bitten Brandy's left breast, leaving the impression of his teeth. He told police that at one point, when Frank left him and Sammy alone with the girl, Sammy told him to get her out of the house.

It was the only suggestion of anyone having a moment's compassion for the doomed girl. But Warren's remark was tempered by an image Uncle Joe supplied of Sammy advancing on the girl with a knife, and then with video-game cords, as if to strangle her.

By now investigators had also talked to Pancho's girlfriend, who'd told them that Pancho, Danny, Sammy, and Frank had showed up at her house around dawn on May 31, 1997. They had cleaned up in her kitchen sink. Later, as Pancho caught a few hours' sleep, she'd washed his clothes and had seen what appeared to be dried blood on his pants and shoes.

Danny's run ended December 30, 1997. Detective Ralph Gagliard of the Trinidad Police Department had been alerted by the Jeffco DA's office to watch for a fugitive wanted on murder and sex-assault charges. Danny Martinez had relatives living in the Trinidad area.

While driving through a grocery-store parking lot late that afternoon, Gagliard saw a car matching the description of one owned by Danny's relatives. He thought he saw a man in the backseat matching the Jeffco alert: Hispanic male, five-foot-eight, shaved head.

Gagliard parked and donned a ball cap and flannel shirt so he could get a better view. He was looking for the tattoo Danny was supposed to have on his neck, one that said "Teresa"—the name of the mother of his children.

Convinced the Jeffco suspect was in the car, Gagliard drove back to the police department and asked his chief, James Montoya, to return to the parking lot as his backup.

When they arrived, the car was empty, so the officers went into the grocery store. They saw their suspect and walked by him several times, trying to spot the tattoo, but he was wearing headphones around his neck. Judging from the photograph they'd been sent by Jeffco, though, the officers had their man.

They followed the suspect as he walked out to the parking lot and got in the car. They approached it with guns drawn, identifying themselves as police officers, and ordered him out.

The suspect got out but began waving his arms and belligerently asking what he had done wrong. Montoya grabbed his arm, and the two officers walked him away from the car in order to pat him down for weapons. But he resisted their attempts.

In the meantime, a woman who'd been in the car approached. "Leave him alone," she yelled. "He didn't do nothin'."

Gagliard feared that the suspect was preparing to run or fight. So he thought quickly and asked why he was making such a fuss over a "shoplifting" arrest. At that the suspect relaxed and allowed himself to be handcuffed.

On the way to the police station, Gagliard finally got a good look at the suspect's neck. *Teresa.* He asked the young man his name and date of birth.

"Henry Vigil," Danny Martinez said but then gave his correct date of birth. February 29, 1972. The police officers knew who they had and told him so. After a moment, Danny admitted they were right.

"How did you find me?" he asked. They didn't respond.

"When are they gonna come pick me up?" Danny was referring to Jeffco authorities, but they didn't answer that question, either. He nodded and said, "I hope they hurry."

CHAPTER THIRTY-FOUR

December 28, 1998

Just three days after Christmas, there are few reminders of the holidays in Maria Simpson's Denver apartment. Although her faith remains strong, she doesn't feel like celebrating.

Danny had been at her house when the news came on about the first arrests in the Brandy DuVall homicide. They were members of Danny's gang. The Deuce-Seven. She'd asked him if he had had anything to do with it. "He said, 'I didn't stab her, Mom.'"

Maria looks down. *No, he didn't stab her, but ...* She had not helped Danny when he was on the run. She'd been too afraid. She wouldn't even let his supporters tell her where he was. She just wanted to know he was all right.

"I understand a lot of people helped him even though they were afraid," she says. "He'd show up and they'd say, 'You can stay today, but tomorrow you got to go. He'd say, 'I understand,' crash for the night and leave the next morning."

During the seven months her son was a fugitive, she'd tried not to think about what he and the others had done to "that little girl." But she knew that couldn't last. "I'm not looking for magic to get Danny off," she says. "If he took part in what happened, then he needs to suffer the consequences.

"All I ask is that the lawyers do their job. And if Danny's convicted ...," she has to pause to keep from crying, "...

and if he's convicted, I hope they can talk the judges out of killing him."

Her entire family is suffering, branded by the monstrous things her eldest son is accused of doing. Her daughter, Raquel, doesn't want to believe what others are saying about her brother. She is angry, mistrustful. But she's also strong and has her own children to worry about, so she will get through this.

It's Antonio who worries Maria the most. Like her, he tends to withdraw and turn inside when troubled. He's worked so hard to move beyond his past, but the connection is not completely severed. There's still danger, and not just from former enemies who would take advantage of the fact that some of his compatriots are dead, the rest locked up.

Guilt is also a danger to Antonio. He has so much guilt that he once told Maria he wished he could be with his brother and friends in jail.

It bothers her when he talks tough, blames the wrong people for what his brother and friends are going through. They have themselves to blame. But she also knows about the nightmares and remembers the time that Antonio broke down and cried, "Mom, you have no idea of the things we've done." At least the tears proved he had a conscience.

She knows enough about what they were capable of just from reading transcripts from the trials of Frank and Pancho. And while they say Danny didn't stab Brandy, for her it's damning enough that he stood on that mountainside while others did and made no move to help the girl.

In this dark time, Maria holds fast to her faith. Whatever happens, it's what God intends. "Even if it's the death penalty, I don't presume to know the Lord's reasons, only that there is a reason ... yeah."

If the state doesn't kill Danny, Antonio has told her what life will be like for him in a maximum-security prison. Twenty-three hours a day in a tiny cell. Only so many photographs of family and friends allowed in the cell. Bad food, bad company. Long days and longer nights spent knowing that there will be nothing better tomorrow.

"It still sounds better than what they did to her," she says.

Although Maria blames rap music for providing a soundtrack for her son's violence, Danny listened to many kinds of music. He was especially fond of ballads. When he called on Christmas Day, he asked her to play love songs. "He was cut off before the second song was over," she says.

Just like his life, like Brandy's life, the lives of all these young people ... cut off before the song was over.

"It's in God's hands now," she says. "I tell Danny, 'Be ready now. If it's your wish in the end to go to heaven where someday we can all be together again, be ready now.'"

CHAPTER THIRTY-FIVE

February 22, 1999

One last trial. Two grieving mothers on opposite sides of the aisle, each aware of the other's suffering. Neither wishing it on the other.

Sitting behind her son, Danny, Maria Simpson tries to tell herself that she is ready for this. She has prepared herself by watching violent movies and reading crime books.

But she knows in her heart that all the preparation in the world won't block out the horror. She doesn't want to watch Brandy's mother, Angela, go through the inventory of her daughter's jewelry for a third time. Hear her describe seeing her child's lifeless body on the coroner's steel table. *"Wake up, baby. Wake up."*

She does not want to see her cry. Does not want her to hurt anymore. But she knows it's impossible for either of them to avoid it.

It was difficult enough sitting through jury selection, listening to some people beg off because they disliked "Mexicans." One man claimed that looking at Danny made his skin crawl. She sat there taking notes, so that she could feel she was doing something for her son—and that frightened one potential juror so much that the judge made an order that no one could take notes in the public courtroom.

Still, Maria likes this judge, Leland Anderson. He's fair, and he treats Danny like a human being ... even if it's just to politely inquire at the beginning of each day if Danny's had something to eat. "Yes, your honor," Danny always says, and the process goes forward.

She's also satisfied with the jurors who were seated—six women and eight men, two of them alternates. They swore they would keep an open mind, that the state would have to prove Danny's guilt beyond a reasonable doubt. And she believes them.

The opening statements had been given on Friday, three days earlier. Nothing prosecutor Ingrid Bakke had said surprised her. It was essentially the same opening she'd delivered at the trials of Frank and Pancho.

"In the early morning hours of the last day of May 1997, a small, four-door wound its way up Clear Creek Canyon. In the backseat are two men; seated between them is a fourteen-year-old girl. She can't see because her eyes are covered. She can't use her hands because they are cuffed behind her back. She's in pain. She is crying, and she is afraid."

This time, though, there was one crucial difference. This time, when Bakke pointed to the man she wants the jury to hold responsible, she pointed at Danny.

Defense attorney David Lindsey followed Bakke. Standing fifteen feet from a young Mexican-American male, he invoked the imagery of "your ancestors and my ancestors" forcing the king of England to sign the Magna Carta to establish the beginning of the American justice system.

He wrapped his opening with a much-used "personal" anecdote. It's a story about how Lindsey and his best friend and his best friend's dog, Charley, used to do everything together. One day the three went to Lindsey's house and discovered that his mother had made two rhubarb pies (sometimes it's blueberry or cherry pies). He and his friend had eaten one pie when they heard his mother driving up. Fearing her wrath, they threw the other pie on the floor and rubbed some of it on Charley's muzzle. The moral of the story, of course, is that the dog was framed.

"It took a long time for the guilt to build up to where I told what really happened," Lindsey said, explaining why he had become a defense attorney, a voice for "Charley and others like him."

The "rhubarb-pie defense" caused a great deal of tittering in the halls outside the courtroom after the jury was sent home for the weekend. "I thought the dog was going to get killed," said one observer.

"I thought the dog was going to be raped and then killed," said another.

They grew quiet when Maria walked by on her way to the elevator. She was so mad she couldn't speak. *A dog? Danny?*

But by Monday she has calmed down. She's known all along that there won't be much of a defense presented for her son. Maybe there isn't one. Maria puts her faith in God and wills herself to accept the outcome.

* * *

Across the aisle, Angela Metzger waits to testify for a third time. Although she can't understand why none of those young men, not one, tried to help her daughter, she places none of the blame for what happened on the other mother, on any of the other mothers or families. The mothers weren't there that night. If they had been, she believes, Brandy would still be alive.

Mostly, she just hurts. She loves her son, Tim, but Brandy was hers. All hers. And then she was ripped away from her.

Angela feels jealous when she sees other women with their children. She gets angry that everyone else still has their daughters. It's not fair. When other parents discuss their kids' activities, she can no longer horn in and boast about Brandy's accomplishments. She doesn't like having these feelings, but she can't help it.

It's not fair. She sees other girls getting ready for prom and talking about graduation. Brandy was so excited that hers would be in the year 2000.

Then she'll see some young girl flirting with boys driving cars on Federal Boulevard, yelling to attract their attention. She wants to ask, *My God, do you know what you're doing? Don't you know what happened?* But she passes them by. They wouldn't listen. ... when do kids ever listen?

A third trial, and it isn't getting any easier. She knows she doesn't have to be present when Uncle Joe or Sammy Quintana describes in graphic detail the torment and death of her little girl. But she thinks that if Brandy had to endure it, she must find the strength to listen. Maybe if everyone—gang members, parents, teachers, kids, politicians—had to hear what happened to Brandy, the whole ugly, brutal truth and not some whitewashed version, then maybe, just maybe, some of the madness could be stopped.

* * *

Others are certainly ready for it to end. Deputy District Attorney Sargent has been on the case the longest. He's tired, emotionally and physically. After fifteen years as a prosecutor, not many cases give him nightmares. This one does.

At one point he had to remove Brandy's autopsy photographs from his office. Even if he didn't look at them, he couldn't handle knowing they were there, knowing what they depicted. It will be a long time before he and his colleagues, Ingrid Bakke and Mark Randall, get over this enormous waste of lives. If they ever do.

Early on, Sargent had hoped that Frank Vigil would turn state's evidence. He was so young, maybe even redeemable.

As the youngest, he could have been the weak link among the four men who drove with Brandy to her death. Maybe they could make a deal. But after listening to Vigil lie for several hours during an interview, Sargent had no longer wanted to make any concessions. Frank might be a kid, but he was a dangerous kid. He didn't feel sorry for Brandy. He only felt sorry for himself.

It was easier for Sargent to prosecute Vigil once he had that insight into who the kid really was: a gangbanger with no remorse. "A real nigga like you and Pancho."

The prosecutors had known that Vigil would be the toughest case to bring before a jury. Not just because of his age, but because there was no evidence that he'd sexually assaulted Brandy or so much as touched her on that mountainside. But he had encouraged the others, then planted the seed that Brandy had to die, and finally had served as one of her guards to make sure she couldn't flee from the car. When the jury came back with a guilty verdict for Frank Vigil, the prosecutors knew the next trial would be a snap.

It was easier to prosecute Francisco Martinez. Pancho was what Vigil was on his way to becoming: a sociopath. In 1994, he'd been accused of shooting and wounding two members of his own gang who had not shown him enough respect. But the two (both of whom were serving time on another murder charge) recanted and wouldn't cooperate with prosecutors.

According to court documents, at the time of Brandy's death, Pancho was a suspect in the shooting of his father-in-law's friend; that man claimed, however, he couldn't identify his attacker. And there were accusations of other rapes; during one, Pancho was said to have slashed a beautiful young woman's face with a beer bottle when she tried to help a friend. But she, too, had been afraid to testify.

If the actions of the others could be explained as twisted self-preservation—murdering Brandy so they wouldn't go to prison for raping her—there was simply no way of understanding what drove Pancho to sodomize her with a broom, or cut her anus with a knife.

Pancho's wife complained that her husband didn't get a fair trial. But witness after witness had testified that on a night of insanity, he was the craziest of them all.

Sammy Quintana was harder to understand. He was the only double-murderer. His part in Brandy's death was second only to Pancho's. And yet Sargent believed his remorse was genuine.

Before this trial was over, Sammy would have one more opportunity to prove him right. But there was a long way to go before then.

CHAPTER THIRTY-SIX

February 1999

The questioning of Jose Martinez, Uncle Joe, falls again to prosecutor Mark Randall. He finds it one of the more unsavory aspects of his job.

The prosecution had heard that Brandy was not the first girl raped by the Deuce-Seven. Stories were rampant about gang members showing up at parties and sexually assaulting young women as an in-your-face challenge to the girls' boyfriends. But most of the informants behind these stories were too frightened to come forward.

In 1997, however, Deuce-Seven member Francisco Guzman had been convicted of raping a twelve-year-old girl at gunpoint. And another young woman, Brandy Cunningham, later told investigators she had been raped by the gang at Uncle Joe's just one week before Brandy's death.

When asked about this, Uncle Joe claimed he'd "rescued" Cunningham by getting her out of the house when one of the younger members of the gang started waving a pistol around. Then again, he claimed to have "fought" Sammy Quintana for the knife and the strangling cords. That he'd demanded they leave his house and do no further harm to the girl. But no one believed Uncle Joe.

In fact, on the night Brandy died, he'd been nothing but a coward. Afraid of the Bloods, his own nephew "Danny Boy."

But there was one extraordinary exception to Uncle Joe's cowardice. When he could have walked away, he'd insisted on testifying.

The prosecution had briefly considered charging him. After all, he had helped destroy evidence. But there were moral crimes and prosecutable crimes. Although he was certainly guilty of the first, proving the second might have been problematic. And they needed him as a cooperative witness. So they told him he wasn't going to be charged no matter what he decided to do. Testify or run, he was free to go.

The prosecutors were surprised when he said he'd testify. It wasn't going to be popular with his family, and it could be dangerous, since it would certainly earn him a "snitch jacket" with the Bloods. But Uncle Joe said he owed it to the girl.

Without him, their cases would have been much weaker. His testimony corroborated—if not exactly, at least in many aspects—that of other witnesses, particularly Sammy Quintana, to whom he had less allegiance than he did to his nephew, Danny, or Frank Vigil, the son of one of his oldest friends.

Now Randall calls Uncle Joe to the stand for a third time. Although Danny is sitting only ten feet away, Uncle Joe doesn't look at him ... or beyond to his former sister-in-law, Maria, and her family.

"How long have you known Danny?" Randall asks.

"Since he was born."

"And Frank Vigil?"

"Since he was born."

"And does Danny have a brother?"

"Antonio. Boom."

"Is he in the same gang?"

"Was," Uncle Joe says. "When all this happened, he was starting to pull away from it all ... and I'm glad of that."

Uncle Joe goes on to accuse Danny of having the most sexual contact with the girl. Of wandering around the house with blood on his legs and boxer shorts. "A sickening man."

Maria tries to listen impassively to Uncle Joe, a man she looked up to like an older brother when she was a teen bride. But as he describes her son's behavior, she covers her face with a hand. Only after she has regained control does she look back up.

Outside the courthouse, after Uncle Joe is through testifying, she says, "I sat there hoping that I could listen to him and hear the truth. I do believe that he was awakened by the noise. I do believe he saw this going on.

"But I also believe that his response was, 'They're raping another girl. Get her out of here.' I don't believe for one minute that he was in fear for his life."

Uncle Joe had told the prosecutors that he didn't see Maria between the time of Brandy's death and when the story broke that Danny was involved. That, she says, is a lie. He used to go to Raquel's house to get clothes for Danny and would run into her there.

"I would sit next to Joe and ask him to help me talk Danny into turning himself in on the drug charges," she recalls. "He knew about what happened that night, but you know what he told me? 'Danny does whatever he wants.'

"His only fear was possibly being connected to what happened. He did not fear for his life then. He does not fear for his life now. There is no one in his family who would harm him. That's just a big story they've all made up to make it look like this gang, Danny in particular, has all this power."

Maria sighs. What does it matter, really?

CHAPTER THIRTY-SEVEN

February 1999

At the trials of Alejandro Ornelas, Frank Vigil, and Francisco Martinez, Deputy District Attorney Sargent has done the questioning of Sammy Quintana. After such a long association with the young man, he's torn by warring emotions.

Danny Martinez's brother, Antonio, questions why Sammy was allowed to wander free for a year after his part in Venus Montoya's murder. But Sargent knows that without Sammy's testimony, they didn't have a provable case against Alejandro Ornelas.

And without Sammy, many aspects of Uncle Joe's testimony in the Brandy DuVall murder trials would have had no corroboration. Worse, there would have been no one to continue the story from Uncle Joe's house up Clear Creek Canyon to highway mile marker 269.5. The jury would have been left to guess what happened between the time the gang left the house with Brandy and a couple of hours later, when four members showed up at the home of Pancho's girlfriend.

After Frank Vigil's trial, Sargent had asked the jurors how they'd perceived Sam Quintana. He'd been surprised when a female juror exclaimed, "I hated him. Just hated him!"

Sargent had worried there might be some backlash about the deal given to a double murderer. That's why the prosecutors in both their openings and closings had called up the old adage about how *crimes committed in hell don't have angels for witnesses.* With no angels for witnesses, the only way to bring justice to Brandy is to make deals with the devil. But still, the woman's vehemence was more than he'd anticipated.

Then Sargent realized she wasn't talking about Sammy. She was talking about defense attorney Randy Canney, who'd thoroughly grilled the witness, accusing him of the murder. "I hated the way he picked on him," she said.

Sammy's testimony had really shaken up some jurors. Intellectually, they'd understood that gangs were no longer just an inner-city problem. But here was this kid, the son of a Denver sheriff's deputy, raised in middle-class suburbia with all of the comforts and advantages that offered. And yet he'd wound up in a gang and involved in two of Jefferson County's most senseless, brutal murders.

Sammy was a charismatic, intelligent, well-spoken young man—and he had killed two young women. For Sargent, perhaps the most frightening thing about Sammy Quintana was that someone who did not come across as a monster was capable of such monstrous deeds.

He'd tried testing Sammy in their various discussions between trials. He wanted to see if he'd take an opportunity to minimize his actions. David Warren had testified that Sammy told him to get the girl out of the house. But when Sargent asked Sammy about this, he said he didn't remember making any such gesture.

In testimony about the Montoya homicide, Sammy had said that if his gun hadn't malfunctioned, he would have "shot at the door," even though there was a young woman behind it. To some, that seemed like a copout. But Sargent believed the statement was a typical gang viewpoint. In a drive-by, the object was to fill a space with as many bullets as possible—there was a better chance of hitting someone and less opportunity for the target to shoot back.

Sargent couldn't help but wonder what might have become of Sammy under other circumstances. The young man had told him he wanted to become a deputy like his father. After getting out of high school, he'd applied but admitted to smoking marijuana and was rejected. He could have stopped smoking dope and reapplied in a year.

Instead, he turned to gangs and became his alter-ego. Zig Zag.

The day before this final trial, Sargent had spent three hours talking to Sammy. During that time, they'd talked about his upcoming testimony for perhaps twenty minutes.

The rest of the conversation focused on the emotional difficulty of this particular appearance on the witness stand and what Sammy's life was going to be like from here on out. He knew that not only would he be facing a cousin he professed to still love, but that he was also likely to see his cousin Raquel and his Aunt Maria, who'd given him a place to stay when his parents were divorcing.

"This trial, I'm not testifying for myself," Sammy told him. "And I don't see it as being for or against Danny. It's about what I feel I owe Brandy's family."

Sargent can never be sure how much of what Sammy says on the witness stand has to do with self-preservation and how much with his conscience. But the prosecutor has dealt with thousands of defendants and witnesses, and he finds it hard to believe that anyone could fake the empathy that Sammy exhibits toward Brandy's family, fake the contrition over his role in their suffering. He's often told his colleagues that Sammy is either the best actor he's ever met or sincerely remorseful.

Others have also wondered. Becky Estrada, the grandmother who'd raised Venus Montoya, had attended part of Francisco Martinez's trial just to hear Sammy testify again. She'd told Sargent that she wanted to know if this one of her granddaughter's killers had fooled her with his tears the first time. If not, she was considering testifying on his behalf at Sammy's sentencing, after the last of the three trials for Brandy DuVall's murder.

When he and Sargent talked about what his life was going to be like, Sammy was under no illusions about what lay ahead. Part of his deal is that he will be allowed to serve his sentence out of state. But for the rest of his life, he will be looking over his shoulder and wondering when someone will learn his identity. There are Bloods in every prison system in the country, and Sammy has provided information not just about his local subset, but about members of the larger organization in Colorado.

And Bloods or not, anyone known as a snitch is always in danger from other prisoners. Sammy's time will be very, very hard.

The prosecutors have told each jury that they will be asking for the maximum sentence for Sammy: ninety-six years. But Sargent has now decided he has become too close to his witness to do what is necessary, to remember that ninety-six years is not too much to ask for the lives of two young women. He's asked Mark Randall to handle Sammy's sentencing.

CHAPTER THIRTY-EIGHT

February 24, 1999

The spectator gallery is nearly full when Danny's sister, Raquel, rushes into the courtroom for the first time. Her mother has urged her to stay away. She has a new job and can't take the time off.

"I'll handle this. You take care of your responsibilities," Maria told her. She would like to protect her daughter from the reality of what's to come.

But Raquel has to hear Sammy's testimony. She needs to hear her cousin's condemnation of her brother from his own lips.

The Danny she knows was the loving, protective brother. Yes, he was in a gang, and violence between gang members was something to fear. She'd narrowly escaped it herself when others had come looking for her brothers and shot up the house at 2727 California while Raquel cowered with her newborn daughter in her arms.

But there's no way to come to terms with this, except to hear it for herself.

Sammy's father has not yet arrived. He has attended all of the other trials. A shamed, terribly hurt man, a sheriff's deputy whose son is proof that gangs can reach into any neighborhood, into any family, no matter what measures you take to escape them.

The witness is brought into the courtroom. Sammy is wearing glasses with black frames and silver rims that give him a studious appearance, despite the orange jail jumpsuit, the leg shackles, and handcuffs. He does not look at his cousin or beyond Danny to the rest of the family as he begins his testimony.

In May 1997, he says, he had a three-year-old daughter and was part of a gang, a subset of the Crenshaw Mafia Gangster Bloods known as the 27th Street Gang, "or Deuce-Seven."

"Where did the moniker for the set come from?" Sargent asks.

"It's a home my family owned for a long time."

"Who lived there?"

"My grandmother, Mary Rodarte," Sammy answers.

"Who else lived there?"

"My cousins, Danny and Antonio. My Auntie Maria."

Maria looks straight ahead, holding her eyes wide open to stop the tears. Raquel isn't as successful.

"When did the Deuce-Seven start?" Sargent asks.

"My cousins started the gang in 1988."

Sargent asks if he's aware of his aunt and cousin in the spectator gallery.

"Yes," he answers softly. He looks down at his feet.

"Is this easy for you?"

"No."

"Why not?"

Sammy's voice cracks. "Regardless of what took place, they're still family. This is difficult to do however you look at it."

Sargent asks about the inner leadership of the Deuce-Seven, the crux of the prosecution's case against Danny. That he called the shots. That there is no rhubarb-pie defense.

Sammy says the top members were Danny, Antonio, and Francisco. "Bang and Boom. And Pancho. I was right up there, also."

"Who was at the top?" Sargent asks.

"Danny and Antonio. I see Danny as having more authority."

Sargent asks who gave Frank Vigil the nickname "Little Bang."

"Danny did."

"And what does that signify, 'Little Bang'?"

"Within the gang world or on the streets, names carry weight with other individuals doing the same thing. To be called 'Little Bang' gets respect, an extra card."

"Did Danny have the ability to tell others what to do?"

"His word would not be questioned too often," Sammy answers.

Sargent asks if Danny had the influence to stop something he didn't approve of.

"Yeah."

"Are you still a member of the Deuce-Seven?"

"No."

"When did that change?"

"At the exact moment when I chose to do what I'm doing."

Sammy admits that when he was first arrested, he chose not to talk. But after two days in jail, he had a change of heart and told the authorities that he would talk with a lawyer present.

"I made the decision to come clean regarding all aspects of my life."

"Are you aware of the potential consequences of your cooperation?'

"It could put numerous people in danger."

"Who?"

"My family. Myself. Possibly my own cousins who are still with the gang. I think about that every day. I've had to weigh it against what's right."

"Why are you cooperating?"

"It's what needed to be done," Sammy replies. "It took all of this to make me find myself, to leave the gang life."

Sargent notes that Sammy made a deal that eliminated the possibility of the death penalty. "Is that the only reason?"

"No. I wanted to be able to look in the mirror and know I had a conscience."

Sammy testifies that the girl he now knows as Brandy was brought to the house by David Warren. "He was the first through the door. He said he had a girl who was down to have sex with everyone."

"Any idea of when they met her, how they got her into their car?"

"No."

"What happened then?"

"Two seconds afterward, other members of the gang came in, and one had his arm around Brandy."

"Did you know her name?"

Sammy shakes his head. "I didn't know her name until I read it in the newspaper."

Sargent asks about the position of Brandy's head as she entered the room.

"Downward," Sammy recalls. "As if she was blocking her face. She was led toward the bathroom."

"She introduced to the other two girls?"

"She wasn't introduced to anyone." In the bathroom there was a discussion about who had cocaine.

"Why?"

"Because she wanted some." Earlier in the trial, David Warren had testified that his cocaine was given to the girl. But Sammy claims it was his.

Sargent asks if the cocaine was for his own use.

Sammy shakes his head. "No. I bought it earlier to sell." Although gangs like the Bloods and Crips sell cocaine for their livelihood, Sammy says it is a "violation" for members to use it.

"How is the word 'violation' used in gangs?" Sargent asks.

"It means not acceptable."

After Brandy was given cocaine, Francisco Martinez took the girl's clothes off and carried her into Uncle Joe's bedroom and put her on the bed.

"Does Brandy say something?"

"She says that before she does anything, she wants to make a phone call."

Sammy was the only one in the house with a telephone. He asked her for the number and began dialing, then "made a decision not to let her make a telephone call."

"Why?" Sargent asked.

"I don't know," Sammy shrugs. He'd loaned his telephone to another girl at the house that night, and she had used it to call some other guy. "I didn't know who she would call, and I chose not to let her."

Sargent asks if his refusal seemed to frighten Brandy.

"There was a change in her demeanor," Sammy concedes.

"Did somebody then have sex with her?"

Sammy nods. "Yes, at that point I took the initiative and had sex."

"What kind?" It is important for the prosecution to establish this for what will come later.

"Vaginal sex," he says. He used a condom and when he finished he left the room.

The jury is beginning to look uncomfortable as Sammy's testimony moves inexorably toward the horror they've already encountered through Uncle Joe's account.

"You drinking?"

Sammy again nods. "Yes. Beer. Some hard alcohol. There was a lot of alcohol being drank." The television was on loud. A radio in the kitchen was turned up. People were yelling and crashing around.

"So much alcohol that you had no control?" Sargent asks.

"No."

"So much that you were not responsible for your actions?"

Sammy shakes his head and looks down at his feet. "I'm still responsible for my actions."

Brandy was kept in the back bedroom for an hour and a half, maybe two hours. By then the other two girls had left. Sammy was out in the living room when Pancho went after Jacob "Smiley" Casados. "Francisco concluded that Smiley was not 'down'—that he hadn't been beaten into the gang. He decided to 'quote' him right there."

"What do you mean, 'quote'?"

"Initiate into the gang."

Pancho punched Smiley in the face, knocking him down. When the younger boy got back up, "I socked him, and he went back down again," Sammy says. Two other young men, Eddie and Mikey—who'd arrived at the house with Casados, the Warrens, and the girls—took off.

Later that night, Sammy says, he explained to Smiley the great honor of having been beat into the gang by two gang members as far up the totem pole as Pancho and Zig Zag. Smiley was instructed on the difference between "being down for the gang and just being a wannabe."

"Does who put you into the gang carry significance?" Sargent asks.

"Yeah," Sammy says. "It carries weight."

They all troop back to the bedroom "to see what's going on." There Sammy instructed Smiley to "go receive oral sex."

"Why?"

Sammy shrugs. Smiley was now a member of the gang entitled to all that represented. And it was important that he understood they were "all playing a part in what was taking place."

"Somebody else get oral sex?"

"Myself." Meanwhile, Pancho was behind the girl "trying to have sex anally. She asked him not to do that. 'Anything but that.'"

As at the other two trials, Brandy's family members sit with their heads bowed, tears running down their faces. This time, the family on the other side of the aisle is also crying for the lost girl. The prosecutor's questions keep falling like the tolling of a bell.

"What then?" Sargent asks.

"I remember Francisco attempting to shove a broom up in her."

"Where did he try to shove the broom?"

"Up her anus."

Sargent asks Sammy what he did at that point.

"I got up and left. I did not agree with what he was doing ... I didn't think it was proper to try to use this kind of object on her."

"In what manner did he use the broom?"

"A forceful manner."

"Where was your cousin?"

"I don't know if he was present or not."

But when Sammy returned to the bedroom fifteen minutes later, Danny was again having intercourse with Brandy, who was now on her back.

"Did you notice anything unusual?"

"There was an odor in the air, the smell of feces. I was aware it was coming from her."

Brandy's family looks beaten. But they stay in their seats, silent witnesses one last time. The jurors, who had thought it couldn't get worse than Uncle Joe's testimony, realize they were wrong.

"What about blood?" Sargent asks.

"I believe there was blood at that time."

Danny and Pancho took Brandy to the shower. "You go to the bathroom?"

Yes. He saw Brandy lying on the floor. There was a lot of blood on the floor. The testimony of David Warren comes flooding back to mind ... the girl bleeding from her rectum and a bloody knife on the bathroom counter.

Sammy says he saw Pancho kneeling by the girl. A toilet plunger was in his hand or near it.

"You see anybody use a knife?"

"No."

"Were you able to see what caused the blood?"

"No," he replies. As soon as he saw it, he went back into the living room. "I don't enjoy looking at blood."

And still the nightmare continued for Brandy. Later, Sammy saw her back in the bedroom, on her hands and knees having sex with Danny.

"She seem to be enjoying this?"

"No."

"Anybody having more sex than the others?"

Sammy hesitates, but only for a moment. "Yes. My cousin Danny." He says he was aware of blood on his cousin's legs and on his boxers. Danny, who had been listening intently, shakes his head.

"Can you tell where it was coming from?"

"No." The girl was taken back into the shower by Danny.

At this point, Sammy says, Frank Vigil told him, "Man, we got to kill her. She's seen our faces. We'll all wind up in prison if we let her walk out." That same message was "conveyed" to all the others.

After taking the girl back to the bedroom, Danny emerged and took control, Sammy says. His cousin asked, "Who's got a gun?" But they were all aware that "she had to go."

"Did you ever think, 'No, this is crazy. We don't have to kill her.'?"

"Not verbally," Sammy says. "But I was thinking to myself, 'How do I get out of this?'"

Brandy's stepfather is weeping steadily now. It's too much, and it never seems to end. One day he went up to the cross the family had erected in the mountains where Brandy died and discovered that someone had written "bitch" on the memorial. Where are these kids' consciences?

At last, Sammy's father enters the courtroom. His black deputy's shirt is partially hidden beneath a blazer. At first he sits on the defense side, but the reception is cold. He quickly gets up and moves over to the prosecution side, taking a seat where his son can easily see him.

"Did anybody say anything in this girl's defense?" Sargent asks.

"No."

Brandy had been brought out of the back bedroom by Danny. She was wearing only a baggy pair of blue jeans, and her hands were cuffed behind her. Danny placed a hooded T-shirt over her—backward so she couldn't see. She was forced to sit by the front door and listen to her tormentors discuss ending her life.

No one had a gun, so the gang began discussing other means of "taking her out."

"Anybody controlling that discussion?" Sargent asks.

"Everybody was giving their opinion, but my cousin is in control."

At one point, there's a council meeting in the back bedroom between Sammy, Pancho, Frank, Danny, and David Warren, where they discuss also killing Smiley. David sticks up for his pal. But later, the others will consider killing the Warrens as well. However, Sammy pointed out that Eddie and Mikey had already run away and might talk if their friends disappeared.

Danny decides that to ensure Smiley's silence, they'll make him kill the girl. Sammy recalls that it was Pancho—not Little Frank, as Uncle Joe testified—who asked the girl if she knew where she was.

"I don't know if it would have changed anything," Sammy says, "but she gave the wrong answer ... she knew where she was, 60th and Federal."

"What happened?" Sargent asks.

"Francisco socked her in the head."

"And what is she doing?"

"She's asking just to be let go. For somebody to take her to a hospital," Sammy replies. "She was told to be quiet. 'Don't say anything!'"

Uncle Joe had claimed he'd been yelling at the gang from the beginning, but Sammy says the older man mostly wandered around during the rape. He didn't start complaining until he heard them discuss killing Brandy—and then it was to tell them to "not do anything here."

Sammy concedes that he had the knife and then the video-game cords. In the earlier trials, he said he got the knife because he grew tired of everyone talking and no one taking any action. This time his explanation is somewhat different. Now, he says, he was just suggesting ways someone else could kill her. He was letting it "be known that this was a way a life could be taken."

When at last the gang left the house, the plan was for Brandy to get in David Warren's car along with his brother and Smiley. They were told they should follow Sammy's car into the mountains. But David said he was going to have to stop and get gas, which might put them at risk of discovery.

So instead, Frank and Danny put Brandy in the tiny backseat of Sammy's car, still hooded and handcuffed, while they crammed in on either side to prevent her escape. At some point, the car with the others turned off and didn't follow.

"Was there a different status between the gang members in your car and the people in David Warren's car?"

"The people in my car I would have trusted with my life," Sammy says.

"Was there any doubt in your mind about what was going to happen?"

"No."

"And what was going to happen?"

"Her life was going to be taken."

The car with the four young men and one frightened girl rolled toward the mountains. The radio was on, loud rap music. The bass was beating the inside of the vehicle like a drum. But not so loud that Sammy couldn't hear the girl begging in the back. "I won't say anything. I don't know you. Please don't do this."

Now Sammy, too, is in tears. "She was pleading, crying for her life not to be taken."

Brandy began to struggle. While her escorts restrained her, Pancho leaned back from the passenger seat and began stabbing her in the stomach with a knife.

"Did the stabbing stop at some point?" Sargent asks.

Sammy nods. "I told him not to." But like Uncle Joe, who was worried about his clothes, Sammy admits, "I did not want to get blood in my car."

Pancho cooperated by attempting to strangle Brandy instead. At last she stopped struggling.

"She still alive?" Sargent asks.

"Pancho said, 'It's not working,' so I guess she must have been still breathing."

As they headed west on Highway 6 out of Golden, Sammy kept asking his homeboys where to pull over. At first they couldn't agree, but finally they settled on a pull-off across the highway. Highway mile marker 269.5.

Sammy made a U-turn so that the car was pointed back down the highway, with the passenger side closest to the creek that rushed through the canyon.

"What happened?" Sargent asks.

"Everybody in the car got out," Sammy replies slowly, reluctantly. He didn't see, or can't remember, who pulled Brandy from the car. By the time he got out and around the back, Pancho had forced the girl to the ground, face down, her head toward the river.

"What did Francisco do?"

"He began to stab her," Sammy says, choking over the words, "in her neck."

"Where were Danny Martinez and Frank Vigil?"
"Just standin' there."
"How far?"
"Five feet."
"Were they in a position to see?"
"Yes."

Sammy says he was told to hold the girl still. "I kneeled down and held her head," he says, his breath trembling, "by her hair."

"What did Francisco do?"
"He continued to stab her?"
"How many times?"
"Numerous times."

At last he stopped. Then "myself and Panch picked her up and threw her down the side. Five, maybe ten feet."

"Did you believe that she was still alive?"
"I didn't know."

The four young men got back in the car, only for Pancho to announce that he'd dropped the knife. "Danny went back out, retrieved the knife and came back and gave it to Pancho. We drove away."

They left Brandy alone in the dark.

Brandy did not give up. She stood and fell, stood again, but the steepness of the slope she'd been thrown down propelled her backwards, toward the creek. Until finally, she fell on her back and closed her eyes for the last time.

The gang members who were now her killers cruised back toward the gray dawn. "Anybody say anything that stuck in your mind?" Sargent asks.

"Yes," Sammy says. "My cousin Danny said, 'We're serial killers now.'"

CHAPTER THIRY-NINE

February 25, 1999

Maria sits outside the Jefferson County courthouse. It's an unseasonably warm day and the bench is in the sun, but she shakes as though cold.

She thanks God that only one autopsy photograph was shown on the television monitor. She had prayed, *"Please, Lord, don't make me see this,"* and the judge had ordered that only the jury be shown the rest.

The trial is over, except for closing arguments. And, of course, the jury's decision.

Danny's lawyers took a few obligatory jabs at Sammy's testimony. Noting, as had all the other defense lawyers, the deal he'd received. Questioning why he hadn't revealed such details as how he held Brandy's head while Pancho stabbed the girl—until after a deal was in the works.

"I wasn't ready to reveal the extreme details," Sammy replied.

Maria doesn't believe that Sammy testified out of conscience. "He did it only to save himself," she says. "He didn't have this attack of conscience until he was sitting in jail, wondering how he was going to get out of two murder charges."

Still, she says, she doesn't blame him. In fact, she wishes Danny would have had the sense to do the same. "I have no animosity towards him or his family," she says. "I miss my sister. We weren't that close before all this, but still, we should have been able to comfort and support each other at this time."

For Maria, it doesn't matter if what each of the witnesses said was completely true or not. "What is true is he was there," she says of her eldest son. "And he didn't try to help her or try to get himself out of the situation. He made a decision in that house and then again on the mountaintop that night. Now he has to deal with the consequences."

When all is said and done, she blames her sons for what they've put her through. Her lament is one that every mother, wife, sister, and child of a gang member knows—when a boy joins a gang, like it or not, so does the rest of his family. Their lives are put at risk. They become outcasts in their own neighborhoods.

"They don't see what they're doing to us," Maria says as the tears tumble from her cheeks, dotting her pantsuit. "I'll tell you what's in the purse of every gang mother. It's filled with paperwork from courts. And there's a calendar full of when their sons have hearings or trials.

"We can't keep good jobs, because what kind of a job is going to let you have all that time off so that you can go to court to support your son? But they don't have to see their mothers or children struggling to get by on food stamps and welfare, wondering where they're going to live tomorrow. They get to sit in a warm, comfortable place with all their buddies, color television, and three hot meals a day.

"Every one of those boys in this case is getting off easy compared to the destruction they've done to their families."

Maria stops. She doesn't want anyone thinking that she's feeling sorry for herself. Not when the families of Venus Montoya and Brandy DuVall have suffered so much worse. But still, it frustrates her that nothing has been learned from this tragedy.

"Eight young lives were lost that night," she says. "And more will be lost."

Yet someone like Lonnie Lynn, who rescued Antonio with his Amer-I-Can program, can't get enough funding to offer more than a class here and there. Even a few volunteers to help him with paperwork while he reaches out to kids would be something.

Before Venus Montoya was killed, when Danny was in the halfway house on a drug charge, he'd contacted Lynn. He'd seen what the program had done for his brother, and now, under forced sobriety, he asked about getting into Amer-I-Can. Maybe, Danny said, he could get some of the other guys interested. But at the time, Lynn had no funding for the program. And so when Danny got out, it was back to the bottle and back to the streets.

"Here is a man who has mortgaged his house to try to keep his program alive. A man who wants to work with these kids. But we'd rather throw all these young men and women into a prison, where we don't have to worry about them ... until they get out."

CHAPTER FORTY

February 26, 1999

One more time, a fifth-floor courtroom is filled to capacity as everyone awaits a verdict. Brandy's family members sit on one side, holding hands, glad the trials will finally be over.

Angela plans to speak at Francisco Martinez's death-penalty hearing in May. Not to call for retribution and a lethal injection, but just to tell him about her little girl and how much she misses her.

Before this, Angela was against the death penalty. Now she has mixed feelings. But while they've put her through hell, she doesn't hate the young men who killed her daughter. Like Maria, she feels there were many lives lost that night, many families shattered. She is not alone in her grief.

Angela feels only an emptiness that was once filled by a daughter's love. While other parents have scrapbooks detailing their children's accomplishments, she has one filled with newspaper clippings. While other parents can touch their children, hold them close, she has to visit a steel cross at highway mile marker 269.5.

She knows that as the blood poured out of Brandy, her last thoughts were that if she could just get to her mother, she would be all right. Brandy was always worried that something would happen to her mom. Just the other day, Angela had found a note Brandy wrote. *Please God, don't ever let my Mom die.*

But the hill Brandy had to climb that night was too high. Sometimes Angela goes there and a butterfly circles her head or a warm breeze caresses her cheek, and she chooses to believe that it's Brandy saying hello. It's no replacement for a lost child.

* * *

Across the aisle, Maria has let friends and family members know that regardless of the verdict, she doesn't want any outbursts. Out of respect for Brandy's people.

Raquel hurries in, late, trembling and fearful that it is already over. Her mother calms her. Antonio wanted to be here, too. But Maria wouldn't hear of it. Instead, she put Patricia on a plane so that she could visit him while the trial was going on. She smiles, recalling her granddaughter's two favorite memories of the trip: The sand was soft, and she saw sharks at an aquarium.

Danny used to see the world like that ... as a great, big, wonderful place that demanded he be up and out of the house at the crack of dawn. And now look ...

The jurors enter the courtroom. The judge has allowed Maria and Raquel and a few other members of the family to sit in the first row close to Danny. Her boy leans forward in his chair, his hair in a ponytail, his elbows on the table and hands clasped in front.

As her family and friends draw closer, all holding each other, struggling for control, Maria is ready. You carry them in your womb, you love them, you set them on the road and hope. She trusts that whatever this jury's decision, God will see that it is the right one. She couldn't ask for more ... except, perhaps, for the opportunity to reach out to Brandy's mother. The judge is handed the verdict forms. "In regard to counts one and two, first-degree murder ... we the jury find the defendant Daniel Martinez ... guilty."

The word drops into silence. Heads on both sides of the aisle bow, hands reach out to each other.

With the judge's thanks, the jury is excused. Danny stands and the handcuffs quickly circle his wrists. Before he's led away, he turns and tells his family, "I love you."

"We love you," they respond quietly.

"Thank you, Your Honor," Danny says.

"You're welcome," the judge replies.

And then Danny is led away.

CHAPTER FORTY-ONE

March 1999

The ride of the Deuce-Seven has come to an end.

Of the seven original defendants in the Brandy DuVall homicide, by late April only two were still waiting to learn their fate—the two facing the death penalty: Danny Martinez Jr. and Francisco Martinez Jr.

The other defendant who'd gone to trial, Frank "Little Bang" Vigil, had been automatically sentenced to life in prison without parole following his conviction in February 1998. Although there was no evidence that he'd sexually assaulted Brandy or raised a hand in her death, he had been the first to suggest she had to die and had then helped escort her into the mountains for her execution. Only his age, sixteen at the time of his trial, had saved him from a death-penalty hearing.

The four remaining defendants—those who had testified against Frank, Danny, and Francisco in exchange for plea bargains that dropped the first-degree-murder charges—had been sentenced in March by Judge Michael Villano. The first of these had been the most important to the prosecution: Sammy Quintana.

Quintana had pleaded guilty to two second-degree-murder charges: one for Brandy DuVall and the other for his participation in the murder of nineteen-year-old Venus Montoya, the unintended victim of a gang quarrel in July 1996. Without Sammy, it was doubtful the authorities could have made a case against the other gang members involved in the Montoya homicide—brothers Alejandro and Gerard

Ornelas. Nor would the prosecution have been certain of winning the DuVall cases without his corroboration of other witnesses' testimony. And Sammy was the only witness to say what happened after they left the house of "Uncle Joe" Martinez.

Sammy was proof that gangs could reach into any neighborhood, into any family. His parents had moved from their old Five Points neighborhood to the suburbs in an effort to get away from the crime- and drug-riddled streets. His father had become a deputy sheriff in Denver, his mother an executive secretary. They had given their children all the right tools for success—music lessons, soccer clinics, good schools, and a safe environment. Still, it had not been enough to save their son.

At Sammy Quintana's sentencing, members of Brandy's family had asked for the maximum. As they had promised three juries who had heard Sammy testify against other defendants, the prosecution also asked for the maximum in both cases—forty-eight years to run consecutively.

Venus Montoya's grandmother, however, had told the judge that she had forgiven Quintana and would accept whatever punishment he deemed necessary.

Sammy's weeping parents had pleaded for mercy, citing their son's efforts on behalf of the prosecution, efforts that might cost him his life in prison. They blamed his "loss of direction" on three factors.

First, their own divorce in 1991, which had left Sammy depressed and looking for a sense of belonging that he found in the gang. Second, his rejection by the Denver Police Academy after he revealed that he had smoked marijuana. And third, the influence of his cousins Danny and Antonio Martinez.

Sammy's attorney, Jim Aber, the chief deputy for the state's public defenders' office, praised Sammy's "truthfulness" on the stand. "Mr. Quintana has really brought down the Deuce-Seven gang and the CMG Blood gang," he said. In Sammy, he added, he'd seen "more remorse and more rehabilitation than I think in any other client I've ever seen."

Aber requested that the judge impose "an appropriate sentence of something less than ninety-six years ... If the Court imposes a ninety-six-year-sentence, everything that he's done for the last two years doesn't really buy him anything, because he will die in prison. He should receive less than the co-defendants who have received life sentences, Your Honor."

And then Sammy Quintana, handcuffed, shackled, and in tears, asked that his efforts to "make things right" be considered. "It's not going to bring any closure," he said as families on both sides of the aisle wept. "But I've tried to make it so that there's no unanswered questions. That they won't have to ever wonder what happened that night.

"There's going to be hundreds of whys. I ask myself why every day. Every day I wake up, I ask why, why my life had to turn out like this. But it's because of decisions I made. There's nobody to blame except myself.

"I know one day there's going to be a lot of questions that I'm going to have to answer to my little girl. She's going to wonder why her dad's in jail. She's going to know that her dad made a lot of mistakes in life, and he made some bad choices, and he caused a lot of pain to a lot of people. But she's going to also know that in the end her dad did what's right and that he changed his life, and he did his time a lot different than a lot of people.

"I'm ready to accept whatever sentence you give me. Thank you."

Villano's twenty-six years on the bench had ended with Francisco Martinez's trial. But he'd agreed to come out of retirement as a senior judge to handle the sentencings, and then again in May for Francisco's death-penalty hearing. Now he told Quintana that although he recognized his efforts had helped resolve the two cases, there were some things that no amount of remorse could make right.

"I can't think of any more horrible acts than have occurred in these cases," Villano said. "You've affected the lives of a lot of people, as well as the lives of the attorneys, the lives of the jurors that heard the cases. Nobody can imagine this type of thing happening until they actually listen to the telling of the events through the testimony of witnesses."

He then sentenced Quintana to two forty-eight-year sentences to run consecutively— ninety-six years all told. "Let me say that I hope you do well for people," the judge added, "because you owe it to society to do that."

The sentencing hearings of the other defendants—David and Maurice Warren and Jacob Casados, all of whom had pleaded guilty to first-degree sexual assault—went much the same way. Their attorneys pointed out that they, too, were abused as children and lacked parental guidance and good role models. But they'd all since found Jesus and changed their wicked ways.

David Warren, who had been the one to bite her on the breast, even fell to his knees, crying and apologizing to his victim's family. "I pray to God to someday ease my mind, because this will always be a cross I have to bear," he said.

Villano was not impressed. "There's a basic decency that we expect in all people," he said at David Warren's sentencing. "It's not hard to know that hurting or killing someone is wrong. It's not hard to know that taking advantage of a fourteen-year-old girl is wrong, and these are basic things that aren't the result of your upbringing."

David Warren was sentenced to thirty-two years in prison. His brother, Maurice, described by defense attorneys as one step shy of being declared mentally incompetent, received sixteen years. And Jacob "Smiley" Casados, who was beat into the gang that night, got twenty for his one evening as a member of the Deuce-Seven.

None of them had been with Brandy when she was stabbed, "just" when she had been raped and tortured.

CHAPTER FORTY-TWO

April 27, 1999

"The presumption of innocence is gone, Mr. Martinez sits before you, a convicted murderer."

Tall and business-like, Deputy District Attorney Ingrid Bakke delivers for the fourth time the prosecution's opening statement in the DuVall case. But when she reaches her conclusion a few minutes from now, she won't be asking a jury to convict the defendant of Brandy's rape, kidnapping, and murder.

Bakke will be asking the panel—Judges Leland Anderson of Jefferson County, who presided over the trial, Timothy Fasing of Arapahoe County and John Coughlin of Denver—to sentence Danny "Bang" Martinez Jr. to death by lethal injection. Nancylly assigned to the unit that deals with sex crimes against children, this has been Bakke's first murder case. And so this will be the first time she will ask a judge for another human being's execution.

It is time for the court to "shift its focus from what crimes were committed ... to what evils have been suffered," she tells the judges. The words, on the more than 750 pages of transcripts from Danny's trial that the judges have been given to assist with their decision, "fall short of describing the indescribable."

A pall hangs over this courtroom that goes beyond the terrible business at hand. It's only been a week since twelve students and one teacher were murdered by two gunmen at Columbine High School in Jefferson County. The blue-and-silver-ribbon remembrance emblem is everywhere.

It adorns lapels and blouses of men and women in the audience, of prosecutors and defense attorneys, of the deputies who stand guard.

Members of Brandy's family also wear a button promoting Victims Rights Week. The buttons read: *Victim's Voice. Silent no more.* But the family sits quietly, knowing, dreading what is to come. Angela and her husband, Carl Metzger. The grandchild Brandon, named after his murdered aunt, in his stroller. Angela's friend Amy. Grandmother Peggy DuVall. Grandparents Rose and Paul Vasquez and several more relatives. As Bakke begins her opening remarks, the older members of the family adjust the headsets provided by the court.

Al Simmons, the short, tough Jeffco sheriff's investigator who took the lead in the DuVall homicide, listens at one end of the prosecution table. He'd been working on the Columbine case, but he had to drop that for this—from one horror involving kids to the next. It will be his job to guide the judges through the evidence that was presented to the jurors at trial in January.

Danny Martinez sits quietly, staring down at the space beneath the defense table he shares with his attorneys, Forrest "Boogie" Lewis and David Lindsey. The long, flowing hair he wore at trial is gone, shaved to boot-camp length.

When he first entered the courtroom in handcuffs and shackles, Danny smiled briefly at the rows filled with his supporters and rolled his eyes as if to say, Can you believe this? His father is there, but his mother and sister wait in the hallway, sequestered because they will be called as witnesses.

Bakke doesn't spend a lot of time making an emotional pitch. These are not jurors she needs to win over. And judges aren't supposed to be swayed by such courtroom tactics—that was one of the arguments for the legislation that took responsibility for the death-penalty decision out of the hands of jurors and gave it to a panel of three judges.

Instead, Bakke lays the groundwork for the first in the four-step process that the judges will follow to reach their decision. Step one requires the prosecution to prove any one of seventeen possible statutory "aggravators" that essentially define why a particular murderer should be killed for his crime.

Bakke tells the judge that the prosecution intends to prove five things: that Danny Martinez caused the death of Brandy DuVall "in the course of or in furtherance of or flight therefrom" a felony—in this case, assault, sexual assault, and sexual assault on a child using force; that Danny intentionally killed a kidnapped person; that Danny was party to an agreement to kill Brandy; that Danny killed Brandy to avoid lawful arrest or prosecution; and that the murder of Brandy was "especially heinous, cruel, or depraved."

To make her point, Bakke tenders photographs—a set for each judge—of how Brandy, "a child by her nature and by legal definition," looked before she met members of the Deuce-Seven. And "how she looked when they were done with her."

As two of the judges see the horror for the first time, she tells them that they will have no choice but to sentence Danny to die.

The statute establishing the three-judge death-penalty panel was passed by the Colorado Legislature in 1995 and went into effect for murders committed after July 1996. The panels consist of the trial judge and two selected at random from surrounding districts.

Prosecutors had pushed for the new law, saying it would bring "consistency" to sentencing. Defense attorneys had decried it, claiming it would be easier than ever to impose the penalty.

Convicted in September 1998, Francisco Martinez was originally scheduled to be the first Colorado man to go before such a death-penalty panel. But when his case was continued until May, that distinction went to Robert L. Riggan, convicted in November, also in Jefferson County, of the murder of a young prostitute. His case went before a panel in mid-April in a Jeffco courtroom that had been modified to allow the three judges to sit in a row on the dais.

At Riggan's trial, the jury had hung on the question of first-degree murder and whether he'd "intentionally" killed Anita Paley. Instead, the jurors had settled for felony murder, determining that Riggan had killed her in furtherance or to cover up another crime—in this case, sexual assault.

No jury in Colorado had ever sent someone convicted of felony murder to death row, although the option remained on the books. Nor would the panel of judges assigned to Riggan's case. On April 16, they'd unanimously decided against the death penalty, citing the absence of intent. Riggan was then automatically sentenced to life without parole.

Afterward, even Jefferson County District Attorney Dave Thomas conceded that his office had not expected to win that one. But it was necessary to test where the panels, as opposed to juries, would set the death-penalty bar.

Danny Martinez's hearing was the second to go before a panel, but only by a matter of days. In Denver, another panel would soon begin hearing the case against Jacques Richardson, the rapist who'd murdered Capitol Hill resident Janey Benedict.

Both of these cases represented further steps up the ladder in terms of culpability. As with Riggan, the jurors in the Richardson case had not been able to decide if he'd intended to kill Benedict when he hog-tied her, leading to her death by strangulation. Unlike Riggan, however, Richardson had a "serious" criminal history as a serial rapist—such histories being one of the aggravators judges can use in making their decision.

Danny Martinez presented another problem. He had been convicted of first-degree murder after deliberation. However, the prosecution theory presented to the jury was that while Danny had participated in the rape and torment of Brandy DuVall and had "called the shots" as the gang's leader, it was Francisco Martinez who'd stabbed the girl to death. The wording in the first-degree-murder count included the "complicity instruction," which meant the jury didn't have to find that Danny had actually done the stabbing.

In the past, Colorado juries have been reluctant to sentence so-called "complicitors" to death. The question was whether a panel of judges would follow suit.

Danny's life would hang on that issue.

* * *

Forrest Lewis makes the opening statement for the defense by trying to shift the responsibility for Brandy's death onto Sammy and Francisco.

It was Sammy who gave her cocaine when she was brought into the house and Sammy who was the first to have sex with her, he says. And Francisco, he reminds the court in a soft Southern accent, was the brute who shoved a broom into her anus, kicked her "like a football," and eventually stabbed her in the neck while Sammy held her head down.

Danny hangs his head as his lawyer smears his friend Francisco. In the months preceding his trial, he'd told his mother that he couldn't accept a plea bargain that would spare him the death penalty (a deal that was never formally offered); he couldn't leave his childhood friend to face such a consequence on his own. Especially because Danny's lawyers had told him that any such agreement would hinge on him giving a statement implicating Francisco.

Danny now sits silent as Lewis, an experienced attorney respected on both sides of the aisle, paints Pancho as the evil instigator of all the worst atrocities while describing his own client's actions during the murder as essentially those of a drunk bystander. "The only evidence of any weapon in his hand was after the fact," Lewis notes, when Danny retrieved the knife that Francisco had dropped. Or so Sammy Quintana had claimed.

Lewis quickly moves on to Danny's tough childhood in Five Points. Both of his parents were drug users. Danny Martinez Sr., in particular, was "a bad influence" who lured Danny away from a program in Arkansas where he was doing well and had just completed his GED.

At this, Danny's father, a short, stocky man, stands up in the middle of a pew. "Well, excuse me!" he says loudly, then stalks from the courtroom.

Lewis takes no notice. He says that others, including a teacher and probation officer, will be called to the witness stand to talk about Danny's good points. The panel will hear that Danny's sister, Raquel, and brother, Antonio, had dreams and "got out ... but Danny did not believe that he could get out."

None of this will be used to excuse Danny's participation in some of the horrible events of the night in question, Lewis notes. "He is guilty of complicity," the attorney concedes. But the "blood of Brandy ... is on the hands of Francisco.

"He'll never get out of prison. He'll never see his children except through bars. He should be in prison for the rest of his life, and he will be ... but the death penalty ... is excessive."

CHAPTER FORTY-THREE

April 27, 1999

"Brandy was only fourteen years old, and she was shy."

Once more, Angela Metzger finds herself standing at a podium trying to describe to strangers the little girl she remembers, not the wayward teen the defendants and their lawyers made her out to be. "When she went swimming, she would wear jeans and almost drown rather than show her body," she says. "She was wise and smart ... I used to say that when I grew up, I wanted to be just like her."

Once more, Angela begins to cry, her voice becoming high and tight in an effort to keep control. She stamps her foot as she gathers herself together. Danny, who has been watching her, looks quickly away.

"I was robbed," Angela says. "She didn't do nothin' to deserve this ... and when she died, the best part of me died along with her."

This time, Angela's testimony has a new twist. She recalls her horror when the Columbine shootings came on the news. "I was thinking about the parents waiting to find out if their children were okay. I remembered what it was like, waiting for Brandy to call, and my heart went out to those people. Unless you've gone through it, there are no words for it."

As she describes seeing her daughter's body at the coroner's office, Angela closes her eyes and reaches a hand toward the judges, trying to grasp something that is no longer hers to hold. *Wake up, baby. Wake up.*

In his seat, Danny blinks rapidly and rubs at his eyes. There are some things that no amount of remorse can make right.

"You know, I never thought I would ever have to stand up and try to convince people how much I loved my daughter," Angela says quietly. "I wish to God you all could have seen us together, and there would be no question about how we felt.

"She was my life ... and I would give my life for just five minutes, right now, to tell her how much I love her."

Angela takes her seat, and Judge Anderson announces that the court will be in recess through lunch. It's a little after 11 a.m. At 11:20 a.m., he, and many others in the city, the state, and the country, will observe a moment of silence for the Columbine victims.

Angela will sit in silence, thinking about her daughter as well.

* * *

When this horrible thing happened," says the tiny old woman, "I couldn't speak for a while. My God, it was like a madness."

Somehow the woman, Rose Vasquez, and her husband, Paul, have made it through all the trials and sentencings, but it has taken an enormous toll. Of all of their granddaughters, they had been the closest to Brandy.

Brandy had been staying with them until the night she disappeared, waiting to move into a new apartment with her mother the next day. They'd dropped her off near Federal Boulevard earlier in the evening so she could catch the bus to her friend's house, as Brandy had done many times before.

But for some reason, Rose recalls, she'd felt uneasy and sent a prayer after the retreating form of her granddaughter, "asking the good Lord to take care of her."

Now nothing will ever be the same. Friends and neighbors no longer come by, and "everybody is afraid to say the wrong thing," she says, then sadly adds that "Angie and I don't communicate anymore. I guess she's struggling with herself.

"I did not realize how quick a life can go and leave such an emptiness."

Some of her memories she won't share with the judges, like the times her five-foot-tall granddaughter would sit her down for a woman-to-woman talk. But she does tell the panel about Brandy's first rose, just a few weeks before her death, given to her by a sixteen-year-old boy who'd driven her home from school.

"The rose and the boy were soon gone," she says. As was Brandy.

The family could have lived with Brandy's death, "would have missed her, but we would have gone on." But the manner of her death—the horrible things that were done to her, the humiliation and shame she must have felt—was impossible to get past.

Brandy's body was identified by her mother on a Sunday. The next day, Rose says, the telephone rang, and when she answered it, "I heard little Brandy's voice. She said, *'Bye, Grandma,'* then the phone went dead and there was no other sound."

Rose pauses a moment. Her thin shoulders shake as she cries, and Sargent puts a hand on her arm to steady her. She takes a deep breath and goes on.

Now, when she dreams of Brandy, "I can't see her face," she says. "I can't touch her or hear her or hug her. All I can do now is pray and cry and visit the cemetery. But a cold stone does not satisfy the arms of a seventy-four-year-old lady."

* * *

Brandy's grandfather, Paul, is next. A friendly man with a gravelly, lightly accented voice, he is nearly as short as his wife.

"She was my youngest granddaughter," he begins. "I needed her, and she needed me. We were friends and companions."

His memories are of bicycle rides to the ice-cream store and watching movies together. Brandy, he says, was free to ask him for money. But she always insisted on earning it with odd jobs and chores.

It was their dream to go to Disneyland. Her brother, Tim, and a cousin had gone years ago, when she was too small to make the trip. "But I told her that one way or another, we would go in 1998."

That dream had died with Brandy. Two years later, a good and decent man is reduced to tears, wishing they had gone sooner.

"If I could have only been there," he says brokenly. "I would gladly have given my life to save her."

When Brandy was alive, out visiting one of her friends at night, he would lie awake, listening for her footsteps, waiting for her tap on the window to be let back inside. Now when he sleeps, he swears he still hears her footsteps and jumps out of bed to greet her. "But nobody's there," he says.

Harder still are the nights when his sleep is interrupted by cries from Brandy. *"Grandpa, help me, help me."* But after he's awake, there is only silence - as he lies still, listening.

CHAPTER FORTY-FOUR

April 28, 1999

After opening statements, followed by the testimony from Brandy's family, it took the prosecutors just the rest of the day to wrap up their case. This morning, it's the defense team's turn.

Danny enters the courtroom looking tired, as though he didn't sleep well after the previous day's emotional testimony from Brandy's family. He asks supporters if his mother is in the courthouse and smiles only after he's told that she is waiting in the hallway.

It is up to the defense to present step two in the death-penalty process, to discuss any of the eleven statutorily allowed "mitigators" that may apply. Mitigators are essentially anything in the defendant's favor that might excuse his behavior somewhat and balance out the aggravators—such as the defendant's age, whether the defendant was under duress, or whether the defendant's participation was relatively minor, though not so minor as to be a defense from prosecution.

While aggravators must be proven beyond a reasonable doubt, there is no burden of proof regarding mitigators, which can include the rather open-ended "any other evidence, which in the court's opinion bears on the question of mitigation." The only caveat is that the evidence is supposed to be relevant to the defendant's character, background, and the circumstances surrounding the crime.

It is this last point that comes into contention after Lindsey calls defense investigator Pamela Ferguson to the stand and asks her about death-penalty statistics that she obtained from the NAACP Legal Defense Fund.

Sargent objects, saying the information is not relevant to Danny. But Lindsey counters that such statistics provide a "moral sense" of what has occurred. Anderson, who as the trial-court judge rules on the nitty-gritty of this hearing, calls for a recess to confer with the other two judges.

Back in session, Anderson overrules Sargent's objection and allows Ferguson to make her report under the "any other evidence" portion of the mitigation statutes. The statistics, Ferguson says, show that of the 6,331 people sentenced to die since the U.S. Supreme Court reinstated the death penalty in 1976, only seventy-six were "non-triggermen."

* * *

"If Danny needed anything, he'd ask me. If I needed anything, I didn't even have to ask. We were just there for each other."

Danny's sister, Raquel, clutches a tissue as Lewis gently guides her through his questions. The hearing has reached the stage where the defense is trying to highlight Danny's good qualities while emphasizing his difficult childhood.

Raquel is Danny's older sister. She works for a communications company and has three children. She clearly loves her brother despite the crimes he's been convicted of, and it isn't difficult for Lewis to wring out the tears—particularly when he shows her photographs of Danny with his twin sons.

There are more tears when Lewis mentions the time when they were children and their mother placed them in foster care while she straightened out her own life. Danny and Raquel had been sent to one home and their baby brother, Antonio, to another.

"We lived terrible," she cries. She and her brother were kept in a basement, sleeping on mats, and forced to use containers when they had to go to the bathroom. If they got into trouble, they had to lie on the ground while their caretaker spanked the bottoms of their feet.

The ordeal didn't last long. Raquel managed to relay the abuse to a social worker, who placed them in the same home as Antonio. "I never talked about it with Danny," she says. "I don't know if he remembered."

Once reunited with their mother, they all moved into their grandmother's house, at 2727 California Street in Five Points. It was a neighborhood in which crime and drug use was rampant. Both of their parents were users.

There was a brief reprieve when Maria married Bill Rollins, a good man who was the first decent role model the boys had known. "That's my dad," Raquel tells Lewis. But her mother's drug problems cost Maria that marriage.

As Danny grew up, he got involved with gangs and selling drugs. No, Raquel says, she wasn't aware that he sold drugs to his own father. But yes, she did know he sold them to his uncle Jimmy.

It was while living at 2727 California that Danny met his friend Francisco. They were soon inseparable. "Without being biological brothers, they were brothers."

"Was the loyalty factor strong?" Lewis asks.

"Obviously," Raquel answers. "It's why we're here."

Raquel testifies that she and Antonio had dreams of getting out of the neighborhood and eventually made it. Danny had dreams, too, "but they just didn't come fast enough."

Before he turns her over to the prosecution for cross-examination, Lewis asks if there's anything she wants to say to Brandy's family. Raquel nods and dabs at her tears.

"I am sorry," she says. "I have two daughters and can't imagine what you are going through. But I know my brother probably better than anybody. He's not this terrible person he's been made him out to be. He's not."

Sargent stands to question Raquel. His praise of Raquel is so effusive that, if you didn't know better, you would be surprised by what side of the aisle he sits on. But that's the prosecutor's point: Despite what the defense wants to imply, Danny came from a loving, supportive family and had his chances to escape the hole he dug for himself. After all, Raquel did.

"You tried to help Danny?" he asks.

"We help each other," she replies guardedly.

"You tried to keep him straight?"

"Yes."

The prosecutor notes that Raquel had written a letter of support to the judge in Danny's last drug case, a letter in which she promised to help her brother. "You wanted him to succeed?"

"Yes."

"You did not have a wonderful childhood?" Sargent asks.

"No."

"Despite that, you chose to get out and you did."

"Yes."

"And you have a job of which you're proud?"

"Yes."

"And your brother, Antonio, chose to get out and did?"

"Yes."

"And again, that's something to be proud of?"

"Yes."

But Danny didn't make that choice, Sargent points out. And wasn't it true, he asks, that anyone who stays mixed up in gangs was essentially looking at one of two ends: death or prison?

Although Raquel disputes this, she can't come up with other options. She also avoids Sargent's question about Danny's role as the leader of the Deuce-Seven. "He had the respect of his peers," is all she admits to. "He earned their respect."

Sargent asks about the origin of the Deuce-Seven name.

"It was just an address—that's all it was," Raquel replies.

"But it was an address he chose as the name of his gang," Sargent notes. He'll leave it for closing, but one of the points the prosecution wants to make is that Danny and Antonio chose to establish a Bloods gang in the middle of a Crips neighborhood. That sort of in-your-face attitude reflected the boys' aggressive nature.

Referring to a defense investigator's report after an interview with Raquel, Sargent points out that she'd said Danny wouldn't fear Francisco. It's an important issue for the prosecutors, because it contradicts the defense's contention that Danny couldn't have stopped Francisco from killing Brandy.

"Correct," Raquel replies.

The issue of mitigators' relevance becomes a hotter topic when Danny's defense team begins calling witnesses—not to discuss Danny's character or background, but to contrast him with the "evils" of Francisco Martinez.

The first of these witnesses is Doug Moore, one of the Jeffco sheriff's investigators who'd worked the DuVall case from the beginning and had been present in the courtroom during Francisco's trial. Lindsey wants to inquire about an incident during that trial.

Moore testifies during a recess on the first day of his trial, Francisco had smirked and laughed at Brandy's family and mouthed the words, "Fuck you."

The defense also calls Brad Clemens, a former counselor at a Department of Corrections facility called Independence House. Under questioning by Lewis, Clemens testifies that he'd known both Danny and Francisco when they were living there and says he considered Danny "a follower" who never ordered Francisco around.

By comparison, Pancho was "a monster," Clemens says, who'd once told a therapist that his hobby was shooting people "because he liked to see their bodies jump."

In fact, Francisco was the main reason he got out of counseling, Clemens adds. Not out of fear, but because "dealing with Francisco made me understand the near hopelessness of community corrections.

"Inmates like Francisco Martinez are hardly far and few between. They have no will, no desire to change."

* * *

"Your honor, I want Brandy's family to know how very sorry I am."

At long last, Maria Simpson has what she's been waiting for: the opportunity to apologize directly to the girl's loved ones, especially to that other mother who sat on the opposite side of the aisle.

During Danny's trial, Maria had purposely avoided forcing herself on Angela Metzger. She had wanted desperately to tell Angela that she in no way excused the actions of her son, that she was ashamed and deeply offended by his part in what happened to Brandy. But she didn't know if such contact would be permitted or appreciated.

So she had insisted that her family members go out of their way to be courteous to the other family. Hold doors open. Allow them to enter and leave the courtroom unimpeded.

Even during this hearing, when her former husband, offended by the defense attorney's criticism of his influence as a father, stormed out of the courtroom, she'd kept her focus. "This isn't about you and me, Dan," she'd lashed out at him. "This is about our son." And ever since,

Danny's father had been quiet when he entered and left the courtroom.

Now, Maria will get to say what's in her heart, and she's been told she can do so at the podium without fear of cross-examination. "Not a day or night goes by without you all in my prayers," she tells Brandy's family. "I am tired of being strong and long to grieve with you."

She keeps it short, not wanting to say too much, and turns her attention to the panel. "Judge me with my son," she says. "I contributed to the problem." She is ready to sit down, but there's a surprise.

Prosecutor Bakke wants to question Maria as a rebuttal witness, to contradict the testimony about her failings as a mother. Judge Anderson agrees, and a very frightened Maria suddenly is sworn in and steps up into the witness stand.

Across the courtroom, Angela Metzger bends over and places her face in her hands. At the defense table, for the first time during this hearing, Danny looks visibly angry at Bakke, the woman who wants to torment his mother.

"I apologize," Bakke says.

But Maria is too petrified to respond. What if she says something that dooms her son? There is no helping it now, she'll have to answer as honestly as she can and pray she does no harm.

Bakke is counting on Maria's honesty. In yet another ironic twist, it's the prosecution that's been defending Danny's family.

When Danny's aunt, Nancy Laes, had testified earlier about problems in her sister's household and life—the drugs and volatile relationship with her first husband—it was Bakke who got her to concede that the children were clean and well-cared for by the larger extended family. And that after Maria kicked her drug habit, she had fought courageously, if futilely, to get her boys out of the gang.

While her nephew may have had a rough childhood, his aunt conceded, it was "not one that leads to this," not to rape and murder.

Now it's Maria's turn to be rehabilitated. Under Bakke's questioning, she admits that she changed her lifestyle in order to help her sons.

"You tried to learn about gangs?" Bakke asks.

"Yes."

"You attended every neighborhood meeting to learn what you could?"

"That's correct."

"You got an apartment in Aurora to get your sons away from 2727 California?"

"Yes, I did."

"You placed yourself in a dangerous situation to get your sons away from a gang member's house?"

"I did. They got up and left."

The questioning goes on and on. Maria warned Danny about the dangers. She kept warning him after her brother was shot at 2727 California and again after Raquel and her baby were in the house during a drive-by shooting.

She did her best to help Danny. She'd even made the fateful mistake of getting him into a drug rehabilitation center rather than sentenced to prison: He was on the run from the center when Brandy was killed.

"Is it true that Danny Martinez made choices that led him to where he is today?"

"Yes."

"He had his chances, just like Antonio?"

There it was. The heart of her family's tragedy. Two sons. One who made a conscious decision to do something more with his life. The other who had given up.

"Yes," says Maria. Because it is the truth.

CHAPTER FORTY-FIVE

April 29, 1999

It's the third and final day of Danny's death penalty hearing. The defense begins by calling one of Francisco's former therapists, Stacy Pike, the one who told Clemens about Francisco's hobby of shooting people.

The defense contrasts that with two witnesses who speak on Danny's behalf. One is the teacher in Arkansas who encouraged him to get his GED. Nearly ten years later, she still remembers him. "I liked to teach, and Danny liked to learn," Ann Whitis says. He also talked with her about getting out of the gang lifestyle but said it was difficult back in his old neighborhood.

She and another teacher were so excited for Danny when he passed his GED that they went to find him. But he was gone, and she never saw him again—until coming to court today. She smiles at Danny, and he smiles back.

Danny had gone back to 2727 California, according to the next witness, juvenile probation officer Beverly Hobbs Porter. She had been Danny's probation officer on a drug case when she and Maria came up with the idea of sending him to Arkansas to get him away from the gangs.

When Danny returned, though, she knew he was running with the Bloods again. This was about the time that he, Antonio, and Pancho formed the Deuce-Seven subset of the Crenshaw Mafia Gangster Bloods.

Danny, Hobbs Porter says, treated her with respect. In fact, he sometimes would caution her when not to visit his home.

"Why not?" Lewis asks.

"I got the sense he wanted to protect me, and sometimes maybe there was something he did not want me to see," she replies. If she'd showed up during a drug transaction or when a large group of guys were hanging around, she could have been in danger.

Hobbs Porter echoes earlier testimony from Danny's uncle Jimmy, the man the Crips mistook for Danny and shot while he was sleeping on the couch at 2727 California. Jimmy had talked about a neighborhood where 95 percent of the male population used or sold drugs. A neighborhood so tough that when Maria forced nine-year-old Danny to go back outside and fight a neighbor boy, it was "the right thing to do. If you didn't fight, the other kids would think you were weak and take advantage of you."

The last time she had seen Danny had been several years ago, Hobbs Porter testifies. She had been walking down the street when a car pulled up. It was Danny, and he wanted her to see his twin boys.

On cross-examination, Randall gets the probation officer to acknowledge that boys don't join gangs just for a replacement family. They also do it for money and power.

Even ten years ago, Danny made a choice to leave Arkansas, where he was doing well, "and he chose his friends," the attorney suggests.

"True," she says, and shrugs.

Hobbs Porter steps down from the stand. The defense's case is over.

The prosecution presents a brief rebuttal, calling two Jefferson County deputies to the stand to testify about behavioral problems Danny's had in the jail.

After all the testimony in this trial, these difficulties seem minor. In one instance, Danny was upset about not being allowed to take a shower after playing basketball. "Paybacks are a bitch, as you and your homosexual partner will find out," the deputy recalls him saying.

In a second incident, he got angry about a jail rule concerning the correct wrist for wearing identification bracelets and warned a female deputy, "I'm not in here for selling crack."

"How'd you take that?" Sargent asks.

"As a threat."

* * *

At last, both sides rest and it's time for closing arguments. But first Lewis formally announces that his client will exercise his right of allocution—to speak on his own behalf without being sworn in.

While his mother, sister, and other relatives weep, Danny shuffles to the podium. A few days earlier, he told his mother that he wanted to apologize but didn't know what to say. "The words won't come," he said. To which she replied, "It only takes two to say, 'I'm sorry.'"

In the end he does a little better than that, without asking for leniency or mercy. "Your Honors, I just want to apologize to both families—my family, Brandy's family—for what has taken place. Also to Your Honors about putting them in a position like this.

"I know it's not easy for nobody, and there's really not no words." Danny chokes up and has to start again. "You know, there ain't no words that could really just explain anything about this. But, you know, I just want you to know whatever happens, that's the Lord's will.

"So, you know, there's no—any hard feelings against anybody, no matter what happens, and I'll just make the best out of whatever happens. And thank you for being respectful to my lawyers. Thank you."

CHAPTER FORTY-SIX

April 29, 1999

"Members of the panel, there are no words that can describe the horror of this crime."

It has fallen on prosecutor Randall to make the closing remarks for the state. "There are no ways to have three judges understand the terror that a fourteen-year-old girl went through," he says, pausing to turn and point at Danny, "at the hands of that man. There's no way to explain his crime.

"But through words and the evidence that we have left of Brandy, the evidence that he left is bloody jeans that she wore when she died, bloody handcuffs that that man placed on her that she wore when she died, bloody jewelry her mother had to identify at the coroner's office, and ..."

Randall continues, as he walks over to the backseat taken from Quintana's car, "... a bench seat where she last sat next to him.

"I don't have Brandy here to try to show you what is left of her," he says, but the panel has "the photos of how he left her. And they are horrible, and they are graphic, but they are this crime. They are his crime."

Once again, like a snuff film that keeps rewinding and playing itself, Randall recounts the horror of what happened to Brandy—and Danny's role in it. "Blood is pouring out of her anus, and that man has his penis inside of her. He gets off of her, and he's covered with blood from the waist down.

"That's who Bang is. Actions speak louder than words, and that speaks volumes of who he is. Even the ultra-evil Pancho didn't do that."

Randall notes that the panel is here to judge the defendant's character two years ago, when the crime happened, not ten years ago when Ann Whitis knew a different young man.

"We don't like to think that that type of horror can take place today, but it does, it did, and she went through it. Put yourself in her shoes. An ongoing spiral of terror, an ongoing spiral of pain, suffering, slow death."

The prosecutor recalls the image of Danny handcuffing Brandy and placing a hood over her face. Danny calling the shots. "They get to the canyon, and everybody gets out. Everybody. And they stand five feet from her. Five feet.

"Pancho's got her down. Someone says, 'Hold her head.' Sam does, and they stab her. And then they throw her down the ravine like so much evidence."

After the gang members get back in the car and Pancho announces that he forgot the knife, it is Danny who gets out and retrieves it. "Knew right where to look," Randall notes.

"He brings it back and gets in the car. What's his comment? 'We are serial killers now.' Not 'you guys.' But 'We are serial killers now.'"

Later, Danny boasts to a sheriff's deputy, Randall recalls, referring to the incident at the Jefferson County jail. "He says, 'We're not in here for selling crack.'"

Randall moves to what he knows will be the crux of the defense argument: That Danny was not the man who actually stabbed Brandy.

"He intended her death after her torture. And because he is not the quote, unquote, triggerman, he doesn't die for this? He is involved in every brutality inflicted on this girl—all through the house, the worst one with the sex, in the car, in the canyon.

"The only thing that he does not do is physically place the knife into her body. He has Francisco for that."

Because of Danny and Francisco, all Brandy's family has left are memories. "And as Rose so eloquently stated, 'A cold stone does not satisfy the arms of a 74-year-old lady.' Because if you sentence this man to life, he will be in prison for sure, but he will be able to see his family. He will be able to see his boys. He will be able to see his mother."

One by one, Randall addresses the aggravators for which he says there is a "landslide of evidence" proving each beyond a reasonable doubt.

First, that Brandy was killed in furtherance or flight from the commission of a felony. First-degree sexual assault. Sexual assault on a child by use of force. First-degree assault. He doesn't dwell on this; he feels he doesn't have to.

The next is that Danny killed a kidnap victim. Randall cites the Colorado Supreme Court's rulings on aggravators that sprang from the case of Gary Davis, who kidnapped, then raped and killed a woman. In October 1997, Davis became the first person executed in Colorado since 1967.

"The legislature reasonably can view as particularly cruel the suffering to which a kidnap victim is subjected through the criminal's calculated terror as the victim is forced to accompany him to her own execution."

The third aggravator is that Brandy was killed to prevent arrest and prosecution. "This factor includes the killing of a witness," Randall says, also noting that at one point in the evening, Danny had even discussed killing Jacob Casados, and possibly the Warren brothers, because he didn't trust them.

"Was she killed because she was a witness to a crime? Certainly," he says. Brandy was asked if she knew where she was and had made the mistake of giving the right answer. "She knows too much. She knows too much. She'd heard their names, seen their faces. She had to die."

The fourth aggravator asserts that Danny was party to an agreement to kill another person. Again, Randall cites the state Supreme Court ruling on Davis regarding the legislature's intent for this aggravator: "The legislature might have concluded that the involvement of two or more persons in a plan to take the life of another multiplies the evil and the depravity of mind requisite to take innocent human life."

Randall returns to the case at hand. "Was there an agreement to kill Brandy DuVall? How many meetings did they have to talk about the death?

"*'Should we bury her in the back?' 'Should we kill her with Sega cords?'* It was clearly an agreement that this young girl—when they were done with their fun with her, when they were done with the sex they were having with her—she didn't matter anymore.

"She had to die to protect the heart of the Deuce-Seven."

Finally, Randall reaches the fifth aggravator, "that the offense was committed in an especially heinous, cruel, or depraved manner." And one last time he cites the Davis ruling that defines "cruel, heinous, or depraved" as "those murders which are conscienceless, pitiless, and unnecessarily torturous to the victims.

"Those words are the very heart of this case, because there was no conscience there. There was no pity there. It was only torture for Brandy DuVall."

Randall knows he must also address the defense's mitigators. First, that Danny was a "minor" participant simply because he didn't actually stab Brandy. "He is in this everywhere, through everything," Randall counters.

Second, that his background explains, perhaps even excuses, his behavior. But it is not fair to blame any of this on Danny's mother, Randall says, or on anyone other than Danny himself. "There is no doubt that Maria Simpson is hurting, too. There's no doubt that she saw her son going down the path of gangs and drugs and did what she could to turn it around.

"A lot of people stepped up to the plate, and he chose to go the other direction. That's his choice. He made it. He can live with it. The blame is not hers. It's not his sister's. It's not the neighborhood he's in.

"As his aunt stated, he had a hard life, but not one that leads to this. He chose his friends, and he chose the friend that would be with him throughout his life—all the way through the death of Brandy DuVall: Francisco Martinez. Pancho."

Others survived life at 2727 California, got out of the neighborhood. "The neighborhood was tough, in part, to be sure, because of the Deuce-Seven," Randall says. "But what does a tough neighborhood have to do with the torture of a fourteen-year-old girl in 1997?

"Everyone we heard from was able to choose to get out of that life. Uncle Jimmy. Raquel. Maria. And even his brother, fellow Deuce-Seven gang member Antonio, gets out.

"He doesn't. He doesn't want to."

Randall notes that step three in the four-step death-penalty process requires the panel to weigh the aggravators against the mitigators. Only if the aggravators outweigh the mitigators is the defendant declared eligible for the death penalty. That weighing would be up to the judges.

But in step four, all legal arguments are dropped, and the judges are asked to make what the Colorado Supreme Court called "a profoundly moral decision" on whether the defendant deserves to die.

At last Randall turns to this step. "Why should this defendant die?" he asks, then answers:

"Some crimes are simply so shocking that society insists on the adequate appropriate punishment. He should die because of every horrible, torturous act that he did to that girl.

"Mr. Lewis stated in his opening: The blood of Brandy Duvall was on the hands of Francisco Martinez. To be sure, it is on the hands of Francisco Martinez. And Sam Quintana, and Frank Vigil.

"But you know something?" Randall asks before pointing one more time at Danny. "The blood's on his hands, it's on his legs, it's on his genitals. It's everywhere that he got the blood of that young girl on him that night. It's not washing off.

"The standard of the death penalty is not Francisco Martinez. The bar is not Francisco Martinez. Francisco Martinez may be a hundred miles above the bar. There are other people that go over that bar, too, and he's one of them.

"Sentence him to the only appropriate sentence there is: Death."

* * *

There is hardly time to absorb the impact of Randall's statement before Lewis stands to deliver his closing. This will be his only chance. Because the burden of proof is on the state, the prosecutors will get the chance to rebut him.

"I'm so tired of seeing the carnage in these cases, and there is much in this one," Lewis says, shaking his head. He sounds tired, and with good reason—he was also the attorney for Nathan Dunlap, a nineteen-year-old who executed five pizza parlor employees and was currently on death row. It was the appeal of the Dunlap case that affirmed the four-step death-penalty process.

"This is the story of a beautiful little girl whose life was taken needlessly and brutally. And it's easy for all of us on both sides of the courtroom to be angry, and to be frustrated, and to feel sympathy, as we should, for her family.

"It's easy to see mothers from both sides of the courtroom wishing they could have done more for their children—one wishing they could have saved her life, one wishing that she could save two lives.

"It's also the story of two brothers and the road that they took, and the forks in the road. We make choices in our lives, for which we are responsible. But there are many factors that go into those choices, and some of them are very strong.

"We don't choose where we're born. We don't choose who our parents are. We don't choose where we live. We don't choose what's going on in the world around us."

But why, he asks, "would anybody choose ... I'm sorry, Danny ... why would anybody choose Francisco Martinez as a friend?"

Danny shows no reaction, but Lewis hasn't waited for one. Instead, he turns to the judges and asks, "How many times have you seen a young person in front of you and you said, 'You know, young man, young woman, you've got to change your friends. You've got to get away from these people.'

"They don't want to listen. So few of them are ever able to break free. He didn't choose for Francisco to be right next door to him, but Francisco was there. And no matter how evil someone is, there is a loyalty that develops with family and friendship, a loyalty that's hard to break, a loyalty that's misguided, a loyalty that's destructive, a loyalty that's dangerous, a loyalty that's not logical or analytical. But it's strong."

Danny has many good qualities, his lawyer asserts. "Would the real Danny Martinez please stand up?" But he made bad choices, especially when he chose to leave Arkansas and return to Denver.

"Oh, God, what a horrible choice," Lewis says. "He's not a killer. This man was not on the road to killing anybody. He's no Francisco. He's not an evil person." Except for a prior drug conviction or two, Lewis notes, Danny qualifies for the "no serious prior criminal history" mitigator.

And now the defense attorney moves closer to the argument that he hopes will sway at least one member of the panel: that Danny was not the principal player in Brandy's death. That even if Antonio had persuaded him to leave when he did, the same atrocities and murder would still have occurred.

They would have occurred because Sammy and Pancho would still have been there, he says. Particularly Pancho, who turned the sexual assault of Brandy DuVall from "inappropriate and disgusting" to "the unthinkable."

Even though Danny stayed, Lewis adds, he was not the leader. "There's a train that Francisco set in motion, but no one's at the wheel," he says. "This was a bunch of people who made unthinkable choices, who had blind loyalty to each other, who didn't have courage enough, guts enough, to get out of a situation or to stop a situation that they wouldn't have started."

He wishes "no harm to anyone," Lewis says, and does not want to "bash Francisco." Then he proceeds to do just that: "This is not a person who needs to be encouraged or assisted in doing the most evil you could ever imagine in your whole life.

"This is a person who, even in the solemnity of the courtroom, cannot hide his evil side and his anger ..." I mean no harm. I mean no harm ... but this is an evil man.

"This, I suggest to you, was going to happen. If Danny had left with Antonio, these fates were already in place. It wasn't Danny who started anything that night. It wasn't Danny who took this to a level of no return. If Danny had gone with Antonio, these events would still have happened, probably just the way they happened.

"His influence was minimal. These forces were set in motion. You had the personality and the evil of Francisco. You had Sammy Quintana, who was willing to hold her by the hair. You have Frank, who said, 'Let's kill her; she knows where we are.'

"You want to list them one, two, three, four; I'm not so sure that you wouldn't put Sam Quintana up there right below Pancho."

Lewis is at the critical point of his defense, the bar Colorado juries have not crossed—and, he hopes, the one judges won't, either. "Do we kill a person who did not themselves kill this little girl? Or should the death penalty be reserved for those worse cases, for the worse people, for those by whose hand the death of sweet, innocent people was caused?"

Turning to Danny, Lewis winds up by saying, "I am proud of the statement you made to the Court. I have no words that eloquent. The boy Danny Martinez had good qualities. The man Danny has demonstrated that he is capable of the atrocities that happened to that child."

* * *

On rebuttal, Randall responds to Lewis's portrayal of the defendant with anger. "The man Danny Martinez has demonstrated that although he is twenty-five years old with a GED, he chooses to possess more than thirty grams of crack cocaine, threaten police officers, murder, rape, torture a fourteen-year-old girl.

"This is not about sex. He had a girlfriend. She was in the house when Brandy was brought in. This is about his desire to torture and brutalize a human being."

Danny could have left that night, Randall points out. But he didn't. "It is Danny who was orchestrating her death."

Randall attacks the NAACP statistics. "We don't know the facts of the cases. For someone who's standing right next to a person that's being stabbed, and orchestrated, and participated in, and took place in everything leading up to the death, intended for her to die, can very well be considered a triggerman.

"But what those statistics do tell us is that there are some cases in which it is absolutely appropriate for even a non-triggerman to be sentenced to die, and Colorado is now facing one, right here and right now.

"How many forks in the road did he come to? There's not one fork in the road. There is not one great fork in the road that created this case. This defendant was thrown lifeline after lifeline after lifeline, choice after choice after choice, chance after chance after chance, and he always chose the wrong one.

"Why? That's what he wants to do.

"He comes out of that neighborhood as the evil murderer that he is, and other people do not. Why? Because he's different. Because he's capable of what he did to Brandy, and the others are not.

"There is only one punishment appropriate for the horror of this crime. It must stop. It must stop. He's been given enough chances. No more.

"Brandy's now dead. Danny Martinez must be sentenced to death."

CHAPTER FORTY-SEVEN

May 7, 1999

After a week of deliberation, it is clear that the panel in Danny Martinez's case did not have an easy time making their decision. But finally, the word comes down that the judges are ready to announce their verdict.

The courtroom quickly fills.

Angela Metzger enters with her family. She doesn't think Danny will get the death penalty, but she will not be disappointed. Either way, his life has already been forfeited.

There is no winning here. Apparently not even any lessons learned. Just a few weeks ago, she noticed a small newspaper article—only a few paragraphs, really—about a fourteen-year-old girl who had been picked up on Federal Boulevard and raped by three men. Unlike Brandy, though, this girl was released several hours later. Hasn't anybody been listening?

If Angela feels anything about this moment, it is her heart going out to the woman across the aisle. She'd been sickened by the way the defense attorneys had attacked Danny's mother. Maria wasn't perfect. But her son was a grown man. He'd made his own choices that night.

Twenty feet away, Maria Simpson tries to control her own fear as well as that of her daughter, who is already in tears. Maria's mouth is set, and she holds her eyes open wide to keep herself from crying.

She has prayed all night. *Please, don't let them kill my son.* But she isn't asking for any miracles. Danny should spend the rest of his life in prison for what he did. That, she believes, looking at the back of her son's head, is justice.

Before the verdict was announced after Danny's trial three months before, she told her family and Danny's supporters that she didn't want any outbursts—however the verdict came down—out of respect for Brandy's family. She has repeated that request, but this time it is Judge Anderson who makes it official for both sides.

When the panel enters, Anderson instructs the audience, attorneys, and defendant to remain standing. He thanks the Martinez and DuVall families for preserving the decorum of his courtroom throughout the proceedings.

He recognizes that emotions are high, however, and so takes the unusual step of saying that he won't tolerate any "outbursts, cursing, clapping, cheers, or obscene gestures" at the announcement of the verdict. "If any person here feels they are inclined to lose control or have any doubts about their ability to remain courageous, silent, and responsible in this kind of proceeding, I ask you to leave now, while we're still standing."

Anderson peers around the courtroom. When no one leaves, he says, "Those people of courage, respect, and civility are welcome to sit with me at this time."

The moment of truth has come. Danny sits with his elbows on the table and hands templed in front of his face. Hands on both sides of the aisle reach for those of a neighbor. Heads bow.

Anderson clears his throat and announces, "We cannot reach a unanimous verdict." It takes a moment to sink in. To send someone to their execution, the verdict must be unanimous. The tension leaves the courtroom like water running down a drain.

A moment later, Danny's family learns how thin a thread his life hung by. The judges had split. Coughlin against the death penalty; Fasing and Anderson in favor.

"Lacking unanimity, the only lawful penalty is a sentence to life imprisonment for Daniel Nieto Martinez Jr."

With that, Danny stands. He is handcuffed, then led away through a side door. He does not look back.

The death-penalty bar had been set higher than Danny Martinez. The question now is whether it will fall on the head of his best friend, Francisco.

CHAPTER FORTY-EIGHT

May 10, 1999

"Now that the facts have been determined, the presumption of innocence is gone, and Francisco Martinez Jr. sits before you a convicted rapist and murderer."

Deputy District Attorney Ingrid Bakke catches the people gathered in the courtroom in mid-murmur, like a play's narrator just before the curtain rises. Those in her audience—the families and friends, the attorneys, the judges, the defendant, and the curious—grow silent as they turn their eyes to her. Many already know Bakke's next line, having heard it just a few weeks ago:

"The court must now shift its focus from the crimes committed to the evils that have been suffered."

This is the fifth time Bakke has opened the prosecution's case against a member of the Deuce-Seven Bloods, who raped, tortured, and murdered fourteen-year-old Brandy DuVall. In three weeks, it will have been exactly two years since the girl's savaged body was found next to Clear Creek a few miles up the canyon from Golden; it's been almost a year and a half since the first trial of one of her killers.

This is the second time Bakke has made her pitch to a three-judge panel that the death penalty be imposed for one of the killers. In April she uttered the same words at a hearing for Francisco's childhood friend and fellow Deuce-Seven member, Danny Martinez Jr.

Barring a conviction or sentence being overturned at the appellate level, this is the last time Ingrid Bakke will have to deliver a speech on behalf of Brandy DuVall. And for that, she is glad.

"Words fall short to describe the terror and the horror" of Brandy's last few hours, "what this man," she says, jabbing a finger toward the defendant, "did to a fourteen-year-old girl." A murder that was preceded by acts committed to "humiliate and torture Brandy and satisfy the twisted whims of Francisco Martinez."

A slight shudder runs through Brandy's relatives, seated in the first pew behind the prosecution table; arms drape protectively around shoulders, as if preparing for impact. Here it comes again. In the spectator sections on both sides of the aisle, hands wipe at the first tears of the day.

Twenty-five-year-old Francisco displays no emotion as Bakke condemns him. His dark-brown eyes show neither anger nor denial nor bravado. Only occasionally does he glance at his accuser, and then he looks away again, as though he doesn't think this conversation has much to do with him.

Of all the gang members involved in Brandy's rape and murder, he has been portrayed as the most vicious and cold-blooded. Even Danny's lawyers labeled him "an evil man," as their own client—his friend—sat mute. Although he doesn't look particularly evil, some women in the spectator section claim they can see it in him. But there are women on the other side of the aisle—sisters, girlfriends, his wife—who say that's not their "Pancho"; his mother, Linda, grieves for him in the hall.

* * *

For two years, this drama has been filled with images of good and evil, of heaven and hell. Of angels and devils.

A large steel cross, erected by Brandy's family, stands at highway mile marker 269.5 in Clear Creek Canyon, where the gang stabbed and dumped Brandy's half-naked body on May 31, 1997. And many in the courtroom today recall the dusty image of outstretched wings on a fifth-floor courthouse window during Francisco's trial last August—surely left by a pigeon attempting to fly through the pane, but viewed as a sign by some leaving the courtroom, who, when they saw it, crossed themselves.

The religious imagery started with Jose Martinez, the infamous "Uncle Joe," at whose Adams County house the gang members brutalized Brandy. When confronted, Martinez told the police that the young men who committed the acts "was possessed by the fuckin' devil." The only piece of physical evidence tying Brandy to that house and the gang was a prayer card that the girl's grandmother, Rose Vasquez, had given her, which Jose hid after the gang left with Brandy. The card depicted a hand punctured by a nail wound, with the inscription: *See, I will not forget you. I have carved you in the palm of my hand.*

The prosecution had seized on the theme. To explain to jurors the deals given to some of the gang members in exchange for their testimony, they'd relied on an old adage: *Crimes committed in hell do not have angels as witnesses.* And without angels for witnesses, the only way the government could secure justice for Brandy was "to make deals with the devils."

They'd made their deals and then tried the three remaining defendants who neither asked for nor were offered plea bargains for the hell they put Brandy through. Frank "Little Bang" Vigil Jr., now seventeen years old and in prison for the rest of his life. Twenty-seven-year-old Danny "Bang" Martinez Jr., in prison for the rest of his life. And now, finally, Francisco "Pancho" Martinez Jr., who, one way or the other, will spend the rest of his life in prison, although if the prosecutors have their way, it will be a short stay.

When this hearing is over and the judges have rendered their opinion, there will be no more devils to deal with for the murder of Brandy DuVall. Instead, those who've lived with this case, who've spent two years in judicial purgatory, will be left to deal with their own private demons.

* * *

To do what she is doing now required a lot of soul-searching for Bakke. As a young prosecutor in the division that deals with crimes against children, she'd convinced herself that she could ask for the death penalty without batting an eyelash. But that was before she'd been assigned to her first capital murder case. This case.

Suddenly, she'd realized she didn't know where she stood on the death penalty. In the nearly two years she'd worked on the case, Bakke had gone back and forth; she hadn't really resolved the issue until shortly before Danny's sentencing. But as she assembled the so-called aggravators—those particularly cruel or unusual aspects of the murder that the government uses to spell out the need for a lethal injection—with her two colleagues, she came to believe that the punishment fit the crime.

By the time she wrote the opening for Danny's sentencing, Bakke saw little difference between Francisco and Danny. Like everyone else, she initially had been caught up in the "co-conspirator" issue: Was Danny as culpable—and therefore as deserving of death—as Francisco, the man who'd actually inflicted the fatal wounds?

But no more. Ultimately, Bakke realized that whatever he'd derived from the crime, Danny's participation was simply different from Pancho's. The words came from her colleague, Mark Randall, spoken during a meeting to coordinate her opening with his closing, but she agreed that comparing Danny to Francisco was like looking at "different shades of black."

Still, she'd told friends, it gave her a strange feeling when she wrote down the last line of her opening: "The People respectfully request that you sentence Danny Martinez Jr. to death." And though she'd felt comfortable delivering that line, there was no joy in the asking.

The three deputy DAs—Bakke, Randall, and Hal Sargent—were worn out from the workload, particularly keeping up with the several hundred motions filed by Francisco's lawyers, more than ten times the number filed by Danny's. Most of the motions contested the constitutionality of the three-judge panels, attacking from every conceivable angle the 1995 Colorado statute that had established them. Others seemed frivolous, such as one motion concerned with any "known side effects" of the drugs used for lethal injection and whether those drugs had been approved by the Food and Drug Administration.

The defense won perhaps half a dozen of its motions, although none that challenged the panel's authority or greatly affected the prosecution's strategy. Yet each issue had to be researched and answered. The prosecution's workdays had begun at six in the morning and continued until ten at night. There was never any downtime; another hearing or trial or sentencing always loomed just a week or two away. None of them had taken a real vacation in nearly two years. Even weekends were spent working.

The emotional demands were just as wearing. The lineup of three trials and many other hearings brought the prosecutors closer to the victim's family than they Nancylly would have been. It was hard trying to keep the family's spirits up while working to stay focused.

The prosecutors had all had dreams and nightmares about the case. The crime. The people. The testimony. All of it looped through their minds on automatic rewind.

Doing what needed to be done had grown progressively harder. Just looking at the photographs of Brandy's mangled body brought back all the horrors.

The case had even changed the way some people looked at them. Bakke noticed that defense lawyers she'd once been friendly with were going out of their way to avoid talking to her. She and her partners had crossed some line from adversary to enemy.

They all have their own devils to deal with.

But now Bakke puts them aside as she tells the judges that the state will be trying to prove, beyond a reasonable doubt, five aggravators. They are the same five it attempted to prove for Danny: that Francisco caused the death of Brandy "in the course of or in furtherance of or flight therefrom" a felony—in this case, assault, sexual assault, and sexual assault on a child using force; that Francisco intentionally killed a kidnapped person; that Francisco was party to an agreement to kill Brandy; that Francisco killed Brandy to avoid lawful arrest or prosecution; and that the murder of Brandy was "especially heinous, cruel, or depraved."

Then she outlines the atrocities the state will lay specifically at Francisco's feet. It was Pancho who removed Brandy's clothes, picked her up, and carried her to the back bedroom after she was "delivered" to 3165 Hawthorne. It was Pancho who sexually assaulted her with a beer bottle. It was Pancho who tried to get Danny's uncle to participate. "Want some head, Uncle Joe?" Bakke mimics the man sitting twelve feet to her right.

It was Pancho who tried to have anal sex with Brandy. And when the girl complained, her anus was sliced open in the bathroom while she was alone in there with Danny and Pancho. Then it was Pancho who took her back to the bedroom and shoved a broom handle into her bleeding rectum.

"He put it in her hard," Bakke says, "and Brandy screamed." When Brandy lost control of her bowels, it was Pancho who declared—and here Bakke nearly yells—"'You shit on my homeboy's shoes, bitch,' and kicked her in the chest."

The little cries, sniffles, and sounds of misery in the background at all these legal proceedings have begun again. Brandy's mother, Angela Metzger, sobs, her shoulders shaking, as Bakke recounts how Pancho kicked her daughter in the head when she made the mistake of admitting that she knew where she was. And still the prosecutor goes on.

It was Pancho who, tired of Brandy's pleas for mercy, began to stab her on the drive into the mountains. Pancho who tried to strangle her into silence. And, at last, Pancho who finished the job by stabbing her repeatedly in the neck while Sammy Quintana held her down.

Bakke quickly outlines the testimony that Villano and the other judges on the panel—Robert Hyatt of Denver and Deanna Hickman of Arapahoe County—will hear during the prosecution's case. The victim-impact statements. Pancho's other crimes, including the beating of a former girlfriend just three days before Brandy's death. His continued penchant for violence even while incarcerated. And his harassment of Brandy's family during the trial.

If there is no joy in her voice when Bakke at last comes to her final line, there is also no hesitation. "The People respectfully ask that you sentence Francisco Martinez Jr. to death."

The first time Bakke made that request, two of the three judges agreed. Because one did not, Danny Martinez Jr. was spared the death penalty.

CHAPTER FORTY-NINE

May 10, 1999

"You don't know whether the jury convicted Francisco Martinez of first-degree murder as a complicitor or the principle. Because of a lack of evidence in this case, you," defense attorney Patrick Ridley says, pointing at the judges, "don't know if it was Francisco Martinez," he says, now pointing at his client, "who stabbed Brandy DuVall to death."

Ridley must counter whatever impact Bakke's opening had on the panel. It may not have been much: Dramatic opening statements are for jurors who can be counted on to let their emotions govern them as much as the law. Not judges.

Judges are supposed to be able to put aside not only improper legal arguments, but their own feelings while making decisions following the stone-cold letter of the law. They aren't supposed to be swayed by impassioned pleas that have no legal merit. They may, in fact, become irritated by over-exuberant lawyering, and there are few things an attorney fears more than an irritated judge.

Then again, and despite any seeming evidence to the contrary, judges are human. So both Bakke and Ridley, a tall, Ivy League-looking sort, have seen fit to add a dash of melodrama to their statements.

Ridley, however, begins by concentrating on two arguments. The first is that Francisco was just one of seven gang members who all had a hand in Brandy's death and that to single him out for the hardest punishment would be "morally and legally" unfair.

And second, that the prosecution wasn't sure enough of its theory that Francisco, not Sammy Quintana, inflicted the fatal wounds to leave out the "complicitor language" when they asked the jury to convict Francisco of first-degree murder after deliberation. Such language, he notes, allowed the jury to hand down a conviction without having to decide that Francisco did the stabbing.

Before opening statements, deputy DA Sargent had successfully countered a similar argument by legal expert Dean Neuwirth, who demanded that the judges stop the proceedings and sentence Francisco to life in prison. It had always been the government's theory, the prosecutor said, "that Francisco Martinez is the one who stabbed her to death," and that was the way the case was presented to the jurors.

The judge had agreed. But now, Ridley raises the argument again. All through this case, the defense has refused to give an inch.

* * *

It's been a long haul for the young defense attorneys, too. While Ridley and his colleagues, Dave Kaplan and Neuwirth, have had only one trial and now this sentencing in the DuVall homicide, they've been up against the considerably larger resources of the Jefferson County District Attorney's Office. In fact, Neuwirth was brought in to combat the presence of an attorney from the Colorado Attorney General's Office as well as the Jeffco DA's appellate expert, Donna Reed, at the prosecution table.

Someone had to research, write, and argue those hundreds of motions the prosecutors complain about. But throw enough stuff at the wall, and something might stick.

The case against Francisco had been overwhelming, as evidenced by the fact that it only took two hours for the jury to convict him. The arguments stacked against him at the death-penalty hearing looked almost as insurmountable.

Even the prosecution had never said that Danny stabbed Brandy. Then there was all that stuff about the broom handle, the bloody knife in the bathroom, and kicking the poor girl. Even a judge was going to have a hard time blocking that out.

But the defense attorneys would throw all they could up there. Danny's case was proof that it only took one judge to see things a little differently. For example, maybe one of the three on Francisco's panel would hesitate to make such a decision based on the accusations of Sammy Quintana, one of the "devils" who'd gotten a deal in exchange for his testimony.

The defense wasn't counting on it. If something stuck, great, but in every motion turned down, every objection overruled, there might be something that would catch the eye of a judge at the appellate level. The lawyers were trying to ensure that even if the panel sentenced Francisco to death, the fight would not be over.

Emotionally, the defense team hadn't had an easy time of it, either. They weren't immune to the tears shed by the victim's family; they'd had to look at the photographs and listen to testimony describing their client's monstrous acts. The images and words would remain with them long after their case files began gathering dust in some storage room.

Still, this was about whether the state should be in the business of executing one of its citizens. It was a battle they fought with the zeal of those who believe they hold the moral high ground against overwhelming odds. And if some people didn't like the way they did their job, too bad—those people weren't trying to save a young man's life.

CHAPTER FIFTY

May 10, 1999

That young man now watches his attorney, turning occasionally to look at the judges as if to gauge their reaction. The day had begun with Francisco asking the judges, through his attorneys, for permission to return to his cell; he didn't want to hear the testimony.

Although some of that testimony would be presented on his behalf, Kaplan had noted that it "is not particularly flattering to his family or upbringing" and that Francisco would be uncomfortable listening to it.

Several members of Brandy's family shook their heads at this request. They suspected that what Pancho really didn't want to hear was how the girl's death had affected them. That didn't seem fair. It certainly hadn't bothered him to hear Brandy's screams and pleas for mercy before he stabbed her. And then this man had smirked and laughed at them, mouthing obscenities during his trial.

Deputy District Attorney Sargent had objected to Francisco's request. "He has no constitutional right to be absent," he told the court. "What we're going to hear throughout these proceedings will be painful for everybody."

Kaplan countered by contending that a defendant's right to waive his presence was up to the court's discretion. But Villano, who'd come out of retirement to preside over this hearing, said he wasn't prepared to rule. Francisco was going to have to stay and listen to the opening statements.

In their effort to execute his client, Ridley now says, the prosecutors "want to demonize and dehumanize" Francisco Martinez. But after the judges get to know his client and the life he lived since childhood and "the forces" that formed who he became, they will realize Francisco had "a relatively small amount of moral culpability" compared to the others.

"How do you take into account so many intangibles?" Ridley asks. What role did alcohol play? What part could be attributed to "another drama" that was taking part in the house—the "quoting," or beating into the gang, of Jacob Casados? How much did all that "testosterone" have to do with what happened to Brandy DuVall?

Ridley points a figurative finger back at Danny Martinez, just as Danny's lawyers had done a few weeks earlier to Francisco. "How do you account for the leaders who make the decisions and call the shots? ... No one disputes that Danny Martinez was the leader and founder of the Deuce-Seven with his brother, Antonio.

"Given the madness, complexity, and chaos of the evening," he warns, "it would not be legally or morally right to pick out one to punish with death."

Like Danny before him, Pancho sits quietly and listens to his attorney badmouth his best friend. Back when it might still have been possible for Danny to plead guilty in exchange for life in prison, thus avoiding a potential death sentence, Pancho had told his attorneys to tell Danny that it was all right with him if Danny cut a deal.

Although prosecutors never made the offer, anyway, Danny balked at letting his friend face a death sentence alone. During the hearings when their lives were on the line, though, neither man protested their lawyers' condemnation of the other.

Danny, says Ridley, echoing the prosecutors' arguments from the last hearing, was "throwing the party at Uncle Joe's house. He was the one who had the most and greatest variety of sex."

Ridley also condemns Sammy Quintana, noting that he'd already killed another young woman, Venus Montoya, before Brandy was murdered. Venus was an unintended target, he adds. "He intended to kill Salvino Rojas," another Bloods gang member, "because Salvino snitched on the leader of the Deuce-Seven, Danny Martinez."

Sammy killed two girls and got off with ninety-six years in prison by turning state's evidence. Francisco, he points out, killed "only one." There is even evidence—a cut mark on Sammy's hand—that he stabbed Brandy himself, Ridley says.

As Ridley labels Sammy a killer and a liar, Jim Aber, the chief deputy state public defender, listens in the spectator gallery with his head bowed. He was the lawyer who put the deal together for Sammy Quintana, whose "truthfulness" on the witness stand he'd praised at Sammy's sentencing. In fact, he'd told Villano that he'd seen "more remorse and rehabilitation than I think in any other client I've ever seen." And yet he now sits on the defense side of the aisle as his client is vilified.

"We're not telling you that Francisco Martinez is not legally responsible for the death of Brandy DuVall. He's been convicted," Ridley says. "Mr. Martinez should spend the rest of his life in prison." (This is just posturing, of course, since an appeal of Francisco's conviction is already in the works.)

But what put Francisco in that position? Ridley says the defense will offer an overview of his client's wretched childhood as a mitigator, although it's "politically unpopular" to make such a connection for why boys join gangs. Such testimony will include his mother's suicide attempt in a local church. "Think of the impact on an eleven-year-old Catholic boy who had just had his first Holy Communion."

Francisco was not "bad at four, not evil. When he was eight or nine, he was not a demon," Ridley says. He outlines a childhood marred by violence between his parents, the family's abandonment by his father when Francisco was four, his witnessing of a murder at eight, and finding the nude, dead body of woman in a neighborhood dumpster at ten.

The boy slept in his mother's bed until she remarried when Francisco was twelve. After that, he curled himself up on the floor outside her bedroom and cried himself to sleep. And soon, Francisco moved out of his house and into the home of Danny and Antonio Martinez, "neighborhood friends whose mother was a heroin addict, and that was still better than his own house."

Turning slightly toward Brandy's family, Ridley says he would be remiss if he did not comment on the "unfortunate incident" during Francisco's trial. His client's behavior was defensive and born of frustration after hearing so many bad things said about him in the prosecution's opening statement.

"I don't think he was meaning to be disrespectful," Ridley now says to Brandy's mom, Angela. The actions stemmed from the depression and post-traumatic stress syndrome from which Francisco suffers—conditions psychologists will address during the hearing.

A sentence of life in prison without the possibility of parole—the sentence received by Danny Martinez and Frank Vigil—would be just punishment, Ridley says. It would be vengeance only "that requires he die by lethal injection."

CHAPTER FIFTY-ONE

May 10, 1999

After lunch, Francisco is granted his wish to wait out the hearing in his cell. Before he is handcuffed and led away, Villano assures him that he's free to return to the courtoom "anytime you want."

Now Sargent begins calling up members of Brandy's family to express what her death has done to them. But the one person who should listen to them is gone.

Brandy's grandfather, Paul Vasquez. "I needed her, and she needed me."

His wife, Rose, for whom Brandy received her middle name. "I loved her deeply and miss her terribly."

At Danny's trial, the defense lawyers pretty much sat in their seats during the victim-impact statements and listened politely. But these are different lawyers.

As Rose begins to talk about how painful it has been for her to imagine what Brandy suffered, Neuwirth objects. Such statements should be limited to the sort of person the victim was and what her loss meant to the family, he argues, not about the crime itself. That would be a violation of his client's right to due process.

Sargent counters that the horrific nature of the crime is part of what the family has to deal with: Not just Brandy's murder, but how she was murdered.

Judge Villano agrees with Neuwirth, however. Whatever Rose's mind has *"conjured up"* about Brandy's suffering will be considered speculation and ignored by the judges.

Tiny and in tears, Rose hesitantly—as though waiting for the defense lawyers to jump up again—finishes her statement for the last time. "A cold stone does not satisfy the arms of a 74-year-old woman."

* * *

Just getting through the first day of testimony is an ordeal. After the family members speak, the prosecution calls on witnesses who can detail Francisco's many encounters with the justice system.

These include probation officers, halfway-house counselors, and cops. They often are reading records written by others, provoking numerous objections from Neuwirth about the hearsay nature of such testimony. It doesn't allow Francisco, through his lawyers, his constitutional right to confront his accusers directly through cross-examination.

The prosecutors note that the rules of evidence don't apply at sentencing hearings. That means a certain amount of hearsay is allowed.

The objections are overruled. Neuwirth's frequent return to the same subject finally irritates Villano, who testily notes that he'd already ruled on the appearance of these witnesses prior to the hearing. "Let's get on with it," he says.

And they do.

Theodore LeDoux, a probation officer with Denver Juvenile Court, testifies that Francisco seemed to have a good relationship with his mother, Linda (combating the expected defense allegations that she was a bad mom), and that she tried to get her son out of the neighborhood after Crips shot at him in 1988.

Neuwirth gets LeDoux to acknowledge that Francisco had been called "Pancho" since he was a little boy and that it was not a gang moniker. He also gets him to admit that when Francisco was in detention, his mother had her telephone service blocked so he couldn't call home.

John Malloy, a former youth corrections caseworker for the state Department of Corrections, testifies that when Francisco was in detention in 1989 after his part in a gang shooting by Antonio Martinez, the young man had stated that he "likes to hurt people." Francisco "believed in gang ideation," he adds.

Malloy is uncooperative when Kaplan, on cross-examination, tries to point out that Francisco had "done well" in the structured environment of the detention facility. This would go to the defense argument that Francisco would not be a problem if allowed to live in prison. But Malloy will concede only that the first three months were "the honeymoon period," after which the defendant "slacked off."

Detective Joseph Catalina of the Denver Police Department relates how Francisco was the prime suspect in the March 23, 1993, shooting of two fellow gang members, Sam Garcia and Gary Rodriguez. The shooting had been witnessed by David Warren, a co-defendant in the DuVall case.

Garcia had positively identified Francisco from a photo lineup, Catalina says, recalling Garcia's comment: "I'm almost dead, and that's the guy who tried to kill me. Yeah, Pancho. Francisco Martinez."

But the men had later recanted, and Francisco was never prosecuted.

CHAPTER FIFTY-TWO

May 11, 1999

The sullen young Hispanic man in the orange jail jumpsuit shakes his head. "I'm not going to talk. I want to go back to my cell."

David Warren has been called to talk about the 1993 shooting discussed the day before. Although he'd testified against Frank Vigil, Danny, and Francisco at their trials, he's now refusing to say any more.

Sargent gets him to admit that he's not happy. He thought his deal was that he got to do his time out of state—a matter the prosecutor is still trying to arrange—and he wasn't pleased when Villano sentenced him to the maximum, thirty-two years, in March.

But his current stance has more to do with fear than petulance. It was one thing to be a "snitch" at a trial; testifying against another prisoner at a death-penalty hearing takes matters to another level.

In their seats, Brandy's relatives groan. They recall that just two months ago, this man was on his hands and knees, crying and begging their forgiveness, telling Villano all the things he'd tried to do to make up for his crime (which had included biting Brandy's breast while she stood in terror, handcuffed and hooded).

Now Warren won't budge, even when Villano threatens him with contempt of court. Finally, he's allowed to step down from the witness stand and is marched back to his cell.

The prosecution calls a more agreeable witness, Stacy Pike, a therapist who treated Francisco while he was residing in a halfway house after getting out of prison in 1995. She says that Francisco had been sent to her needing therapy for "alcohol abuse and anger management." Pike has worked with many violent offenders in her two decades as a therapist, she says, but Francisco was in a league by himself.

Early in the group sessions, she says, the participants were working on issues regarding their belief systems. They were asked questions that required yes or no answers. One question was: Do you believe you will be famous?

Francisco answered yes. When she asked him what was going to make him famous, Pike testifies, "He said he was going to blow away an entire gang."

With that in mind, Pike listened even more closely to Francisco's responses at the next session. This time the participants were asked about their favorite hobby. "He said his favorite hobby was shooting people," Pike recalls. "I hadn't heard that one before, so I asked him what it was about shooting people that he liked. He said that after he shoots them, he likes to watch their bodies twitch." Pike asked Francisco if he would shoot her. His response: "Oh, no, Miss Pike. I like you."

In another instance, the participants were asked to pick out nicknames for themselves; it was a way for them to get to know each other. The nickname had to begin with the letters of their real names. Francisco, however, chose "P" for Pancho. And he said he wanted to be known as "Psycho Pancho."

That was enough for Pike. She called Francisco's caseworker at the halfway house that allowed him out during the day to work and attend classes, and, she says, told him to have Francisco picked up by the Department of Corrections. In her opinion, he was homicidal and did not belong on the streets.

Over the course of her career, how often had she called a caseworker to have someone "taken off the streets?" Sargent asks.

"This was the second time."

"Do you scare easily?"

"Not after nineteen years," Pike replies.

"Did Mr. Martinez scare you?"

"Yes, he did."

On cross-examination, Kaplan notes that Pike didn't write on her report that she felt Francisco was "homicidal."

"I stated he was very dangerous," says Pike, who looks at Kaplan with what appears to be distaste.

"Right," Kaplan says, ignoring her hostility, "but not 'homicidal.'"

"I thought he was homicidal," she says.

Kaplan also observes that she never wrote anything down about "Psycho Pancho."

As Pike shrugs, Kaplan points out that according to her reports, Francisco got good marks for participation and cooperation in the group session. The caseworker's report noted that Pike had suggested Francisco get intensive individualized counseling, as well as continue in group therapy.

"I do not agree with the statement," Pike sniffs.

"He never got physically aggressive with you or anybody in the group," Kaplan says.

"No, he did not," she admits.

On redirect, Sargent asks if there was a reason she specifically remembers the nickname incident.

"Yes," Pike says and smiles. "I was surprised he knew that 'psycho' started with a 'P.'"

Another witness, a Denver police detective, recalls how Francisco and other members of his gang robbed two younger boys. Francisco, he says, was the first to pull a gun. A second detective testifies about a case concerning Francisco and a friend robbing two men of a keg of beer.

Then witnesses are called to testify about a May 1, 1997, shooting incident in which Francisco was the main suspect. Francisco's father-in-law, a man named Chico, had discovered that Francisco was carrying on an affair with his niece, Gina Ynostrosa, the first cousin of his daughter, Nicole.

According to testimony, Francisco had persuaded Chico's nephew, Toby Archuleta, to accompany him to Chico's home. There they were told by a roommate, Pedro Medina, that Chico wasn't home, and they left.

A short time later, someone came and shot Medina from behind in the left shoulder and lower back. Medina now tells the judges he never got a good look at the person who shot him.

But the police believed it was Francisco, who went on the run. By the end of the month, Brandy DuVall was dead.

During a break in the testimony, a catfight erupts on the defense side of the spectator section. There have been two camps of Francisco supporters over there: his family and a couple of girlfriends who have borne him children in one; his wife, Nicole, and her mother in another.

Nicole and one of the girlfriends get into it when the latter asks, "What you lookin' at, bitch?" George Anders, a retired bailiff who occasionally works when needed, has to separate them.

The deputies who provide court security request the women's presence in the hallway. There they lodge complaints against each other. One had slashed the other's tires. The other was giving dirty looks.

Nicole produces paperwork for a restraining order against the other woman. The wrong girlfriend's name is on the papers.

Villano is apprised of the situation, and he sternly warns the women to sit apart and not so much as glance in each other's direction. Otherwise, he says, they will be ejected from the courtroom for the rest of the hearing.

Gina Ynostrosa is called to the stand. She seems an unlikely candidate for an affair with a gang member. A pretty girl, she is studying criminal justice in college. Her father, now deceased, was a state trooper; one brother is currently a state trooper, and another is in the police academy.

She says a male cousin introduced her to Francisco—who was going by the first name of "Leroy"—in 1996. At the time, she didn't even know he was living in a halfway house; it wasn't until long after they'd become lovers that she realized who he really was: the husband of her cousin Nicole.

When she confronted Francisco, she says, he denied it at first. She stopped seeing him, but Francisco was persistent, and they resumed their relationship in January 1997.

In response to questioning by Randall, Gina testifies that Francisco was "very close" to his mother, who had a huge photograph of him on one wall and smaller photos of her son on the other walls. He'd never confided anything about any childhood traumas, she says.

She knew he was a gang member. For one thing, he had tattoos proclaiming that fact all over his body. But he didn't bring the gang over or use gang lingo around her. In fact, he became something of a school project for her ... firsthand insight into a street criminal.

In late April 1997, Nicole learned about the affair, "which opened a can of worms." A few days later, Gina came home to find a nervous Francisco pacing around. He said the police were looking for him because of a shooting ... the Pedro Medina incident.

After his mother called to say the police had been by her house looking for him, Francisco left. Gina didn't see him again for a couple of weeks, but he called plenty. Only this time, the nice-guy routine was missing. If she didn't answer the telephone, she says, he left "crude messages," such as "Who you out fucking? Bitch, where are you?"

On the evening of May 26, she was home alone with her son, asleep on the couch, when Francisco broke in. He straddled her and began punching her in the face and strangling her. "It was 'bitch' this, 'bitch' that," she recalls.

Gina blacked out. When she came to, her nightshirt had been torn off her body and was in shreds. Francisco was still in the home; when she asked, he let her see that her son was all right. But soon he left the apartment and got into a car with other young men.

Gina says she drove to Francisco's mother's house. "Look what your son did to me," she told her. But although her face was bruised and swollen and there were obvious finger marks around her throat, Linda "was not supportive ... she said the bruise on my throat looked like hickeys to her."

But the cops believed Gina Ynostrosa.

Now Francisco was on the run for assaulting her as well. But he continued to call, asking what he had done that was so bad she felt she had to betray him.

Later, when she heard about his possible involvement in the killing of Brandy DuVall, she'd asked Francisco about it. "He said, 'Fuck that bitch. She deserved what she got.'"

"Did he say whose fault it was?" Randall asks.

"Her own," Gina replies. "He seemed bitter and angry about it."

On cross-examination, Kaplan points out that before the assault, Francisco was "trying to be a better person." Gina agrees. He was good with her son, she says, and often sent her flowers.

On redirect, Randall asks, "So Francisco was capable of behaving well?"

"Sure," she says.

"And he was also capable of assaulting you?"

"Correct."

The boyish-looking Randall practically blushes as he asks if Francisco made any peculiar sort of sexual requests.

"On a few occasions, he asked for anal sex," she replies. But she wouldn't agree to it.

Randall asks if Francisco's demeanor changed after she told the police about the assault. Her former lover became more gang-like, Gina concedes, and his language was filled with gangster talk. He reminded her that he had taken her address book following the assault. "He said, 'I know where your family and friends live. Make this hard for me, and I'll hurt you or someone you care about.'"

She pauses, then concludes, "He scared the shit out of me."

CHAPTER FIFTY-THREE

May 11, 1999

Once more. Just get through this one more time, Angela Metzger thinks, as the prosecutor announces that Brandy's mother would "like to make a statement to the court."

"Had to" would be more accurate. How can she "like" baring her soul, exposing wounds that never get a chance to heal before they're ripped open again? "Like" does not describe the feeling of standing in front of strangers, unable to control her tears, choking over the words of her misery.

Somehow, somewhere, Angela Metzger always finds the strength to do what must be done. She had bared, ripped, and cried through three murder trials and half a dozen sentencing hearings of the young men who had raped, tormented, and killed her daughter. But it was not something she wanted to do—not even for revenge.

When the morning of each new trial or sentencing arrived, she only wished she could stay home, cloistered as she was most of the days between court appearances. She didn't want to see people. Or talk to them. She wanted them all to go away and leave her to her grief.

She wanted Brandy ... but that wasn't going to happen.

Now her obligation was to bear witness. So Angela would get up, dress, and head to the Jefferson County courthouse to listen one more time to what members of the Deuce-Seven Bloods gang had done to her little girl.

Then it would be the defense lawyers trying to excuse what had happened, blaming childhoods of abuse, bad neighborhoods, peer pressure, too much alcohol, and testosterone ... and, of course, negligent parents. They'd argue that the "tragic incident"—or some other generic term that blew past the reality of what was done to Brandy—was someone else's fault. Not their client's.

In the two years since she'd identified Brandy's body on the coroner's table—*Wake up, baby. Wake up.*—this was all that remained of Angela's life.

In a way, the slow machinations of justice had given her something to keep her going. There was always another hearing, another trial, another sentencing—another step as she fought to keep her head above the still-rising tide of her grief. She had no idea what would happen when the last of the legal proceedings was finished and there were no more steps.

Nor did she care.

Angela had no illusions that it would soon "be over." It would never be over. Some members of her family talked about getting on with their lives once Francisco was sentenced and urged her to do the same. She had her friends and family who loved her. And there was her new grandson, Brandon, named after the murdered aunt he would never know.

She loved them all and knew they meant well. But they weren't Brandy. Nor could they lift the enormous weight of guilt she felt. Discussion about what Angela should do "when this is over" had led to arguments, and she'd withdrawn even further into her shell. She came out only when she was called back to court.

At prosecutor Sargent's bidding, Angela now rises from the pew where she'd been sitting with her family. Once again, she'll try to explain the impact of a never-ending nightmare. She doesn't care what decision the judges reach. She hadn't been disappointed with the panel's decision to spare Danny; such things were in God's hands. And she feels for both of the mothers on the other side of the courtroom.

Either way—life without parole or a lethal injection—Francisco will not be hurting any more little girls. But Sargent, whom she trusts implicitly, has told her it's important. One last time.

As she stands trembling next to Sargent at the podium, Angela clutches the paper on which she's written what she wants to say. It will soon be two years since Brandy was killed. Sometimes it seems like a long time ago, but in May, the last month of Brandy's life, it always seems like yesterday.

Angela keeps her eyes on the judges. The prosecutors have told her not to state what penalty she thinks is appropriate or to address Francisco personally. But avoiding Francisco won't be difficult: He isn't here. Instead, Francisco is represented by three lawyers and an empty chair.

Angela doesn't want Brandy to become just another victim in one of those textbook cases the lawyers are so fond of spitting back and forth at each other. She doesn't want them to forget that Brandy was once a real little girl.

Already she can feel the tears, never more than a memory away, waiting to spill over. So she begins while she still can. "I want to tell you a little bit about Brandy," she says, looking up at the row of impassive judges.

"She was fourteen years old, and she was a shy person."

This is the only good thing about testifying: It gives Angela an opportunity to talk about the little girl she knew. The good student. The athlete. The teenager who was still shy about her body.

"And now I go to the mountain where she died," Angela says. "I pick up the rocks that have dried blood on them, and I put them in my yard, because I don't want them up there. I don't want people seeing them or walking on them or driving on them.

"And I have there to go, and I have her grave to go to and just sit there and talk to her, and I don't get to hear her calling me 'Mom' anymore, hear her voice or see her or hug her or ...," she wraps her arms around herself and weeps, "Oh, God, she had the best touch."

With an effort, Angela moves on to thank God that the last words she and her daughter said to each other were words of love. "She loved me a lot. That girl loved me a lot, and I could feel it, and now I don't feel it no more. And now I don't even care about life. I don't care about nothing."

Her husband has had to suffer the loss of both his wife and stepdaughter. "I look at him and his boys," Angela says, "and I think, 'Why? Why do you get your kids?' Why does he get them, and I don't get mine? What did I do? She didn't do nothin'. She's just a little girl. And how come everybody else gets their kids, and I don't get to see mine, or touch mine, or tell her I love her?"

Failure eats at her every day. Parents are supposed to keep their children safe, and she didn't. "Everyone knows that that's the way it is ... but I couldn't save her. I couldn't help her. I couldn't comfort her."

Maybe, she says, if she's good, there'll be a chance to atone in the future. "If I'm lucky enough, I'll be with her again, because I know she's in a good place, and I got to work real hard so I can be with her, and that's the only thing I think that keeps me going ... that I get to see her again.

"I got to tell her I love her, and I just got to hold her, and I got to apologize to her for not helping her, for not being able to do something, and that's my hell."

Angela reaches the end. But, as always, she has the feeling that there's something else she should have said, some word to describe the emptiness. She wipes away a tear. "I wish I could make you understand."

CHAPTER FIFTY-FOUR

May 12, 1999

The prosecution wraps up its case with a few last witnesses. A parole officer who testifies that Francisco was wanted for the shooting of Pedro Medina and the assault on Gina Ynostrosa. Two deputies who relate an incident at the jail when Francisco, upset about not being allowed to go immediately to his cell following a hearing, picked up a heavy metal shower grate and seemed ready to attack.

Jacob "Smiley" Casados, another young man in an orange jail jumpsuit, is brought in to testify about an occurrence during Francisco's trial. Another co-defendant who testified for the prosecution, Casados accidentally crossed paths with Francisco, who told him: "You won't be Smiley anymore." But like David Warren, Casados now refuses to talk.

"Why don't you want to testify?" Bakke asks.

"My life would be in danger," he says.

Casados is sent back to his cell. But a deputy who heard Francisco's statement to Casados tells the court all about it.

The rest of the afternoon is consumed by Jeffco sheriff's investigator Al Simmons, who reviews the evidence from the trial.

At the end of the day, the prosecution rests. Tomorrow the defense will get its turn.

CHAPTER FIFTY-FIVE

May 13, 1999

The defense spends its first day of testimony trotting out witnesses to testify about Pancho's childhood.

Francisco's father, Francisco Martinez Sr., testifies that he used to beat his wife, especially when she "talked back" about his womanizing and drinking. One Christmas, he tossed the turkey and the Christmas tree out the door.

The violence went both ways. His wife once took a shot at him, and later, after he'd forced his father-in-law off the road, his wife's family had come gunning for him. He'd taken off for California and never returned. At the time, Francisco was four.

Jacqueline Baros, Francisco's aunt, testifies about fleeing her own abusive husband and moving in with her sister, Linda, and Linda's three children. For the first few months, they lived crowded together in a portion of their parents' former home; Linda had blocked off the rest of the house to conserve heat. Jacqueline recalls that they'd see mice crawling over the children, who slept on the floor. "We thought it was funny, but, you know, it's not."

Jacqueline testifies about the day that Linda, who was on anti-depressants, pulled Francisco and his younger sister, Monique, out of school and took them to church. In the front pew, Linda explained to then-eleven-year-old Francisco that he would have to be a man now and "take care of things," then pulled out a gun and aimed it at her head. Fortunately, Linda had called the police in advance, and they showed up in time to wrestle the gun away.

After the turkey incident with Frank Martinez Sr., Linda refused to celebrate Christmas until 1997, Jacqueline says. Noting the date, one member of Brandy's family whispers to another, "only after Brandy was killed."

On cross-examination, Bakke gets Jacqueline to concede that the kids celebrated Christmas with other members of the extended family. "And you made sure the children were never neglected?" Bakke says.

"Yes, I did," Jacqueline admits.

"And didn't you tell a defense investigator that after the church incident, Pancho seemed 'more concerned than upset?'" Bakke asks, reading from the investigator's report.

"That is true."

It's late afternoon when Nicole Martinez takes the stand. She's faithfully attended every day of the hearing, watching sullenly as Francisco's girlfriends testified about what a good father he was to their children.

She'd met Francisco when they were both young teens. She was soon pregnant, but Francisco and his family were unhappy when she had a baby girl instead of a boy.

Nevertheless, she says, Francisco was always a good father to the three children. He'd come by to see them, even when they didn't live together, as often as two or three times a week.

Francisco's mother didn't like her. "She'd rather see him with his friends than his family," Nicole says. Linda would even invite Francisco's girlfriends and children to dinner with them.

"She was always interfering," Nicole says, and forever making up ways to get Francisco to come home. "She was always dying of cancer or some other sickness."

On August 19, 1994, Francisco was shot by members of the Crips gang. After he recovered, he was sent to prison in Buena Vista, where Nicole visited him with the kids every weekend. He was in prison when they married, in February 1995.

They married because they loved each other, Nicole says. But Linda didn't like it. She would tell Nicole's children, "'I'm not your grandmother,' and 'Your mother's a bitch,' which is not something you tell a two-year-old boy."

When Francisco got out of prison and went to the halfway house, things went well for a while. But gradually Nicole began to see less and less of him. She didn't know he was carrying on with her cousin Gina.

On cross-examination, Randall comments that Francisco was often unkind to her.

"Quite a few times," she concedes.

Once, Randall continues, when Nicole found out about a pregnant girlfriend and confronted Francisco in tears, "his reaction was to laugh."

"That's true."

Randall points out that while Francisco was living in the halfway house, she was supporting their three children alone—even though she was sick with lupus. And during this time, Francisco took her rent money.

"We had an argument," Nicole says in Francisco's defense. "He just put it in a different place."

Reading from a defense interview of Nicole, Randall notes that she'd said when Francisco joined a gang, "he was proud for doing something he knew he shouldn't."

Nicole nods. "It was the first time he had ever accomplished something on his own."

Randall asks her about a domestic-violence incident on April 21, 1993, during which he struck and kicked her "numerous times" and threatened her with a gun.

They both had been fighting, Nicole responds. She was partly to blame.

Randall asks Nicole if she's aware of comments Francisco made to caseworkers at the halfway house. In one, he said that though he loved his children, he felt no special attachment to them and that they were their mothers' responsibility. In another, he said that if he went back to prison, Nicole would leave him, but that was okay because he'd just start another family.

"Those weren't nice things to say," Randall suggests.

"No, they weren't," Nicole agrees.

In tears, she insists that Francisco always made it a point to see the children. But throughout her testimony, she refers to them as *my* children, never *our* children.

CHAPTER FIFTY-SIX

May 19, 1999

"Your Honors, Judge Villano, Judge Hickman, and Judge Hyatt, I want to apologize to Angela Metzger, and Paul and Rose Vasquez, and say that I am deeply sorry for my participation in this crime. She didn't do anything to deserve what happened. You didn't deserve this."

Francisco Martinez Jr. stands at the defense table, reading from a single sheet of paper. Today, the last day of his hearing, he wears a long-sleeved white shirt over his tattoos, his scars, and the electric-shock control belt.

For the past two days, he'd been out of his cell and in attendance while two defense psychologists contended that he was depressed and suffered from post-traumatic stress syndrome and an antisocial-personality disorder— all attributable to his experiences of an abusive, violent childhood and youth. Now, in just a few minutes, closing arguments will begin and then his fate will be turned over to the judges.

At the sentencing hearing for Danny Martinez, Danny's sister, grandmother. and mother all tearfully apologized to Brandy's family. Danny's aunt, while testifying that he'd had a difficult childhood, also said that it was "not one that leads to this." No one in his family had wanted Danny to die, of course, but they weren't blind to what he had done. And so they'd requested that his lawyers let them make their apologies.

At this hearing, no one from Francisco's side has offered a word of condolence to Brandy's family. His mother and sisters were never asked to give a statement or testify. Two aunts and his wife appeared on the witness stand, but none said a word to Brandy's family.

It is up to Francisco, who makes his remarks in a flat, emotionless voice. He says he's sorry for the harassment incident during his trial. "I was not trying to make it worse for you," he tells Brandy's family.

Then he apologizes to his own family for his actions, "especially my mother, my sisters, and my children, and I want to thank you for staying by my side all the way," he says. He does not mention Nicole.

Francisco looks up and thanks the judges. "Please spare my life," he says, before taking his seat.

CHAPTER FIFTY-SEVEN

May 19, 1999

Hal Sargent wastes little time with his closing arguments. The prosecutor wants this to be over as much as anyone. Preparing for this closing, he decided not to use the photographs of Brandy—in part because he didn't think they would be necessary, but more because he couldn't stand to look at them again.

"We would have to search a long time in the darkest reaches of our minds and imaginations to come up with a crime more depraved than this one," he begins.

Looking directly at Francisco, who keeps his eyes on the judges, Sargent adds, "We've seen hell in its most human form.

"What he did to Brandy DuVall was brutal, it was absolutely merciless and absolutely tortuous. What kind of man does that to a child—intentionally, deliberately, and, the evidence is, even joyfully?"

Turning to Brandy's family, he says, "When he killed Brandy, he did something else. He sentenced these good people to lives of sorrow, grief, and pain."

With that, he goes through the five aggravators he says the prosecution has proved beyond a reasonable doubt. When he reaches the "heinous, cruel, and depraved" aggravator, he points to Francisco and asks the judges to imagine "the terror of that little girl when she felt the knife and then that man's hands around her neck ... knowing he was going to kill her and knowing she could do nothing about it."

The judges didn't have to rely solely on Sammy Quintana's testimony to know who'd really stabbed Brandy, he says. Francisco himself, when questioned by police, had admitted he was in the front passenger seat when the gang left Uncle Joe's house (although he denied that Brandy was with them). The wounds to Brandy's stomach and sides had been caused by the person sitting in that seat.

When the judges reach step three, Sargent says, they will find that whatever mitigators they allow "would pale in comparison to the aggravators." And when they turn to step four, he says, there can be only one sentence: "for the ultimate crime, the ultimate punishment."

* * *

Defense attorney Kaplan waits for Sargent to sit before he proceeds slowly to the podium, as if lost in thought. He is drained. One day during a break in the hearing, he had begged a different judge to reschedule another trial—not because Kaplan didn't have that case together, but because he would be too emotionally depleted by this one to put any heart into it, he said.

"Who should live and who should die is not an easy question for a civilized society," Kaplan now begins. And the judges will have to make their decision not just according to "legal concepts, but moral concepts."

They should begin with "the presumption of life, the value of life. The life of Brandy DuVall," he says, turning to the girl's family, and then pointing to his client, "and the life of Francisco Martinez."

Kaplan revives the argument that all of the evidence pointing to Francisco as the man who inflicted Brandy's fatal wounds came from Sammy Quintana. Recalling Quintana's involvement in the killing of Brandy and Venus Montoya,

Kaplan asks, "Is that the type of person whose testimony you can rely on in order to kill Francisco Martinez?"

The attorney also returns to Ridley's opening statement that the judges couldn't know if the jury convicted Francisco as the principal or the complicitor. In which case, he says, "it would be impermissible to sentence Francisco Martinez to death on a theory of complicity."

Kaplan attacks the quality of the prosecution's evidence regarding its aggravators, particularly those accusing Francisco of crimes of which he was never convicted. Much of it was hearsay, he argues, or blown out of proportion.

"And what of Francisco Martinez, the man before this court? What of his life?" Kaplan asks, then delves into his client's past.

The judges can't just "sweep it off the table like yesterday's news. It was not just like every other hard-luck story." Some of what Francisco went through would have been "okay if everything else was okay. But it was not okay when you have virtually nothing else going for you."

Kaplan ends his remarks by recalling the Columbine High School shootings a month before. A civilized society, he says, needs to ask questions about what events precede "something this horrible, whether Brandy DuVall or Columbine," and what might have been done to prevent either one.

His voice cracking from the strain, Kaplan says that this is the first time he's had to argue about whether a client should live or die, "and I'm not quite sure how to sit down. Tomorrow will be too late." He asks the judges to try to understand the forces that created Francisco, "and hopefully, to understand is to forgive."

Hal Sargent takes a last glance at his rebuttal notes before looking up at the panel of judges. Two years of prosecuting members of the Deuce-Seven Bloods gang for the May 1997 rape and murder of fourteen-year-old Brandy DuVall are nearly at an end. This is not the time to falter.

The task has been monumental. Three murder trials. Endless meetings with attorneys to make deals and get co-defendants to roll over and testify against the others. Innumerable hearings to quibble with other attorneys over legal technicalities.

Then four sentencings. And finally, two death-penalty hearings, including this one for Francisco "Pancho" Martinez Jr., who sits twelve feet to Sargent's right, staring sullenly up at the three judges who will decide if he lives or dies.

Sargent is young, clean-cut, and, like the other Jefferson County deputy district attorneys who make up the prosecution team, Mark Randall and Ingrid Bakke, deeply tired of the DuVall case. They are all emotionally and physically spent.

It has been difficult to get up each morning and generate the energy necessary to continue this course—and it's been even harder since the first death-penalty hearing for co-defendant Danny "Bang" Martinez Jr. in late April. Not that Sargent believes any less in what he is doing, but like an actor in a play that keeps going, night after night, he finds the material has grown old, flat. He feels the danger of Brandy becoming two-dimensional, a footnote in the law books—instead of a young girl who died so horribly at the hands of these young men.

Now, less than two weeks shy of the day two years ago when Brandy DuVall's savaged body was found alongside Clear Creek, the finish line is in sight. Lead defense attorney Dave Kaplan has delivered his closing arguments, but the last word will be Sargent's.

* * *

"Mr. Kaplan ended with a point that I think deserves some comment," Sargent says. "Can we explain? Can we understand Mr. Martinez?

"One of the things I think we do in courtrooms is, we lose sight of the focus. I have great respect for what mental-health professionals do in attempting to understand behavior, understand causes so that it can be treated. But that is not the focus here.

"To understand does not mean to excuse. Mr. Martinez has told everyone who would listen what he's about, who he is. He said in 1989 to John Malloy, 'I enjoy hurting people.' He told Stacy Pike, 'I want to be famous for killing people.' He told her that his favorite hobby was shooting people because he 'liked to watch the bodies jump.'

"We can hope to understand and to explain what combination of forces make Francisco Martinez the man he is. But when we're done with that, when we're done with explaining who he is, the question is: So what? What do we make of it? Do we excuse him?"

As Sargent speaks, twenty-five-year-old Francisco keeps his eyes averted. His mouth hangs slightly open; he looks like a man who realizes this is it. The end. He no longer has the demeanor of the gangbanger who at his murder trial last August smiled and smirked at Brandy's family, then told Sargent, *"Fuck you, you pussy,"* when the prosecutor intervened.

Francisco's hair has been shaved to a dark stubble that matches his goatee. He wears a long-sleeved white dress shirt that hides the gang tattoos on his arms and covers the long, ugly scar on his belly where a surgeon opened him after he was shot in 1994; the shirt fits loosely, even across his thick shoulders, so that it covers the electric-shock belt that bulges from his lower back.

Francisco wasn't in this Jeffco courtroom for most of the hearing. On the first day, his lawyers had asked that he be allowed to stay in his cell, because he didn't want to hear the bad things they were going to say about his family in their effort to save his life. Of course, that meant he wouldn't have to hear from Brandy's family about the suffering he'd caused them, either.

But Francisco has been back in the courtroom for the last two days, to listen to defense psychologists explain why he had joined a gang, to explain his propensity for violence, and to explain his inability to make good decisions while drunk and under stress.

Francisco's lawyers also look worn out. Pat Ridley slumps in his chair beside the defendant, a pen in his mouth. Next to Ridley, still jotting notes and passing them to his co-counsels, is Dean Neuwirth, a legal expert brought in to counter the lawyer from the Colorado Attorney General's Office who sits with the prosecution to aid on matters of legal precedence in death-penalty cases.

And finally, closest to the podium, is Kaplan, the lead defense counsel who ended his remarks by recalling the shootings, just the previous month, at Columbine High School. A civilized society, he said, needs to ask the questions about what events precede "something this horrible, whether Brandy DuVall or Columbine," and what might have been done to prevent it.

The defense team fought hard and bitterly—some on the prosecution side of the aisle would say they were outright obstructionist—filing more than three hundred motions just between the end of Francisco's trial early last September and this hearing, then jumping up to object at what seemed every comment made by the deputy DAs or prosecution witnesses. But as the attorneys on this side would argue—and argue they do—how much is too much when a man's life is at stake?

And so Kaplan and his colleagues made their arguments that Francisco's abused, violence-marred childhood pushed him into a gang and down a path of violence.

On a less philosophical note, Kaplan also argued that there was no proof beyond the questionable word of Sammy "Zig Zag" Quintana that Francisco was the man who actually wielded the knife and stabbed Brandy twenty-eight times. The jury had not been asked to determine if they believed that Pancho was the so-called triggerman, or just one of many culpable in the girl's death, he noted, and so to single him out for lethal injection would be unfair.

But Sargent now counters that the jury believed Quintana—and so should the panel of three judges. The question, he says, is what punishment fits Francisco's crime and character.

"By whatever combination of forces brought Francisco Martinez to be the man he is," Sargent continues, "he is an absolutely dangerous man ... All you've got to do is listen to him if you want to know what makes him tick, what he is about.

"The experts hired by the defense—and I don't mean to belittle their attempts to explain him—but they carefully avoided asking the direct question 'Why did you sodomize Brandy with the broom?' because they knew the answer.

"You know the answer. It is in his psychological makeup that he enjoys hurting other people."

* * *

The courtroom feels lopsided.

Francisco's family and friends—including at least two girlfriends and a wife who have all borne his children—had filled the second and third pews behind the defense table for most of the eight-day hearing. (For security reasons, only defense-team investigators and defense attorneys who dropped by to watch the proceedings had been allowed in the first pew.) But today just Francisco's mother, Linda, clad in a T-shirt, shorts, and dark glasses, and one younger woman are seated on Pancho's side.

Behind the prosecution table, the second and third rows are packed with members of the press, along with employees of the DA's office and court personnel who want to witness the last great battle in one of the most horrific cases in anyone's memory. The row closest to the prosecution is filled with members of Brandy's family, sitting as close as possible to one another, holding hands, some resting their heads on nearby shoulders.

For the past two years, this has been their life, too. Day after day, week after week, sitting on hard wooden benches that seem designed for discomfort; the thin pillows handed out by victims' advocates provide scant comfort.

But what could comfort them? Physical inconveniences pale beside the ordeal of listening again and again and again and again and again to how members of the Deuce-Seven Bloods raped, sodomized, tortured, humiliated, tormented, and, finally, stabbed Brandy, leaving her to die alone in the dark. As they listened to different young men recall ad nauseam Brandy's screams, her pleas for her life, they were powerless to stop the tears or stifle their sobs.

To add further insult, they were forced to listen to defense lawyers try to lay the blame on one of the others, or contend that their clients were too drunk to be accountable, or too frightened of other gang members to try and stop the insanity.

In March the family sat through the sentencing hearings for the prosecution witnesses, who pleaded for mercy when they themselves had shown none to Brandy. Having now found religion and a conscience, they apologized to the relatives of the girl they'd treated like a piece of meat—one even biting into her breast like an animal. And her family was supposed to forgive them?

Nothing beat the excuses given at the death-penalty hearings. The first had been for Danny Martinez Jr., the reputed leader of the Deuce-Seven, just a few weeks before. Danny was no relation to Francisco, but as Danny's sister had testified, they were even more like brothers than biological brothers could be.

And now here was Francisco, the man accused not only of stabbing Brandy but of being the most brutal during the three to four hours of torture that preceded her death. A man described by prosecutor Randall as *"ultra-evil."*

Francisco, too, had apologized, just before closing arguments, saying Brandy *"did nothing to deserve what happened."* As if that was even a question. But of course, Francisco had also avoided making any admission beyond acknowledging his *"participation"* in the events that night. After all, there are appeals to consider.

For Brandy's mother, Angela Metzger, it was particularly hard to listen to the defense teams talk about Danny's and Francisco's mothers. She'd heard enough mean comments about her own parenting—*What was a fourteen-year-old girl doing on Federal Boulevard at midnight?*—to wish any more anguish on those women. They would have to live with the guilt of hindsight. It was a twisted irony that the prosecutors had tried to point out that those other mothers weren't as bad as their sons' lawyers made them out to be.

* * *

The psychologists who were hired to examine Francisco did not do so thoroughly enough as to ask him what possibly could have been going through his head that night. "The mental-health mitigator," Sargent says, referring to the defense's arguments used to combat the prosecution, "tells you what to make of this man in this state of mind. But it is only an excuse.

"It only lessens the blame if it substantially impairs his ability to recognize right from wrong. We've got to, if we have any system of laws, start with a basic premise of free will. That we are responsible. We are able to make choices. And we are responsible for choices we make, both good and bad."

Walking over to a large blackboard where the defense has created a timeline showing how Francisco's unhappy childhood impacted his monstrous adulthood, Sargent points to several photographs of the defendant as an infant and boy. "I don't mean to demean or belittle what Francisco Martinez may have gone through as a child," he says.

"I have sympathy for this child of one or three or eight who may have seen more than any child should be exposed to ... and I have sympathy for that child who saw too much, perhaps.

"But again, as sympathetic as you may be for that three-, six-, ten-year-old boy, that's not who stands before you today. In between those early years lay years of intervention, years of alcohol counseling, years of intensive individual mental-health therapy.

"We could hope that he could be given more programs when he was little. But it's not society's fault because we didn't offer him enough programs. It is his fault. He owes us something as well. That he failed to learn, failed to change his behavior, is not our fault. He has to be held accountable for those decisions he made.

"What role does sympathy play?" Sargent asks. "You're asked to feel sorry for what he experienced in his life."

The prosecutor pulls out a book written by psychiatrist Willard Gatlin, in which Gatlin laments the aftermath of the murder of a young woman named Bonnie Garland.

"When one person kills another," Sargent quotes, "there is an immediate revulsion at the nature of the crime. But in a time so short as to seem indecent to the members of the family, the dead person ceases to exist as an identifiable figure.

"To those individuals in the community of goodwill and empathy, warmth and compassion, only one of the key actors in the drama remains with whom to commiserate, and that is always the criminal.

"The dead person ceases to be a part of everyday reality. She ceases to exist. She is only a figure in a historic event. And we inevitably turn away from the past towards the ongoing reality, and the ongoing reality is the criminal.

"He usurps the compassion that is justly the victim's, and he will steal the victim's constituency along with her life.

"Don't let that happen. He does not deserve your sympathy. He does not deserve your compassion. He doesn't deserve your mercy. And most of all, he does not deserve your leniency."

Sargent closes the book and picks up a photograph. He holds it up as he approaches the judges. "Your compassion," he tells them, "should be justly reserved for this fourteen-year-old girl. This little girl whose life he stole.

"And," he says turning toward the pews behind him, "for the family he left behind with his actions. Imagine the pain that they feel every day. As painful as it was to listen to them in the few minutes they described what her loss has been to them, and how they feel. How that tears them apart. Imagine how they live with that every single day, and will until they die.

"Those are the people who deserve your compassion, your goodwill," Sargent says, then points to Francisco. "Not this man.

"There is no other choice but to give him the ultimate punishment, and that is the sentence of death."

For a moment, the courtroom is absolutely silent. Then a sob escapes from Brandy's mother, a brokenhearted reminder that for some, this will never be over.

CHAPTER FIFTY-EIGHT

May 27, 1999

"I didn't want to come, but Danny asked me to. I told him I don't want to show any disrespect for Angela. But he said, 'Linda needs you.'"

Maria Simpson sits outside the courtroom where, in a few minutes, she'll learn whether the young man she has known since boyhood will be sent to the state executioner. Outside, low gray clouds obscure the tops of the foothills just west of the courthouse—fitting weather for the occasion, she notes.

"I told him I'd come but I didn't want to go in the courtroom," she says of her conversation last night with Danny. "I no more want to hear them hand down the death penalty for Pancho than I did for my own son. But he said, 'You have to go in the courtroom and be there for her.'"

Maria sighs. In the few weeks since Danny had escaped the death penalty by a single vote, she'd felt good. Her prayers had been answered: Her son would live.

But as Pancho's hearing approached, she realized she'd been kidding herself if she thought she could get on with her life. It can only be over if he receives a life sentence without the possibility of parole. That would be justice for what her son and his best friend did to that little girl. "They should have to get up every morning and work hard until night," she says, perhaps building schools or playgrounds.

But if Francisco gets the death penalty, it will not be over. Not for his family, not for hers: The sentence would automatically be appealed, and the legal battles would go on for years. She fears for her son Antonio if Pancho is sentenced to die. Antonio escaped the gang and has a good life far away from Denver, but Pancho was his friend, too. Antonio feels guilty because he walked away but didn't find a way to save Pancho and Danny. It is hard enough for Antonio that his brother will spend the rest of his life in prison; if Pancho is sentenced to die, she worries it will be too much.

"I want this to be over," she says, and gets up to comfort Linda, who has arrived, her face a picture of terror.

A few raindrops strike the window behind the women and run down the panes. The weather seems a portent, predicting the tears of the families waiting in the hall, waiting to be let into the courtroom, waiting for the final judgment.

Angela and her family appear; they are led past the line and to their customary seats. What will she do when this is over? Where will she go? Angela doesn't know. She's purchased books on how to deal with death, but none have helped. Her grief has no structure, no stages to check off. The tide continues to rise. She will heal at her own pace—or not at all.

Shortly before 10 a.m., the rest of the spectators are in the courtroom. Francisco soon enters and appears stunned by the size of the crowd. He sits quickly, without searching out any faces. A few minutes later, the judges come in. As Judge Anderson had done at Danny Martinez's sentencing, Villano encourages anyone who "will not be able to listen to the sentence without disrupting this court ... to go into the hall now."

After the verdict was read at Francisco's trial, his family and friends had erupted in grief, crying "no, no, no" over and over as they wept. But no one leaves the courtroom now, and families on both sides of the aisle struggle to keep quiet.

As he hands packets containing the sentencing order to the attorneys, Villano asks them not to open them or read them until after he announces the verdict.

So no one knows until later that the judges have determined that all five of the prosecution aggravators were proved beyond a reasonable doubt. Of the mitigators, they've accepted just one, the catch-all "any evidence which in the court's opinion bears on the question of mitigation." While the judges largely dismissed the testimony of the defense psychologists, they had some sympathy for Francisco's upbringing.

"The panel finds that this defendant did endure a difficult, disturbing, and unsettled childhood," their decision reads. "He suffered from the absence of positive male role models and the presence of a mother who, though she appeared to love him, suffered from mental disturbances that were, at times, debilitating.

"Although many of the defendant's claims of abuse and neglect were determined by the panel, after hearing, to be less compelling than claimed, the panel does find that the defendant is entitled to mitigation based on the unsettled and disturbing nature of his childhood home."

With that as the only mitigator, the judges had easily decided in step three that the aggravators outweighed the single instance in the defendant's favor. Which brought them to step four.

"In nearly fifty years of collective judicial experience," the judges stated in their opinion, "this panel has never dealt with a more shocking display of conscienceless depravity than that of this defendant.

"Counsel has asked the panel to try and understand the factors that shaped this defendant and led to this crime. That level of comprehension does not assist in understanding the crime.

"Even at trial, a year and a half after the crime, the defendant's conduct was extraordinary. Following the tearful and emotional testimony of the mother of the fourteen-year-old victim, while the court was in recess, the defendant felt compelled to make eye contact with the mother and to laugh and smirk and nod his head at her.

"The defendant's brief emotionless statement of apology to the child's family at the end of the sentencing proceedings seems to pale against the backdrop of his malevolent attitude toward them over the course of this long and difficult process."

Even for a gang member, the panel wrote, Francisco was unique. "While this panel knows all too well the insidious nature of the gang as a surrogate family and the difficulty inherent in resisting its embrace for a man like the defendant, it must be acknowledged that not every gang member rises to the level of barbaric malevolence attained by Mr. Martinez.

"The panel also acknowledges the tragic consequences of this crime for the victim and her family. The death of Brandaline DuVall and the manner of her death will never be understandable or bearable. It is beyond the ability of this panel to alter that tragic fact."

All of this and more is contained in the packets that sit unopened on the tables in front of the attorneys. The details will spill out later. Right now, the consequence of the judges' considerations comes quickly from Villano:

"It is the judgment, sentence, and warrant of the Court that the defendant, Francisco Martinez Jr., be delivered to the Executive Director of the Colorado Department of Corrections to suffer the penalty of death by lethal injection."

A single, desperate moan escapes from a woman on the defense side, then tiny whimpers as Francisco's supporters try to abide by the judge's order. Brandy's family also cries quietly. There is no happiness here.

Francisco shows little reaction, other than the quick tapping of his foot on the floor. When he stands to be handcuffed, he doesn't look back. Not at his family crying in their seats, not at the family of the little girl he murdered. He leaves the courtroom.

Finally, there are no angels. No devil. Only the lost and those who mourn them.

FROM THE AUTHOR

As might be expected, a lot has happened over the years since the sentencing of Francisco "Pancho" Martinez. Significantly, in 2003, the U.S. Supreme Court struck down the use of three-judge death penalty panels; the justices argued that such a decision should be left in the hands of the defendant's fellow citizens, not jurists.

As in other states that had used the three-judge panels, Colorado district attorneys were given the choice to conduct new death penalty hearings in front of a jury, or commute the death penalty to life without parole. In Colorado, the death penalty sentences, including for Francisco Martinez, were commuted to life without parole.

Of those sentenced to life without parole for premeditated murder in the Brandaline Rose DuVall case:

Francisco Martinez is currently incarcerated at the Colorado Territorial Correctional Facility, a medium security prison in Canon City, Colorado.

Frank Vigil, 39, is currently incarcerated at the Arkansas Valley Correctional Facility, a multi-security level prison in Ordway, Colorado.

Although **Daniel Martinez** was sentenced to life without parole, the Colorado Department of Corrections inmate locater system did not turn up a record of where he is currently incarcerated. This could mean several things: that he was transferred to a prison out of state, that he is deceased (though there is no record of this either), or the Department of Corrections website is incorrect. Attempts by this author to reach someone at the Jefferson County

District Attorney's Office to ascertain his status were not returned.

Of those sentenced in the Venus Montoya murder case:

Alejandro Ornelas, 45, is currently serving a life-without-parole sentence at the Fremont Correctional Facility, a multi-security level prison in Canon City, Colorado.

The **Warren brothers, David and Maurice**, who received sentences of thirty-two and twenty years respectively for first degree sexual assault, have been released from prison. **Jacob Casados**, who was beat into the gang that night, was also sentenced to twenty years for sexual assault, and has been released.

The prosecution team of Hal Sergeant, Ingrid Bakke, and Mark Randall have all moved on from the Jefferson County District Attorneys Office. In 2017, Sergeant was appointed Division D judge for the First Judicial District which includes Jefferson County. In 2017, Bakke was appointed Boulder District Court chief judge in Boulder County. Mark Randall is also a district court judge for the First Judicial District.

Sadly, Angela Metzger died in December 2008 of cancer. When Francisco Martinez's death penalty sentenced was commuted, she'd wept as she complained to a newspaper reporter. "They let me down. They let Brandy down," she said. "It makes it like it was a waste of time. It makes it like he got away with it."

It's been more than twenty years since I first wrote about the murders of Brandaline Rose DuVall and Venus Montoya, and the subsequent trials of their killers. It remains one of the most horrific, brutal cases, I've written about before or since. The trials were emotionally and psychologically devastating on so many people, including myself.

In fact, I gave up writing about true crime for several years. I just didn't want to hear any more mothers, or siblings, or spouses, and friends of victims, or children, crying or reliving their nightmares on a witness stand. Or see the psychological damage done to prosecutors and detectives, social workers and witnesses. Or hear over and over, the horrific retelling of a young teen's last hours, or the senseless murder of a young mother.

I felt, however, that this is an important story that should not be forgotten. Not just for Brandy's sake, or the many people who suffered as a result of the actions taken by the gang that night or subsequently. But so that we as a society are reminded that violent crime does not happen in a vacuum, that although one has to wonder about a sociopath like Francisco Martinez, monsters are sometimes created by the circumstances that surround them.

Having said that there is no excuse for what happened to Venus Montoya or Brandaline Rose DuVall. Examining the lives of the young men who committed these crimes explains but does not excuse their actions. Nor does it forgive them.

I've lost track of many of the people involved in the writing of this story, including Maria Simpson, Antonio Martinez, Angela while she was still alive and the rest of Brandy's family, as well as the many professionals in law enforcement and the judicial system I met. I've heard that many of them are still traumatized by this case.

I know how they feel. Eventually I recovered and went on to write other true crime stories and books. But this story will haunt me the rest of my life.

*For More News About Steve Jackson,
Signup For Our Newsletter:*

http://wbp.bz/newsletter

Word-of-mouth is critical to an author's long-term success. If you appreciated this book please leave a review on the Amazon sales page:

http://wbp.bz/naa

AVAILABLE FROM STEVE JACKSON AND WILDBLUE PRESS!

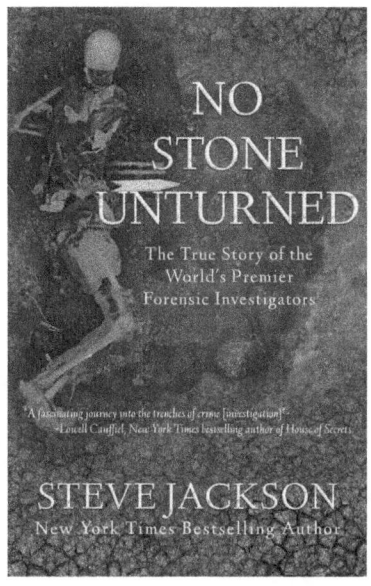

NO STONE UNTURNED by STEVE JACKSON

http://wbp.bz/nsua

Other WildBlue Press Books By Steve Jackson

Bogeyman: For years he stalked elementary schools and playgrounds looking for young girls from low-income neighborhoods to abduct, rape and murder. They were "throwaway kids" to him, hardly missed, soon forgotten. He was every parent's worst nightmare. The bogeyman they warned their children about, who lurked in the shadows outside of bedroom windows. *wbp.bz/bogeymana*

A Clockwork Murder: They thought about their evil fantasy for months. Then wound up like clockwork toys ... they acted. In April 1997, 22-year-old Jacine Gielinski stopped her car at a red light in Colorado. She had no idea that the two young men looking at her from the car next to hers would in that moment decide she would be their target for unspeakable horrors. *wbp.bz/clockworkmurdera*

ROUGH TRADE the story of two people from the seething criminal underworld of Denver, Colorado and how their paths crossed first on the streets and then at a murder trial: Robert Riggan, a violent sexual predator, and Joanne Cordova, a former cop-turned-prostitute, who risks her life to testify against a man she believed killed her friend. *wbp.bz/rta*

Smooth Talker: Anita Andrews, the owner and bartender of her own bar was found raped, beaten, and stabbed to death in a bloody frenzy. She'd last been seen alive the night before talking to a drifter at the end of the bar, playing cards and flirting with her. The stranger disappeared, and two decades later a serial rapist was fingered for a different murder. *wbp.bz/smoothtalker*

AVAILABLE FROM MIKE ROTHMILLER AND WILDBLUE PRESS!

TRUE CRIME CHRONICLES: VOLUME ONE by MIKE ROTHMILLER

http://wbp.bz/tcc1

AVAILABLE FROM SUSAN HALL AND WILDBLUE PRESS!

THE WORLD ENCYCLOPEDIA OF SERIAL KILLERS: VOLUME ONE by SUSAN HALL

http://wbp.bz/tweoska

See even more at:
http://wbp.bz/tc

More True Crime You'll Love From WildBlue Press

A MURDER IN MY HOMETOWN by Rebecca Morris
Nearly 50 years after the murder of seventeen year old Dick Kitchel, Rebecca Morris returned to her hometown to write about how the murder changed a town, a school, and the lives of his friends.

wbp.bz/hometowna

THE BEAST I LOVED by Robert Davidson
Robert Davidson again demonstrates that he is a master of psychological horror in this riveting and hypnotic story ... I was so enthralled that I finished the book in a single sitting. "—James Byron Huggins, International Bestselling Author of The Reckoning

wbp.bz/tbila

BULLIED TO DEATH by Judith A. Yates
On September 5, 2015, in a public park in LaVergne, Tennessee, fourteen-year-old Sherokee Harriman drove a kitchen knife into her stomach as other teens watched in horror. Despite attempts to save her, the girl died, and the coroner ruled it a "suicide." But was it? Or was it a crime perpetuated by other teens who had bullied her?

wbp.bz/btda

SUMMARY EXECUTION by Michael Withey
"An incredible true story that reads like an international crime thriller peopled with assassins, political activists, shady FBI informants, murdered witnesses, a tenacious attorney, and a murderous foreign dictator."—Steve Jackson, New York Times bestselling author of NO STONE UNTURNED

wbp.bz/sea

www.ingramcontent.com/pod-product-compliance
Lightning Source LLC
Chambersburg PA
CBHW051528020426
42333CB00016B/1824